PRIESTLEY PLAYS THREE

J.B. Priestley
PLAYS THREE

Music at Night

The Long Mirror

Ever Since Paradise

Introduction by Tom Priestley

OBERON BOOKS
LONDON

WWW.OBERONBOOKS.COM

Published in this collection in 2012 by Oberon Books Ltd
521 Caledonian Road, London N7 9RH
Tel: +44 (0) 20 7607 3637 / Fax: +44 (0) 20 7607 3629
e-mail: info@oberonbooks.com
www.oberonbooks.com

Visit www.oberonbooks.com to read more about all our books and to buy them. You will also find features, author interviews and news of any author events, and you can sign up for e-newsletters so that you're always first to hear about our new releases.

Contents

Introduction

BY TOM PRIESTLEY

Three very different plays – one so different it is described as 'An Entertainment' rather than a 'play'. *Music at Night* was the thirteenth of his plays to be produced in the 1930s. He was invited to write a new play for the 1938 Malvern Festival and had the idea while travelling in America and began making notes, completing the play in London for production in Malvern. Though it was well received by audiences he felt it needed some rewriting, and after further revisions it was rehearsed and ready for production at the Westminster Theatre in London, but the war intervened and all theatres were closed. In due course permission was given to re-open the Westminster, and it was the first play to be produced in London during the war.

Music at Night is a deliberately experimental play, going well beyond the bounds of a conventional play of the time. But in his own way he was always experimental, and enjoyed the challenge of trying out new techniques. Here, in a definitely non-realistic setting, suggestive of a sitting room, a group of people assemble to hear the performance of a new piece of music. Each act follows a movement in the music, which inspires the listeners to react each in their own way, looking inside themselves for their true feelings and sometimes reliving significant episodes from their past.

Relationships are reviewed, mistakes regretted, emotions expressed; the characters function as if in a dream. As the lights focus on character after character, the attention of the audience shifts from one to another. It builds to the Third Act – Allegro – agitato – maestoso – nobile – where the characters seem to lose their individuality and unite in one single being. It is powerful and strange. This is a play crying out to be rediscovered. Inevitably, as in all Priestley's plays, there is emphasis on Time, when characters remember even relive key moments from the past, and on relations between the sexes.

This is more sharply identified in the other two plays. *The Long Mirror* is a much simpler play, conventional in form – single set, small cast of five, easy to stage if well cast. It was written in Oxford in 1940, where our family was staying during a bitter winter, and staged at the Oxford Playhouse. Despite its simplicity *The Long Mirror* requires the audience to accept the basis of the central situation, the meeting between a composer and a young woman who seems to have been telepathically connected to him for some time, and has thus experienced much of his life before actually meeting him. Her knowledge of his past can help his future as an artist and a husband. Unlikely though this may seem, it is in fact based on the actual experience of JBP's sister-in-law, my aunt Ena, who wrote a fictionalised version of her experience in her novel *The Undercurrent* published in 1926. The play is only loosely based on the novel, being a dramatic reworking of that psychic experience.

He described *Ever Since Paradise* as 'A Discursive Entertainment chiefly referring to Love and Marriage, in Three Acts'. He first wrote it in 1939, revised it at intervals, produced it himself and after a long tour it opened in London in 1947. The cast is made up of three couples, The Musicians, The Commentators and The Example, who present the different aspects of Love and Marriage, sometimes playing themselves, sometimes other characters, with appropriate music played on two pianos. It is quite unlike a conventional play, being more an examination of the various ways men and women connect or misunderstand each other, played in a series of illustrative scenes; argument alternating with romance, affection with disagreement.

Unconventional but entertaining. An unexpected experiment from a master playwright. Three very different plays but enjoyable and engaging for all that, blending human relationships and the subtle illusion of Time in a way that was unusually bold for its day.

MUSIC AT NIGHT

A Play in Three Acts.

Author's Preface

Early in 1938, when I was in America, I received an invitation to contribute a new play to the Malvern Festival of that year. As I strongly approved of the new policy of the Festival, which was to present new plays if possible, I accepted this invitation.

During our trip to Rainbow Bridge, when we were weather-bound up at Rainbow Lodge, in the cyclopean wilds of Southern Utah, I had the idea for an experimental play – and I felt that a dramatic festival offered the time and place for an experimental play – and immediately began making notes for it. I wrote the play soon after I returned to London, in the early summer, and after some heroic rehearsing by H.K. Ayliffe, who was struggling with five new plays at once as well as with a revival of Shaw's *Saint Joan*, this play, *Music at Night*, appeared in Malvern. This production was quite successful (I was told it broke the record for the Festival Theatre), and the play appeared to please rather than puzzle nearly everybody except the dramatic critics, who seemed to be far more bewildered by it than ordinary members of the audience appeared to be. Nevertheless, I felt it ought to be re-written, and I was especially dissatisfied with the third act. So at odd times during the following twelve months I re-wrote it, for a production by the Mask Theatre Company at the Westminster Theatre in London. It was duly rehearsed, but then the war came and all theatres were closed. As soon as we had obtained permission to re-open the Westminster, we produced *Music at Night*, which has, I believe, the honour of being the first play to be produced in London during the war.

In spite of the black-out, which was appallingly thorough in those early weeks and made a visit to the Westminster Theatre something of an ordeal, people came to see the play and were rather touchingly grateful for this opportunity to forget for an hour or two the misery and menace of the war. Afterwards the play was revived in several suburban theatres, and has since been played up and down the country by both professional and amateur companies. The third act still leaves me dissatisfied, and

I think I tried to do in it more than the contemporary playhouse could grapple with or more than my dramatic technique could successfully accomplish. But the play has moments – especially in the second act – that seem to me to be as good as any I have produced in the Theatre, moments that have the strange timeless poignancy of a dream.

J.B. Priestley, 1943

Characters

*The scene throughout is a large music-room in
MRS. AMESBURY's house in London.
The action is continuous, and the time is an evening
just before the War.*

First produced at the Malvern Festival Theatre, on 2 August 1938, with the following cast:

DAVID SHIEL, Robert Harris

NICHOLAS LENGEL, Stephen Murray

MRS. AMESBURY, Jean Cadell

KATHERINE SHIEL, Catherine Lacey

PETER HORLETT, Michael Denison

ANN WINTER, Jenny Laird

PHILIP CHILHAM, Richard Littledale

LADY SYBIL LINCHESTER, Lydia Sherwood

SIR JAMES DIRNIE, Milton Rosmer

CHARLES BENDREX, Mark Digman

PARKS, J. Hwfa Pryse

RUPERT AMESBURY, Nicholas Meredith

MRS. CHILHAM, Maria Ault

TOM, Stephen Murray

DEBORAH, Kay Bannerman

DR. EBENTHAL, Wilson Coleman

ACT ONE

Enter SHIEL, carrying the score and LENGEL, his violin. They are deep in technical talk.

SHIEL: We'll take the whole of the middle section of the first movement faster and harder than we did this afternoon.

LENGEL: All right, David. But I take it from you, remember.

SHIEL: I know. But if I'm still too slow and soft, whip it up.

LENGEL: I'll give it hell. *(Staring about him.)* Where do we play?

SHIEL: *(Pointing to recess as MRS. AMESBURY enters.)* In there.

MRS. A.: *(Rather hastily.)* I'd forgotten you hadn't played here before, Mr. Lengel. I've heard you play so often – and – well – so *many* people have played for me here – that I was forgetting.

LENGEL: *(With a touch of irony.)* And now at last, Mrs. Amesbury – I am honoured.

MRS. A.: Thank you, though I don't believe for a moment you feel honoured. Why should you? Probably thinking, 'Well, the old busybody's got me at last – '

LENGEL: Oh – no – please. Besides, I know what you have done for music – and especially for David here.

MRS. A.: I haven't done much, but at least I've tried. And as I told you, I've been excited about this concerto for weeks.

LENGEL: It's good. One of the best things he has done.

MRS. A.: Splendid! *(Moves towards recess with him.)* I must apologise for putting you in this recess, but I've always kept my piano there – and the platform helps enormously, I always think.

SHIEL: *(Reassuringly.)* I've always liked it.

LENGEL: We're meant to be heard not seen.

MRS. A.: I'll send the others in. I warned you it would the tiniest party – and of course as usual several people let me down at the last minute, telephoning to say they couldn't get back from the country in time – lazy lying brutes! So everybody's here except Charles Bendrex – and I *know* he's coming.

SHIEL: *(Impressed.)* Bendrex, eh?

LENGEL: The Cabinet Minister?

MRS. A.: Yes. He's a very old friend of mine. He always says he adores music.

LENGEL: *(Mockingly.)* Can he mean it – an English politician?

MRS. A.: He says so, and grumbles because he's no longer any time to listen to it. So I insisted upon his coming here tonight. You know, David, he ought to be able to do something for you.

SHIEL: I know. If Bendrex likes the concerto tonight and then I go and die next week, he might be able to get Katherine awarded a Civil List pension of Fifty Pounds a Year.

LENGEL: *(Going towards recess.)* What – fifty pounds of good government money – and they could have bought a nice bond with it!

MRS. A.: *(Quickly, with lowered voice.)* David – I hope you didn't mind my asking Sybil Linchester here tonight –

SHIEL: *(Rather stiffly.)* Good Lord – no! Why should I?

MRS. A.: You see, I didn't want her here – you never know what mood she'll be in, and if she's feeling mischievous, she can just spoil everything – but she wanted to come and bring Sir James Dirnie – you know about those two, of course – everybody does –

SHIEL: Yes. I heard that Dirnie was running her –

MRS. A.: David, what a horrible phrase!

SHIEL: It was the least offensive I could think of.

MRS. A.: Well, as you know, Dirnie's terribly rich – and Sybil's now bringing him out as a patron of the arts – he's just given a few thousand to that opera scheme – and I thought it might help if he heard the concerto –

SHIEL: I hate to admit it, but I think it might.

MRS. A.: So that's why Sybil's here, drinking my best brandy as fast as she can get it down. I'm glad you don't mind her being here.

SHIEL: I repeat, why should I?

MRS. A.: *(After looking at him hard.)* I – seem to have heard something – once – a few years ago.

SHIEL: Ancient history – probably untrue.

MRS. A.: That's my tremendous age. I'm beginning to forget the difference a few years make when you're younger. Well, now – I'll go and collect them –

Enter KATHERINE SHIEL.

KATH.: Mrs. Amesbury, Mr. Bendrex has just arrived. You'd better look after him. He seems dreadfully tired.

MRS. A.: *(As she goes.)* Poor Charles – I'm afraid he *is* dreadfully tired these days. *Goes out.*

KATH.: I didn't realise Mr. Bendrex is so terribly old. He looks – worn out. *(Looks at the two men.)* Well, chaps? All ready?

LENGEL: Katherine my dear – you're nervous.

KATH.: How do you know?

LENGEL: I know that look of yours. And *chaps.* That's not really you. And why be nervous? After all, these people – who are they?

KATH.: Rather grand, some of them, Nick.

LENGEL: You mean, they have their names in the newspaper. So do the tooth pastes and little liver pills.

KATH.: *(Playfully to SHIEL.)* He's very cynical tonight.

LENGEL: Because it is Sunday night. I am always the same on Sunday night.

SHIEL: What do you think you are from Monday to Saturday – a little ray of sunshine?

KATH.: *(Hastily.)* Listen, David, this is important. Philip Chilham's here –

SHIEL: The fellow who writes that awful column in the *Daily Gazette*? What does he know about music?

KATH.: Nothing, probably. But everybody seems to read his column. And he's just told me that Filderberg is on his way over from New York. He might take the concerto back with him, David.

SHIEL: He might, if I can get hold of him.

LENGEL: I wouldn't. You're a romantic –

SHIEL: *(Indignantly.)* I'm not.

KATH.: Of course you are, David. Go on, Nick.

LENGEL: And Filderberg's very harsh and dry. A great technique, of course – but you feel he's mocking the music he plays.

KATH.: But why should he?

LENGEL: He has gone sour. You know what happened to his family in Vienna – terrible! So now he seems to use his great technique to mock at music – at least, all tender, romantic music.

KATH.: But that's – *horrible!*

LENGEL: You may not have noticed, Katherine, but a lot of things now are horrible.

SHIEL: Including our performance of this last movement, Nick. I wish we could have another go at it. Look!

As they look at score together, PETER HORLETT enters.

KATH.: You look rather gloomy.

PETER: I feel gloomy.

KATH.: I ought to warn you, it's my husband's concerto that's being inflicted on you.

PETER: Oh – you're Mrs. Shiel, are you? I'm Peter Horlett.

KATH.: I know. I read some poems of yours the other day.
(Pauses.)

PETER: Well?

KATH.: *(Laughingly.)* I'd better wait until I know what you think of David's concerto.

PETER: That's not fair.

KATH.: All right. I liked some of them – very much. But if they're poems for the people, as you say they are, oughtn't you to write them so that the people will understand them?

PETER: *(Proudly.)* They will understand them one day, when the masses come out of their dope.

ANN WINTER, a pretty young thing, enters hurriedly.

ANN: *(Excitedly.)* Peter – Peter!

PETER: *(With cheerful brutality.)* Shut up, Ann. I'm talking.

ANN: *(Cheerfully to KATH.)* Hasn't he foul manners? *(Addressing them both, very confidentially.)* I say – I don't think Lady Sybil Linchester's *so* marvellous.

PETER: *(With huge scorn.)* Marvellous? She's poison. So's that fellow Dirnie. *And* Chilham. *And* that old stuffed shirt, Bendrex. All poison.

ANN: *(Still confidentially.)* No. Old Mr. Bendrex is sweet. But I really can't see that the famous Lady Sybil –

PETER: *(Cuttingly.)* Snoops! God, what a set! Snoops!

ANN: I really can't see she's so wonderful. To begin with, she's getting ancient –

KATH.: Here, steady. I refuse to be ancienter still.

ANN: You're different. Mrs. Shiel. But don't you think that often girls like that, just by some sort of trick or fluke, persuade a few people they're marvellous, and then after that it goes on for years – I mean, everybody saying they're marvellous – when really they aren't at all. Don't you think so, Peter?

PETER: What?

ANN: Oh – you *are* the limit.

PHILIP CHILHAM, a thin, pale, weary-looking man in his thirties, appears at the entrance and pauses to light a cigarette.

PETER: *(Softly.)* Oh – God – here comes the *Daily Gazette.*

Goes off to sit down on chair L. CHILHAM comes up to the two men L.C. The two musicians are still busy with the score.

CHILHAM: *(Who talks in a quick, staccato manner, rather American.)* If you ask me, there'll be another shuffle in the cabinet soon.

KATH.: Why?

CHILHAM: *(Dropping voice.)* Bendrex doesn't look as if he'll last much longer. He's old, of course, but he looks a sick man too. Heart, I'd say. *(Pauses.)* Give me a line on Mrs. Amesbury. I hardly know her.

ANN: *(Impulsively.)* She's nice.

CHILHAM: *(Drily.)* Thanks very much.

KATH.: *(Rather quickly.)* She's been a widow a long time, and then about six years ago she lost her only son, Rupert – he was in the Air Force – a test pilot – and was killed. She's really fond of music, and she tries to help people like my husband in various ways – like – well, tonight, for instance.

CHILHAM: *(Obviously making mental note.)* I get her.

ANN: *(Brightly.)* And I'm Ann Winter, Mr. Chilham. It's an easy name to remember. And I'm here because my mother is an old friend of Mrs. Amesbury's, and I like music too, and – let me see – what am I good at?

PETER: *(Groaning from his chair.)* Making me feel sick.

ANN: Shut up, Peter.

CHILHAM: *(Smoothly.)* I suppose you'd hate to be mentioned in our capitalist rag, Horlett?

PETER: Please yourself.

CHILHAM: You know your friend Fordley's going to write for us?

PETER: I'm not surprised. I always knew it wouldn't take much to buy Fordley – especially after he married that girl.

CHILHAM: *(Coolly.)* Can we print that?

PETER: You daren't.

CHILHAM: You'll find it in my column in the morning.

PETER: *(Alarmed.)* No – you'd better not. Forget it, please, Chilham.

CHILHAM: Right. But next time don't dare us. We've taken a lot of dares on the *Gazette*. We don't run on tram lines like your poor little Red papers.

PETER: *(Hotly.)* No, you go wobbling all over the town, like a damn carnival wagon with blood on the wheels.

Enter SYBIL LINCHESTER followed by SIR JAMES DIRNIE. She is talking to him in loud, rather insolent tone.

LADY S.: It's one of those houses that are like film studios. You know, they photograph you all the time. You haven't time to *do* anything – only to look as if you're doing it – for the photographers. Audrey says whenever she stays there, she always looks under the bed for a cameraman.

They are now in. Seeing her, CHILHAM has detached himself from PETER and moved to meet her. ANN is talking to PETER. SIR JAMES goes to KATHERINE SHIEL.

SIR J.: *(Pleasantly.)* Let's see – you're Mrs. Shiel, aren't you?

KATH.: Yes – and you're Sir James Dirnie.

LADY S.: *(Loudly to CHILHAM.)* Is it true Verity Astley-Uppingham is still bouncing all round Germany shouting *Heil Hitler* in shorts and showing the storm troopers her very Nordic legs?

KATH.: And I hope you're fond of music.

SIR J.: Some.

CHILHAM: *(The knowing one.)* It's worse than that, our Berlin man says. You see –

SIR J.: I don't know much about it, but I'm trying. Can't say fairer than that, can I?

LADY S.: Who's doing Mercy Beaufort's publicity now – do you know?

CHILHAM: A boy who's just started. No good.

LADY S.: Definitely lousy.

CHILHAM: She's trying to get it on the cheap.

LADY S.: Mercy always tried to get everything on the cheap. She thinks life's one great bargain basement.

KATH.: No, once he's started on something, David goes straight on and he's angelic. The difficult time is just before he begins anything – and then it really *is* troublesome. But of course I'm used to it now, and even the children understand they mustn't worry him then.

SIR J.: He's a lucky man.

KATH.: What? You *say* that! He's had an awful struggle, y'know.

SIR J.: What's wrong with a struggle if you've something worth struggling for? I say, he's a lucky man.

LADY S.: *(Turning.)* That sounds all wrong from you, Jimmy. Who's a lucky man?

SIR J.: Shiel.

LADY S.: *(Looking insolently from SHIEL to KATH.)* Really! *(She gives a short ironical laugh.)* That's very sweet and modest of you, Jimmy. *(Turns to CHILHAM again.)*

PETER: *(Suddenly raising his voice, to ANN, and drawing everybody.)* Well, and why not, you goof? I haven't the least objection to destroying everything and starting all over again.

SIR J.: What's all this?

PETER: I'm saying I've no objection to wiping out Homer and Shakespeare and Dante and Michael Angelo and Leonardo and Bach and Mozart and King's College Chapel and Chartres and the Bodleian and the British Museum and the National Gallery – and the whole bag of tricks. Why not? We'd have the fun of doing it all ourselves then. Starting from the beginning. With a clean slate.

LADY S.: *(Maliciously.)* I'm glad you said *slate.*

PETER: *(Suspiciously.)* Why?

LADY S.: It sounds so suitable.

MRS. A. has now entered up stage of BENDREX, who is carrying a small glass. MRS. A. is bright but anxious.

MRS. A.: Now, Sybil, you're not to be naughty, and Peter you mustn't make so much noise. You're not going to start destroying anything tonight. Now, Charles, you don't know them all yet –

BENDREX: No, but we mustn't hold everything up, my dear May.

MRS. A.: I'll do it quickly. Lady Sybil and Sir James Dirnie you've met already. This is Mrs. Shiel. That's Ann Winter. And that's Peter Horlett, who thinks he's a communist poet. *(The two musicians who have been in the recess now come forward a moment.)* David Shiel, the composer. And Mr. Lengel, who's kindly playing the violin part for us.

BENDREX: *(Graciously.)* This is a great pleasure – to hear such an important new work.

SHIEL: It's good of you to come, sir. *(To MRS. A.)* We're ready, if you are.

MRS. A.: Make yourselves comfortable everybody. Charles, will you sit here.

They begin to seat themselves. MRS. A. attends to BENDREX.

BENDREX: *(With some difficulty.)* Just a moment, my dear May.

MRS. A.: Of course, Charles. But you're not feeling ill, are you?

BENDREX: *(Slowly, faintly.)* Not really. But – I have to take – certain precautions. *(She holds the glass while BENDREX brings out a small box of tablets and takes one or two with the water, taking the glass from MRS. A, then handing it back to her and closing his eyes for a moment while she puts it down. Then he looks rather more alert.)* Now for some music. I like music best these days because it's the only art that's really detached. It doesn't lead you back to the newspapers. It doesn't drag in the rest of the world. You can lose yourself in it.

MRS. A.: That makes it all the more dangerous sometimes, Charles. It can break down those careful barriers we build up inside our minds.

BENDREX: Yes, but nobody knows but ourselves.

LADY S.: Thank God for that! It would be pretty awful if other people knew what sometimes happens somewhere inside our heads, when music gets to work on us.

KATH.: Perhaps other people can know.

LADY S.: My dear – absurd!

KATH.: But it may not be happening inside our heads.

DIRNIE: It couldn't be happening anywhere else.

LENGEL: *(Appearing from recess.)* Why not?

SIR J.: Well – ask yourself, my dear fellow. Impressions, thoughts, fancies – if they're not in your head, where are they?

LENGEL: I don't know, and neither do you. We know nothing of any importance about ourselves.

KATH.: But perhaps what we think is happening inside is really happening outside. We may think about life all the wrong way round.

PETER: Now wait a minute, Mrs. Shiel. We know that what we call thought is only a change in the cell structure of the brain –

SHIEL: *(Right of pouffe.)* You call yourself a poet, Horlett – and believe that dreary rubbish.

BENDREX: *(Half humorously, half wearily.)* Gentlemen! – music please, not metaphysics. Fortunately Mrs. Amesbury won't compel us afterwards to describe what happened in what – with all due deference to you, Mrs. Shiel – I shall persist in thinking are our personal secret little worlds.

MRS. A.: If I did, this would probably be the last little musical party you'd all attend here. Now, David.

SHIEL: *(To everybody.)* You do understand, of course, that this is really a concerto for violin and full orchestra, and that all I can give you is a rough transcription for the piano of the orchestral parts. It's in three movements. And it's not one of those programme works – fate knocking at the door in the first subject, and so on. You can each make your own story for it, if you must have one. Now for the first movement – *Allegro Capriccioso.*

MRS. A.: *(As SHIEL goes into recess.)* Thank you, David. *(Listeners in relaxed attitudes as the concert begins. After music is established, MRS. A. rises and as she speaks, music slowly fades out.)* Begins quite well. But then David Shiel always did begin things well. Can he keep it up – that's the question. I do hope he's done something really good this time, and that they'll like it. *(Looks at BENDREX.)* I'm sure *you* could do something for him, Charles, if you really wanted to. You're looking terribly old and tired tonight, Charles. I'm sorry, my dear, really sorry, though I don't mind telling you that I feel tired too. It's such a bother being loud and bright all the time, and yet if you're not, people don't seem to listen any more. Everybody just shouts. There's no conversation any more, is there, Charles? It might have been better if you and I were having a cosy little talk about old times, because we shan't have many more little talks. But I wanted to help David Shiel. Perhaps the music will make us feel better. *(Looks at PHILIP CHILHAM.)* You could do something for him, too, Philip Chilham, I don't like you very much, and I hate your horrible cheap nasty newspaper – but – well there it is. *(Looks at DIRNIE.)* What about *you?* I don't like you very much, Sir James Very-Rich Dirnie, though of course I don't know you very well, but I suspect you're a bit of a brute. I've only Sybil Linchester's word for it that you like music at all. And you don't look as if you do. And God knows she may have said it just so that you would have to come here with her and be bored all evening. She's quite capable of that. *(To SYBIL.)* Yes, you are. And you know it. At any moment you may start yawning and whispering at the top of your voice that you don't like the concerto, just to spoil everything. And I warn you, Sybil, I'll be furious if you do play any of your tricks tonight, and I'll pay you out somehow. So keep that private devil of yours chained up tonight, please. *(Looks at KATHERINE.)* Poor Katherine. Trying so hard not to look anxious. Pretending you don't care about anything now but the music. Hump!

KATH.: *(In trance-like tone.)* Mrs. Amesbury, whatever happens, we're really grateful.

MRS. A.: I'm glad to do it, my dear. I like you and David, and I also happen to like music.

KATH.: I know you do.

MRS. A.: If I didn't do something of this sort, I'd soon become a useless old thing. If I'm not one already.

KATH.: You know you're not.

MRS. A.: I believe a lot of people say I'm just an old busybody, trying to make myself important.

KATH.: They've no right to say so.

MRS. A.: Of course I *am* an old busybody, and I do like to say, 'Oh he played it for the first time in my studio.'

KATH.: Why shouldn't you?

MRS. A.: And I've sometimes caught these musical geniuses of yours giving each other a look and a wink. And I know what they've been thinking. 'Better humour the old girl – she might be useful.'

KATH.: David doesn't talk about you like that.

MRS. A.: But behind all the busybodying and the boasting and the snobbery and whatever else it may be, there's something real. I do care about music itself. That's real. Sometimes I think it's more real than we are. What are we? We don't know.

KATH.: No, we don't know.

MRS. A.: You're anxious, aren't you, Katherine? Yes, terribly anxious. And I envy you. Just to have something, somebody, once again, to be anxious about.

She sits down, and now KATHERINE comes to life and is urgent.

KATH.: All of you – please, *please* – do listen properly – and then like the concerto, really like it, so that you'll tell everybody about it. *(To CHILHAM.)* You – Philip Chilham – like it – and tell everybody about it –

CHILHAM: *(Without expression.)* Just what I thought. Old-fashioned stuff so far. Hasn't got the modern tempo No modern hardness. Steel. Nickel. Chromium plate. Bakelite. Streamlines. Machine guns. Bombing planes –

KATH.: *(Breaking in impatiently.)* Oh you! *(Turning to others.)* This means a lot to us. It isn't money – though that's important.

SIR J.: *(Grimly.)* You surprise me!

KATH.: But David's put himself – the very best of himself – into his work. I know you've all heard that before, but it really means something. You see, he's not just playing – amusing himself, and hoping to amuse you. It's not like that at all.

ANN: *(Loudly, cheerfully.)* He doesn't look a bit like Beethoven to me. Fancy having Beethoven in love with you! Frightening! But he used to pick his teeth with a fork.

KATH.: David's giving himself, every little secret, in the music of his. I used to be jealous sometimes. There seemed so little left for me. Nothing special of my very own. All going into the music. For everybody. For people who'd say, 'Yes, that's all right. Not bad.' But now I'm not jealous any more like that. I want him to be happy. If he's happy, then I'll be happy – and of course the children will be happy too – we'll all be happy, all the Shiels. And it hasn't been like that for a long time. David's often so worried and miserable. So many disappointments.

LADY S.: Whose fault is that? *(Slowly, clearly.)*

KATH.: *(Fiercely.)* And if *you* start being a nuisance – spoiling everything for us – I'll – I'll *kill* you.

CHILHAM: *(Sitting up, distinctly.)* What a look! I believe she *hates* Lady Sybil. She could *kill* her. That would make a sweet story.

KATH.: *(Appealingly.)* Like the concerto – please – *please!*

Sits. We now concentrate on CHILHAM.

CHILHAM: A swell story. Lady Sybil Linchester murdered! Good idea for a detective yarn. All the set-up here. I could do it in my head. Mystery story – or a play. Better make it a play. More money in a play. And film rights and everything. Bags of money in a good mystery play. Might work some of it out now with these people and this setting. Let's see. Snoops Linchester is murdered. Who did it? I see the final scene.

He points to the others. All except LADY S. who is supposed to be dead, and ANN, who is not in this scene, sit up sharply, in a strong, rather white, light. CHILHAM now plays the superdetective, and the others typical characters in an average mystery play. They should all play in a rather heavy conventional theatrical style, thought not like old-fashioned melodrama.

CHILHAM: *(Continued as MORTON FERRET.)* I have brought you all here again so that we might have a final talk on the murder of Lady Sybil Linchester.

SIR J.: *(With heavy stagy tone.)* Ah – so the mystery's been too much for the famous Morton Ferret.

CHILHAM: On the contrary, Sir James –

SIR J.: You mean – ?

CHILHAM: I mean, I have solved the mystery.

General cries of astonishment, 'What', 'Good God!', etc.

SIR J.: Then where is the murderer?

CHILHAM: The murderer – my dear Sir James – is here.

More 'What!' and a cry from KATH., who collapses.

PETER: She's fainted.

KATH.: *(In faint tones.)* No. I'm – all right.

CHILHAM: *(In self-satisfied tone.)* It has been a most curious and complicated case. I soon discovered that with one exception you all had a strong motive for killing Lady Sybil. The exception was Mrs. Amesbury. But – with one exception – you all had alibis. Again, the exception was Mrs. Amesbury, who admitted that she could have committed the murder. But of course she had no motive. It did not take me very long to establish that your various alibis were false, although very ingenious. You, Mr. Bendrex, could have left – and *did leave* – that train at Surbiton. The figure your butler saw in your library, Sir James, was a dummy. Horlett, you *were* at the dance, as your friends testified, but you were not there *all the time*. The only alibi I couldn't break down was – *(Turning to KATH.)* – yours. Yes, Mrs. Shiel's alibi was apparently perfect. Yet I know that Mrs. Shiel came here – *(A gasp of astonishment. KATH. gives a little cry.)* Well?

KATH.: All right. You've won. I'll confess. I came here and saw her – she was asleep – and I thought of all the horrible mischief she made – something snapped in my brain – I killed her.

CHILHAM: Thank you, Mrs. Shiel. Only – you see – you *didn't* kill her!

SIR J.: *What!*

KATH.: But – that's impossible – I know I did.

CHILHAM: You couldn't have killed her. You see, when you came here, Lady Sybil *was dead.* She had been dead for at least two hours. *(Very gently.)* Mrs. Amesbury you must have had a very strong motive. What was it?

MRS. A.: She had deliberately wrecked my boy's life. I had waited for years for a chance to avenge him. And then at last it came. I have no regrets.

She pretends to take poison from a little bottle and falls back dead.

BENDREX: Why – she's –

CHILHAM: *(In self-satisfied tone.)* Yes, I thought that would happen. Well, that completes the Case of the Four Alibis.

SIR J.: *(In stagy tone.)* God! – Ferret – they were right – you *are* a wizard.

CHILHAM: *(In self-satisfied tone.)* My dear Sir James, merely a matter of adding two and two. And now I'll get back to my bulbs – so much more amusing than human beings. Good night. *(Instantly the light change and all the others go back to their listening attitudes. CHILHAM becomes himself again.)* Yes, I could do it on my head. But after all why should I bother? I'm making plenty of money.

BENDREX: *(Solemnly.)* You can find my salary in Whitaker's Almanac.

CHILHAM: I make more than you do, Bendrex. *And* earn it.

SIR J.: *(Contemptuously.)* Chicken feed! You've never seen any real money, Chilham.

CHILHAM: *(Aggressively turning to him.)* I don't pretend to make it on your scale, Dirnie. But don't forget I go for nothing to places where you've to pay through the nose. And more people run after me than they do after you.

SIR J.: You should see the size of the people who run after me.

CHILHAM: *(Passionately, a man convincing himself.)* I'm somebody in this town, don't forget it. And ten years ago nobody had heard of me.

PETER: *(Scornfully.)* And in another ten nobody'll hear of you.

CHILHAM: *(Same tone as before.)* That's not true – unless I'm dead and done with by then. And if I am, well that'll be that. I'll have had my fun.

KATH.: *(Calmly.)* I wonder.

CHILHAM: *(Annoyed.)* You've no need to wonder. I tell you, if some of you had my life for a month, you'd have to go into a nursing home.

KATH.: So much fun?

CHILHAM: *(Annoyed.)* Yes, yes, yes. But it's got pace, real tempo, my life has. I don't just exist, I *live.*

KATH.: I wonder.

CHILHAM: *(Irritably.)* I know what I'm talking about. If your husband made what I do and had the pull I have in this town, you wouldn't know yourself.

MRS. A.: *(Calmly.)* She likes knowing herself.

CHILHAM: *(Irritably.)* You took damn good care to get me here didn't you, hoping for a little publicity. You're not honest, you people, that's your trouble. Envy me really, only you won't admit it. Oh – to hell!

Stalks back to his chair, and resumes listening attitude. ANN WINTER now trips forward, wearing nothing but a bright South Sea Pareu and a wreath of white flowers. Downstage light should be very bright for this episode.

ANN: *(Brightly, moving about.)* Well, here I am on my South Sea Island again. *(To others.)* And there you all sit, looking so dull, not having any fun at all – stupid, stupid, *stupid.* Yes, even you, Peter. *(Turns away from them.)* It's a lovely little South Sea Island. Out there's the lagoon – bright, bright blue – and full of rainbow coloured tiny fishes. Here are palm trees, of course – and lots of flowers – magnolia and hibiscus and – and – things. Here – all lovely clean sand. The sun shining – or a big moon, just as you like. Nobody to worry me. Nobody saying, 'Ann darling, you really shouldn't, you know.' No, none of that nonsense. The beautiful queen of the island. *(Turns, calling sharply.)* Mr. Chilham!

CHILHAM: *(In trance-style.)* Yes?

ANN: *(Settling herself down.)* You must write in your column about me on my island. Miss Ann Winter on her beautiful little South Sea island.

CHILHAM: Okay. Is the island yours, Miss Winter?

ANN: *(Proudly.)* It wasn't originally, but now I'm queen of it.

CHILHAM: And a very popular queen too, I imagine.

ANN: You are quite right, Mr. Chilham. I *am* a popular queen, the *most* popular queen the island has ever had. As soon as I arrive – because I'm not here all the time, you know, sometimes I'm staying with my mother in Knightsbridge – but as soon as I arrive, all the natives hold a week's festival, with processions and speeches and songs and dances and – and – everything, and they all cry, 'Hail to our beautiful white queen.'

CHILHAM: Does Hollywood know about this, Miss Winter?

ANN: Oh – yes – they're most excited about it in Hollywood, and they've made me a most wonderful offer to act in a film.

CHILHAM: What's the film about?

ANN: *(Proud but confidential.)* Well, you see, in this film Ronald Colman, Clark Gable and Robert Taylor are all madly in love with me, and I have to choose one of them.

CHILHAM: Which do you choose?

ANN: *(Triumphantly.)* That's the point. I don't choose any of them. No, in the end I suddenly tell them I prefer an English boy, not famous at all, thought of course he might be at any time –

CHILHAM: Who is this English boy?

ANN: I don't feel I ought to tell you that, Mr. Chilham. But thank you very much, and please put some very nice photographs in, but don't let my mother give you any of her snapshots of me – they're *awful.* *(Gets up and pirouettes a little,*

humming, then stops near PETER and points a toe.) Peter, Peter –
look – aren't my legs pretty?

SIR J.: *(Coolly.)* Yes.

ANN: *(Indignantly.)* I didn't ask you. You think about your
precious Lady Sybil. And she's not so jolly marvellous when
you have a good look at her. She's *ancient* really – though
not to you, I suppose, because you're ancient too. Peter,
Peter – do look at me. *(But he doesn't, and she is downcast.)* Oh
– well – I think you're mean.

*DIRNIE yawns loudly. ANN hurries back to her chair, where she must
get back into her frock. DIRNIE rises and strolls forward, looking
idly about him.*

SIR J.: *(Yawning.)* Well, it's all right, I suppose, but it hasn't
done anything to me yet, your violin concerto. Nothing's
happening inside. Not one little window's opened yet. My
fault or his? Probably his. No genius. But I dunno – I'm
getting stale here too. Hell – yes – Jimmy Dirnie, you're
getting stale. *(Looks at the others.)* Don't think much of this
lot. Kid's pretty – but insipid – like most of 'em.

ANN: *(Without moving or being seen.)* You liked my legs.

SIR J.: You mustn't attach too much importance to that. Our
minds don't run all the time the way you think they do.
Young Horlett – communist poet from Oxford. They're
three a penny now. Parlour pinks.

PETER: Pink yourself! You wait.

SIR J.: I'll have to. All for the people but can't write anything
they want to read. Awkward that, Bendrex. Well, you're
about through – even if you live much longer. You've
wangled through the last twenty years on a nice committee
manner and dining out with the right people.

BENDREX: *(Quietly.)* There are worse things, Dirnie, than a nice
manner and dining out.

SIR J.: What do you mean? *(After a pause, much louder.)* What the
hell do you mean?

BENDREX: *(Very quietly.)* You know.

SIR J.: I don't know what you're talking about. Great British Statesman! Saving the Empire! You couldn't save a fish and chip shop, Bendrex. You couldn't save a canary from a cat. And don't try to patronise me again tonight, my Right Honourable Friend, or I'll let you have it where it'll hurt.

BENDREX: *(Very quietly.)* I think – you're too late – I can't – be hurt – much more.

SIR J.: *(Looking at him, change of tone.)* Poor old devil! He's about all in. That's what's waiting for me, and even now, already, everything's getting damned dull – *(Yawns and looks at LADY S.)* Yes – damned dull – no lights being turned on anywhere inside – no windows being opened – and I'm not forgetting you, Sybil – *Snoops.*

LADY S.: Leave out *Snoops.* I didn't throw that into the bargain. That's not for sale..

SIR J.: I'm glad to know something isn't. Well, I'm sorry to inform you, Lady Sybil, but nothing happens any more when I look at you.

LADY S.: My God! I've been screaming with boredom at you for months and months.

He ignores this and looks at KATH.

SIR J.: *(Slowly.)* Mrs. Shiel. Sensible woman. Nice woman. Loves her husband, makes a home, produces children. Dull probably, but – I wonder what that would have been like. I wonder…

He moves downstage as he repeats this slowly, and the lights are thrown where he stands. KATH. now comes forward to him.

KATH.: Well, Jim! *(She kisses him lightly, then brushes something off his lapel.)* Have a nice trip?

SIR J.: *(Rather awkwardly.)* Why – yes – pretty good.

KATH.: *(In a very wifely style.)* The children have been worrying these last three days about when you were coming home. 'When is Daddy coming back?' they kept asking, the little stupids. Richard fell rather badly yesterday – cut his knee – but Nanny and I cleaned the cut very carefully and put a big bandage on – and he's tremendously proud of his bandage.

Marjorie wanted one too. Jim, we'll really have to have poor Marjorie's eyes tested. I was talking to Nanny about it this afternoon, and she's certain there's something wrong –

SIR J.: Not seriously wrong?

KATH.: No, of course not, but she might have to wear glasses for a year or two.

SIR J.: She won't like that.

KATH.: That's all you know. She'll love it. They always do, if you tell them that glasses are rather special. You'll see.

SIR J.: What's happening tonight – anything?

KATH.: No, my pet. The Forbes rang up, but I said I knew you'd want a quiet evening at home tonight. That's all right, isn't it?

SIR J.: *(A shade doubtfully.)* Yes, of course.

LADY S.: And there'd be an awful lot of those quiet evenings – little chats about brats – and a soprano or two on the wireless.

KATH.: *(Brightly.)* I'll run up to the nursery and tell them that you're *coming in to see them.*

She hurries back to her seat. LADY S. comes downstage.

LADY S.: *(In a trance tone.)* Well, that wasn't so very wonderful either, was it?

SIR J.: *(Slowly.)* I don't know.

LADY S.: Come on, Jimmy, be honest. That's one thing you can be. You don't usually deceive yourself.

SIR J.: *(Slowly.)* It came too quickly, you see. We hadn't built up to it together. That must make a difference.

LADY S.: Oh, don't talk like a fool – that kind of woman and that kind of life would start you drinking yourself to death within six months. Do you think I don't know you?

SIR J.: I'm sure you don't. Never even expected you to know me.

LADY S.: You're not going to pretend now you haven't been pretty sentimental at times with me, Jimmy?

SIR J.: No, I expect I have. But I think I was talking to myself really, not to you. I was feeling mellow. I'd got what I wanted.

LADY S.: Me.

SIR J.: *(Slowly.)* No, not really you. Less than you, and yet at the same time a lot more than you. I'd been conquering your famous old family and that famous old mansion and that miles of park with the high wall round and the footmen and the gardeners and gamekeepers and all the people you see in carriages and big cars and in the stalls of theatres when you're a poor little devil in the gallery and Mayfair and the House of Lords and Ascot and Cowes. I'd been taken to bed by the whole lot.

LADY S.: In short, the good old inferiority complex having a romp.

SIR J.: Well, you can't grumble. You've done pretty well out of it. You've cost me fifty thousand if you cost me a penny.

LADY S.: And if I could have worked it, that fifty thousand would have been five hundred thousand. *And* I'd show you the door five minutes after you'd written your last possible cheque. *And* – my dear Sir James – if I'd thought you'd gone out to make a pound or two hawking coal or bananas in the street – in other words, if you'd been compelled to go back to where you first started from – I'd have been delighted. What do you think of that?

SIR J.: Doesn't surprise me at all, Sybil. I'm not sure I haven't enjoyed our tussles over the cheque book more than anything else.

LADY S.: *(Coming to life.)* That's lucky, because they lasted longer. And now I'll show you something – and your nice dull friend Mrs. Shiel too. *(DIRNIE steps back towards his seat.)* Five years ago. No, six. But only six. There'd been a charity concert, at the Albert Hall, but this was a few hours after it had finished. You see, a new short work for the orchestra had been included in the programme and had been conducted by the composter – Mr. David Shiel – *(She says this almost as if she were announcing him, and now he enters quickly R. He looks rather younger now, is in full evening dress, but rather untidy, and is at once excited and rather drunk.)* David? I thought you weren't going to see me again.

SHIEL: I wasn't.

LADY S.: *(Mockingly.)* And now –?

SHIEL: Yes, I'm here. I couldn't keep away.

LADY S.: Isn't your wife waiting up for you somewhere?

SHIEL: *(Excitedly, bitterly.)* Yes, yes. This is an important night for us, a new work being played for the first time. We went out to supper, I left them. I said I had to see Duplet from Geneva.

LADY S.: And I'm Duplet from Geneva?

SHIEL: *(Bitterly.)* Yes, I'm having a very important talk with him about a performance of my symphony there. So of course that must come before everything. Only reasonable, isn't it?

LADY S.: My dear David, this mood of self-reproach – you're not tight, by any chance, are you?

SHIEL: Yes.

LADY S.: *(Lightly.)* Thought so. But this self-reproach isn't very complimentary to me, you know. If that's how you're feeling, hadn't you better hurry back and do your little duty.

SHIEL: *(Eagerly now.)* I couldn't keep away. All night I was thinking about you, Sybil. I tried not to, but it was no use. Did you like the work?

LADY S.: Yes, lovely – David.

SHIEL: Do you mean that or is it just politeness?

LADY S.: My dear, I'm the rudest woman in London.

SHIEL: *(Eagerly.)* When you were listening, were you thinking about me, remembering what I'd said to you, what had happened between us?

LADY S.: The whole time.

SHIEL: *(Rather savagely.)* My God – I never know whether you mean a single thing you say, Sybil. I'll admit it, I can't make head or tail or you. And I'm not trying to flatter you. I don't think it *is* flattering. I hate it. Sometimes I hate *you*. But I can't keep away. Sybil –

He tries to take her in his arms but she fends him off.

LADY S.: *(Coolly.)* I may be a nuisance, a liar, and a cheat but – please – may you make love to me – humph? *(He looks sullen and does not reply.)* Don't be sulky, David. That's it, isn't it?

SHIEL: And what if it is? If my arms are round you and I'm kissing you, then you're really there and I can forget the ache and the torment for a few minutes.

LADY S.: Aches and torments? You're not just dramatising everything, are you?

SHIEL: *(After a pause, slowly, miserably.)* Over and over again Sybil, I've wished that I'd never exchanged a look or a word with you, that I'd run for miles that night down at the Abingtons instead of going to your room, that I'd –

LADY S.: *(Cutting in sharply.)* Yes, you needn't enlarge on it. And I wish I felt flattered by being regarded as a *femme fatale*, but the truth is, I find it rather ridiculous that you should come here, not very sober, in the middle of the night, to assure me you wish to God you could be anywhere else –

SHIEL: *(Urgently.)* No, no, no, you know what I mean.

LADY S.: I think you'd better go.

SHIEL: *(Distressed.)* No – for God's sake, Sybil, let me stay now, please – please. You don't know the state of mind I've been in. Forget everything I said. I don't know what I'm saying. I'm bewitched, Sybil. Look – look at me –

He has fallen to his knees in front of her and has taken her hands and is kissing them, a miserable distraught man. CHILHAM now strolls into the scene.

LADY S.: And there he was, you see, Philip, going on like a madman. I was irritated, but I was sorry for him too. I'm sorry for anybody who's compelled to behave like that. Love's just not worth it.

CHILHAM: *(Unreal tone.)* I agree. What happened next?

LADY S.: *(To SHIEL.)* I'm sorry, David, but I really think you're becoming a bore. *(Gives him a hand to rise. He rises slowly and stares at her.)* Now don't start being tragic – and please remember, anyhow, you're tight. *(He still stares at her.)* And if you hurried, you might still catch that conductor from Geneva, Monsieur Duplet. A sensible chat about music instead of making an absurd scene here.

SHIEL: *(Very bitterly.)* Go to hell!

He hurries out R. She turns to CHILHAM.

LADY S.: *(As if being interviewed.)* And that was that. And believe it or not, I was really being rather kind to him. But of course, he was never my sort.

CHILHAM: Right. You like 'em tougher than that.

LADY S.: *(Firmly.)* Tougher and much, much richer.

Sits down on pouffe.

CHILHAM: Of course. *(Taking interviewer's tone.)* Now then, Lady Sybil, you're recognised as being at the head of your profession –

LADY S.: *(Graciously.)* Sit down, Mr. Chilham, won't you? Yes, I think I may say that I'm one of the most successful kept women in London.

CHILHAM: *(Politely.)* Which means now, in the world.

LADY S.: Possibly, I don't know. I've travelled a good deal, of course, and have many friends abroad, but – well – give me a good clean-living Englishman.

CHILHAM: *(Makes a note of this.)* Swell! Now I know that our feminine readers would like your views on what a girl's chances are nowadays in your profession. Can the modern business girl succeed as a kept woman, or is the competition of society and the stage too keen? Is there still plenty of room at the top? Is the life as easy as it's imagined to be?

LADY S.: *(Promptly.)* Certainly not. A girl who merely wants an easy life should keep away. To succeed she will have to have determination, courage, perseverance, foresight, and a cast-iron personal charm.

CHILHAM: *Thank you. Now –*

But they are interrupted. PETER has risen, wearing a Red Army general's cap, and now strides forward. He is followed by ANN, not as herself but as an aide.

PETER: *(Harshly.)* Quiet!

LADY S.: *(Surprised.)* What?

PETER: *(Very harshly.)* I said – *Quiet!*

ANN: What must be done with these two, General?

PETER: *(Considering them.)* The woman can do the washing-up in the lorry driver's canteen –

LADY S.: *(Angrily.)* I won't go.

PETER: *(Thundering.)* Then you'll be sent to the Farm of Correction. Which do you prefer? *(To CHILHAM.)* Let's see, you were a journalist, weren't you?

CHILHAM: *(Eagerly.)* Yes, general, my column in the *Daily Gazette*, you remember was –

PETER: *(Cutting in sharply.)* Report at the Sewage Works. *(To ANN.)* Send 'em off again.

ANN leads them out of scene and they sit down. ANN comes to PETER again.

ANN: The Concrete-Mixers' League of Marxist Youth is waiting to hear your poem, General.

PETER: I'll be ready in a minute. *(Waves her away and she returns to her seat. He paces up and down, after taking off his hat, worried about his poem.)* Damned if it's right yet, though it's good enough for the Concrete Mixers. *(Begins reciting.)*

You, my comrades, iron steps over the mountain, steel turrets
And Pylons for the power line, cables crossing the ice,
The electrified wire round the prison camp of decay and death...

That's not so good – 'the electrified wire – round the prison camp.' Cut it out, I think, Must get the end right, though. As long as that's all right, all the middle part doesn't matter – not for this lot. Let's see – *(He recites with feeling.)*

These also salute you:
The night mail flying blind among the mountains;
The diver groping over the hulks; the iceberg
Defying the Gulf Stream; a seagull in Regents Park;

All men building bridges, all good guys in blue jeans
Lowered five hundred feet down the face of the great Dam:
Amazon salutes you, and Everest, and the Northern Lights,
And diamond constellations that will not let the spaces
Cover and hide them: these too salute you.
The flags are dipping.
The guns shake the air.
Now, lift in return, comrades,
The Clenched Fist.
(Shouts this last phrase, lifting his clenched fist.)

ANN: *(Without moving, calling.)* Ready, General.

PETER: *(Shouting, as he faces imaginary entrance to big meeting.)* Ready!

Walks forward impressively, as if into meeting, but actually returns to seat. All the other characters except BENDREX applaud heartily and this applause can be supplemented offstage. BENDREX, now with light on him, should rise, in the manner of a popular political after-dinner speaker. Clapping ceases.

BENDREX: *(In the manner of such a speaker.)* Mr. Chairman, Your Royal Highness, You Excellencies, My Lords, ladies and gentlemen: I thank you for the gracious manner in which you have proposed and received this toast. I stand here, as the representative of His Majesty's Government, an unworthy representative, no doubt, but at this moment a grateful one. And, may I add, a sincere one. I believe that the government in which I have long had the honour to serve truly reflects the mind and the will of the English People. It is, in truth, *your* government. You do not know, you cannot understand, what is happening in the world. The Government does not know and cannot understand what is happening in the world. Speaking for myself – and after all I have been in office, except for a few short periods, over twenty years – I have not the least comprehension of what anything means anywhere any more. The last time I made any sense at all out of the world was in July nineteen-fourteen. Since then I have not been able to make head or tail of anything that has happened three miles from

Westminster. I might be compared to the driver of a large fast vehicle who, unknown to his passengers, who are busy reading the cricket news, has become paralysed and has lost most of his eye-sight. Ironically enough – and nobody can say I have not always appreciated irony – it is more than likely that I shall be dead before the inevitable crash occurs. But, ladies and gentlemen, if you will kindly remember that you too are among those passengers, and will reflect upon your unenviable situation, you can entertain yourselves throughout the other speeches, which I have no doubt will be even drearier than mine – although the worst of them will be good enough for such an assembly of greedy, guzzling, complacent half-wits as I see before me tonight –

After 'half-wits' there are cries of 'Shame' and 'Order' and 'Sit down' from the other characters. He manages to shout the concluding words above this noise, but has to sit down. The light on him now fades. The music comes through, the concluding bars of the movement being heard. All the characters are listening quietly. When the music stops all of them except BENDREX, *who should seem very tired, move a little in their chairs, as people, always do as they murmur to each other 'Quite good' and 'Not bad' and 'Nice opening movement', 'Excellent', and so on.*

MRS. A.: *(Going to lights and switching on, rather loud.)* Cigarettes on there, if anybody wants them. Katherine – very good first movement. *(Calling to recess.)* Delightful, David, quite delightful.

As soon as she has said this, still standing near lights, the curtain is down.

ACT TWO

Stage exactly as we left it at end of Act One, and MRS. A. is just speaking her last line again.

MRS. A.: *(Calling.)* Delightful, David, quite delightful.

SHIEL: *(Calling from recess.)* Thank you, Mrs. Amesbury.

MRS. A.: *(To DIRNIE.)* Didn't you think so, Sir James – a very delightful first movement?

SIR J.: Oh – yes. Most interesting – *most* interesting. Kept me interested all the time.

LADY S.: *(Impudently to KATH.)* You know, Mrs. Shiel, I remember now – I heard one of your husband's orchestral works once before – several years ago.

KATH.: *(Steadily, knowing what is implied.)* Yes, I'm sure you must have done.

SHIEL and LENGEL appear at the edge of recess.

LADY S.: *(To SHIEL.)* I was just saying to your wife, I distinctly remember now hearing one of your orchestral works – several years ago –

SHIEL: *(Coolly.)* Did you? Well, they *are* played now and then, y'know.

CHILHAM: Tell me, Shiel, do you consider yourself a modern?

SHIEL: What's the answer to that, Nick?

LENGEL: *(With a touch of sarcasm.)* Oh – I think he's about as modern as the *Daily Gazette*, Mr. Chilham. He's alive and kicking, you know.

CHILHAM: So are we, so are we.

PETER: *(Who has been talking to ANN.)* Oh – a lot of fellows are in the movement because they've got large romantic ideas of what it'll turn them into.

LADY S.: *(As if continuing a conversation.)* And what do *you* want then, Mr. Lengel?

LENGEL: Nothing. No, that is not true. The violin occasionally. A bottle of *Montrachet* of a good year. And a little sleep after lunch. That is all.

SIR J.: *(Heavily.)* Wouldn't suit me. Always made my way by my own efforts, and want to keep on making it.

MRS. A.: *(Who has been saying something to BENDREX.)* Are you sure you're all right, Charles?

BENDREX: *(Who isn't.)* Yes, my dear May. Don't worry…a little tired, that's all.

MRS. A.: We'd better not wait too long then. Now, David?

SHIEL: *(Telling them all.)* Now for the second movement then. *Adagio.* Still no story for you as before. You'll have to make you own. But – *(Lightly.)* – being an adagio movement, of course it's all rather sad.

MRS. A. has gone to the light switch on her previous speech and now switches off, as SHIEL and LENGEL go into recess, and she returns to her chair and settles down with the others. Music begins and they listen in silence for several bars. When MRS. A. speaks music fades out, but fades in again towards end of her speech, and fades during beginning of next, and so on. Music should come in and out frequently during this act.

MRS. A.: *(Without moving, very quietly.)* Years ago, when Rupert was about five, we used to go in Spring and stay in a little village in Hereford, not far from the Welsh border, and there it was all white with apple blossom, and when the wind blew through the orchards it would snow apple blossom, and little Rupert, who was a lovely happy child, would run among the trees and sometimes hide and then come dancing out, and laugh as white petals were shaken down…a little boy…in an orchard…years ago… I've been back since, but it isn't the same…there doesn't seem as much apple blossom now…it's changed…it's changed…

SIR J.: *(Same manner as above.)* When I was kid, my old dad would sometimes take me with him for a bit o' fishing Saturday afternoons or Sunday mornings up in one o' the becks where they said you might find a trout. Dad didn't know much about it, but he was always hopeful, and so was I, of course, being only a kid. And I'd go wading downstream, ducking under branches and standing on stone in the water and feeling the mossy stuff between my toes and putting foxgloves on my finger and lying on the bank watching the stream wink at me and then falling asleep till Dad would shake me and we'd walk back to the tram and I'd feel as if I'd been away from the street and houses and mills for years... I'd got clean out of it... I can't get out of it like that any more... I've tried all sorts of places... fairly thrown money away...but it can't be done...funny, but it can't...you're fixed...you're fixed...

LADY S.: *(Same manner.)* When I went to California four years ago with the Shirley-Wilsons, we made a trip into the Painted Desert and the Navajo Indian Reservation in Northern Arizona. The sky was pure turquoise and the colossal sandstone cliffs were like burnished copper, and it was all far away, far away, and very peaceful. The Navajo Indians have song-prayers and they used to invoke the Four Winds – the Black Wind, the Blue Wind, the Yellow Wind and the Iridescent Wind – and they used to cry, 'That is may be peaceful behind me. All is peace, all is peace.' And nobody understood or believed me when I said that I wished that I'd been born a Navajo woman...to wander with my sheep in those lost canyons...under a burning empty sky...crying to the Blue and Yellow Winds...they wouldn't believe me...yet it was true...it was true...

A pause.

PETER: It's all wrong. We sit here listening to sweet slow music, thinking nice sweet low wistful thoughts, simply because our bellies are full, we're warm and comfortable, and in an hour or two we can trot off to a good bed. To hell with sweet slow movements! To hell with wistful little thoughts! To hell with bourgeois sentimental self-indulgence! We ought to be hard – hard as steel – *until the last wrong's righted.*

KATH.: *(Wonderingly.)* He wants a world without tenderness.

PETER: Things like tenderness in the world as it is are just like bait on a hook, the soft juicy worm with the cruel steel barb hidden inside it.

KATH.: We have not enough tenderness, not too much.

PETER: Go on being tender while the possessing classes go on being tough, and all you'll get is still more misery in the world. That's why they encourage you to be soft. Be hard, and then you're dangerous.

KATH.: But if the people merely become hard, and take the power into their hands and have their revenge for what they have suffered, then there will still be injustice and suffering and misery in the world, and nothing will have been really changed, for the world will still be the same kind of world.

PETER: *(Jeering.)* I know. Let's have a nice change of heart all round.

He sits.

KATH.: More tenderness. More people listening to slow movements and being deeply stirred by music.

PETER: That's not going to stop a machine-gun.

KATH.: It would do more than that, it would make machine-guns useless.

The music comes in again, and as they listen without moving, LENGEL enters, without his violin, and the light follows him as he moves restlessly round, an unhappy man.

LENGEL: *(Slowly, bitterly.)* I will tell you something, my friends. All that makes life worth living is magic, any kind of magic, and if you no longer feel that magic is at work, bringing you miracles, then really you are dead. Except during perhaps ten of twelve bars of great music and for a minute when I am half drunk and do not realise I am half drunk, there is no more magic for me, and so I am dead and have been dead for years. *(To LADY S. closely, confidentially.)* Yes, lady, dead, and you cannot bring me back to life, though I saw a look in your eye when you asked me what I wanted that told me you would not mind trying. I am sorry. You are ten years too late. *(Going across to ANN.)* You are very sweet, my

45

child, and I will play so cunningly now that you will have to open wide your heart to yourself and be your own confessor. That may prove a little magic for you. But not for me, not for me. *(Turning to BENDREX, whispering.)* Sir, I think you are right. The very roses are not as red as they used to be. *(To KATH.)* Ah, Katherine, you were magic once for me, do you remember? Then I began to make such a nuisance of myself that I had to go away and fiddle at the other side of the globe. And all the time you loved David so dearly. Once I thought, all this love, a senseless cruel thing, but I did not know then what the face of the world looked like without it, what a vast weary face it wears – *(Turning quickly to DIRNIE.)* – a face rather like yours, you dull rich fool, rather like yours. And now its reflection fills my sky, and not four times a year do I see the sun, moon and stars. *(Angrily to them all.)* You sit there like lumps of clay. By God, I'll fiddle the dead out of their graves– the dead men and women, the great hours that are dead but once were alive – and full of magic. Look out, you clods, the earth's stirring –

Goes into recess. SHIEL's voice, sounding young and gay, is now heard calling, as if from bottom of stairs.

SHIEL: *(Off, but approaching.)* Katherine! Katherine!

KATH. now comes sharply to life, sitting up expectantly.

KATH.: *(Not answering him, for herself.)* David.

SHIEL: *(Off, but nearer.)* Kath–er–ine!

KATH.: *(Rising and answering now.)* David, I'm here. What's happened? Hurry up!

She is all eagerness. SHIEL, singing cheerfully, now bursts in, dressed in tweed coat and flannel trousers, rather untidy, and a much younger and happier man than we have seen before.

SHIEL: *(Excitedly.)* Katie – it's all right. *(Kisses her, then twirls her round, chanting.)* It's all right, it's all right, it's all right.

KATH.: *(Happily, breathlessly.)* Stop it, idiot. What happened?

SHIEL: *(Releasing her.)* You and I are going to live on top of a hill in Shropshire – a Shropshire lad and lass, in fact – and there

I am going to compose *ein Meisterstück, ein Meisterwerk* – a bloomin' masterpiece, kid –

KATH.: *(Excitedly.)* They've commissioned it.

SHIEL: They have, and I'm getting a hundred and fifty pounds *certain* – and Mac's letting us have his cottage in Shropshire for three months and all I have to pay him is one pound per week.

KATH.: *(Gasping.)* But – David – that's marvellous!

DAVID: *(Boyishly chanting.) Wundersam und Wunderschön und Wendervoll!* Honestly, Katie, all the way back I've been touching wood and crossing my fingers and dodging away from ladders.

KATH.: I should think so. When do we start?

DAVID: *(Thundering.)* Tomorrow, woman, tomorrow!

KATH.: David, we *can't possibly!*

DAVID: Tomorrow as ever was.

KATH.: Darling, it simply can't be done.

DAVID: Have I to take some other woman then?

KATH.: I'll kill her.

DAVID: Then tomorrow it'll have to be.

KATH.: I'll have to stay up half the night, there's so much to do.

DAVID: I've known you stay up half the night when –

KATH.: I haven't time to listen to your foul remarks.

DAVID: There was nothing foul –

KATH.: Millions of things to do.

DAVID: *(With mock solemnity.)* And you know what the first is.

KATH.: *(Caught.)* What? *(He holds out his arms.)* Idiot! *(But she goes and kisses him, then stays within his embrace, solemnly.)* We're awfully lucky, y'know, David. I wonder if you realise how lucky we are.

DAVID: Of course I do. *(The lights begin to fade. Gently he releases her, steps back a pace, but stares at her.)* But why are you crying?

KATH.: *(Urgently.)* Oh – David – David –

DAVID: *(Who has stepped further back in the dim light and can hardly be seen. In a far away voice.)* Why are you crying? *(Still further away.)* Why are you crying?

KATH.: *(In terrible alarm.)* David, David, come back. Everything – come back.

She drops down, sobbing quietly. The music comes in softly. The speeches that follow can come through it, but now KATHERINE stops sobbing but remains seated in the same attitude in front of the others.

SIR J.: *(Seated but looking towards the audience, quietly.)* I don't understand why the music should be so sad. I don't understand this elaborate sadness. I believe it's a kind of affectation, like finger bowls after dinner or going to dance in white kid gloves and that sort of nonsense. What really gets a fellow down is staleness, feeling weary and half-dead. I suppose you can't get that into music, but that's the real thing. Staleness. Feeling that nothing's worth the bloody great effort you have to make. I'm stale half the time nowadays. But not sad – no – that's all my eye.

LADY S.: You are sad after you have made love.

SIR J.: No. But I know what you mean. And I'll tell you what that is, now. It's a feeling I have there's a catch in this love-making business. It's like a lot of other things – it's a letdown. There's something about a good-looking woman that makes you feel, if she'll treat you right, that at last you'll get clean out of yourself, like a door suddenly opening into another sort of life. But – afterwards – you see that it hasn't worked – it's just another letdown. Nearly everything's a letdown.

PETER: *(Calmly but forcibly.)* That's your conscience – you old crook!

BENDREX: I once examined the works of Marx and Engels but couldn't find in them any suggestion that Man has a *conscience.* How does matter in motion develop a conscience? *(The light is now focused on BENDREX. BENDREX now rise slowly, and has behind his back a straw hat. The music can still be playing, very softly.)* I remember Ernest Newman saying that a beautiful slow movement of Brückner's – and also, I think, the Elgar cello concerto – were really the final bittersweet laments for a dying epoch, the swan-song of a civilisation. All slow sad music seems that to me. It has done these many years. The world I knew, the world worth living in, vanished in 1914, and since then we've all existed in a series of vast mad-houses, shrieking with hate and violence, stinking of death. *(Listens a moment, then solemnly.)* This music is an elegy for the 'boater' – *(Produces it, and regards it affectionately.)* – the dear old straw hat. *(Puts it on and lights a cigarette or cheroot. He must now be fairly downstage. The light should now suggest strong morning sunlight.)* From Straw Hat to Steel Helmet – or the Return of the Dark Ages. We ought to have realised that the world that could banish such a frail, charming, useless piece of headgear was done for. This was the straw that ought to have shown us which way the wind was blowing. *(Sighs.)* Well, we were civilised and happy once…

PETER: A few of you – the lucky ones.

BENDREX: *(Without turning to him.)* Better a few than none at all. *(Enter L. – PARKS, typical elderly manservant of Edwardian country house.)* Ah! – good morning, Parks.

PARKS: Good morning, sir. And a very nice morning too, sir.

BENDREX: Beautiful! Where is everybody?

PARKS: *(Slowly.)* Well, sire – her grace and most of the ladies and the Colonel have gone to Church. His Lordship and Captain George and the other gentlemen are down at the stables. Mr. Balfour and the young gentleman from Cambridge – Mr. Wilding – are down on the tennis court. Mr. Barrie is in the library – writing –

BENDREX: Good! Have you any idea what Mr. Barrie is writing, Parks?

PARKS: *(With a tiny grin.)* A piece about a member of Parliament, he said, Mr. Bendrex. Something about what women know, he told me. He's a very affable gentleman, Mr. Barrie is, sir.

BENDREX: Very. And if he comes out of the library, tell him he'll find me in the Italian Garden.

PARKS: Yes, sir. Would you like the papers, sir?

BENDREX: *(Taking off the hat, slowly.)* No, Parks, not this morning. *(Pauses.)* Let me see, Parks, it was in 1913 – rather suddenly too, wasn't it – that you died?

PARKS: Yes, sir. I was taken bad two days after Ascot – one o' them meat pies I always say.

BENDREX: I think you were lucky, Parks. You died quickly and in your own world. I have been dying for twenty-five years – in a world I no longer understand. I'm puzzled. I'm sad. I'm afraid… *(Gives him the straw hat.)* No, I shan't want it.

PARKS: Nothing else I can do, sir?

BENDREX: *(Sadly.)* Not just now, thank you, Parks. *(PARKS goes out L.)* May!

MRS. A.: Are you all right, Charles?

BENDREX: No, my dear. I'm not. But don't worry. *(Looks at her affectionately.)* I still think of you as a young thing, May.

MRS. A.: I'm not. I'm old too – and tired, Charles. And now I feel rather guilty because I insisted upon your coming here tonight. Don't bother about the music –

BENDREX: *(Gently.)* I like the music.

MRS. A.: *(Touching his arm.) Rest and be quiet. (BENDREX goes back to his chair. MRS. A. watches him a moment, then sits down in front of the others. Then she calls quietly.)* Rupert! Rupert!

RUPERT AMESBURY, an attractive young man in the uniform of an Air Force pilot of several years ago, appears at the entrance L. He wears no hat, looks rather untidy, and is very pale.

RUPERT: *(Quietly.) Yes, Mother? (She smiles and holds out her hands. He comes forward slowly, with a slightly stiff walk, and takes and affectionate position by her side, with his arms round her.)* Why do you bother about these parties, Mother? They're only a worry and a responsibility, and you're tired out half the time. Why don't you just chuck them?

MRS. A.: It's something to do. It keeps me going.

RUPERT: Is it worth it? You know what some of these blighters say?

MRS. A.: Yes, darling. They say I'm a silly old busybody who wants to keep herself in with the musical crowd and pretends to be important when she must know very well she isn't. Umm?

RUPERT: That's about it, and why you spend time and energy and money on 'em I can't imagine.

MRS. A.: If you were still with me, I probably wouldn't.

RUPERT: *(Disgustedly.)* Snoops Linchester – my hat!

MRS. A.: I know Rupert – thought I don't believe she's as bad as so many people make out. She's always attracted attention – and men always find her attractive – and so the others are jealous – you know –

RUPERT: Is that Tippy Horlett's kid brother?

MRS. A.: Yes – Peter. He's a clever boy – though I can't say I understand the poetry he writes – and he does talk a lot of wild nonsense sometimes – but he's alright really, Rupert.

RUPERT: They're not worth it, Mother. Drop the whole game. Take it easy.

MRS. A.: I may have to soon whether I want to or not. But while I can at all, I must make an effort – and keep going – keep going…

RUPERT: *(With increasing agitation.)* Keep going – keep going – keep going – *(Airplane engine noise now comes in. He shouts above it.)* Keep her going, you bloody fool! That strut's gone! Bank her, bank her!

MRS. A.: *(With terrified loud tone.)* Rupert! Rupert!

He is oblivious to her. The stage is rapidly darkening. The engine noise is louder and with it is a roar of wind.

RUPERT: *(Shouting at top of his voice.)* For Christ's sake – hold her now! Hold her! Hold her! No, no, she's not taking it. *(In a final scream.)* Look out!

The airplane and wind noises increase again. There is a shouting from all the characters and people. Then a terrific crash, and a complete black-out on the stage. In the silence that follows MRS. AMESBURY can be heard sobbing, but as she does this she must make her way back to her chair, so that she is seated listening with the others when

51

lights go up. Music could be faded in here for a while. ANN now rises and comes forward.

ANN: *(Imperiously.)* Peter! *(PETER comes forward. ANN stands before him in a 'take me' attitude.)* Peter – look at me.

PETER: *(After doing so.)* Very attractive young woman, Ann.

ANN: I don't know about the attractive part – though I have an idea you're right, Mr. Horlett – but *young woman* is true. And – *(With a quick change of tone.)* – you remember when you first came to stay with us, and we still had the house in Dorset? I was fifteen then. Geoffrey – I suppose because he was my brother and five years older – was my hero. And you were Geoffrey's hero. That didn't make me jealous. It turned you into a sort of super-de-luxe hero –

PETER: My hat!

ANN: Then afterwards when I went to France, you faded out a bit – but then, a year ago, it all came back – different, of course – I'd grown up and you didn't seem quite so super-de-luxe – but, you see, by then I knew I'd fallen in love with you Peter – and – no, listen – that I'd never be in love with anybody else –

PETER: Sorry, but that's nonsense, Ann. You'll be falling in love with dozens of fellows before you've finished.

ANN: *(Gravely.)* No, I shan't.

PETER: How d'you know?

ANN: I just do.

PETER: That's silly.

ANN: It may seem so to you, but it wouldn't to a girl. She'd understand. You really do know. It's something you feel – deep inside you. And – Peter – if you didn't want to be married – if you don't believe in marriage – *(Nervously but bravely.)* – that wouldn't matter – I mean – I'd come to you – without being married – or do – whatever you liked –

PETER: *(Rather gruffly.)* No…no…no…

He turns away and moves restlessly.

ANN: Listen, Peter – please!

PETER: *(Same tone.)* I am listening.

Stands still.

ANN: *(Continuing bravely.)* I read all your poetry – but I don't
understand it very well – though perhaps I will in time.
I'll try. And I don't really care about communism and
revolutions and the proletariat and all that – it never seems
quite real to me, and somehow I don't like most of the
people who are mixed up in it – the girls are *awful* – but
I'd try to care about it – and if you wanted me to, I'd got
to meetings and walk in processions and everything, if you
really wanted me to. And I don't care at all about not having
much money. I'm quite good at making do with things – ask
Mummy. With you there, I think it would be fun. Why are
you shaking your head? Don't you believe what I'm telling
you?

PETER: Yes, it's not that. Only –

Hesitates.

ANN: Only – it's hopeless? Is that it?

He does not answer, but looks away.

PETER: *(Rather impatiently.)* No, of course not.

ANN: You needn't say 'of course not' like that – as if falling in
love was something quite ridiculous and fantastic! People
have been doing it for thousands and thousands or years.

PETER: And there's been a lot of bilge talked about it. You see,
Ann, we're not interested in this romantic love business.
A good deal of it seems to us just affected nonsense, and,
anyhow, it's liable to get in the way of more important
things.

ANN: That seems to me a very queer thing for a poet to say.

PETER: *(Rather impatiently.)* There again, that's only because
you've got an old-fashioned bourgeois notion of what a
poet's like. A poet isn't a pretty-pretty ass writing elaborate
drivel about some idle girl's left eyebrow. *(In ringing tone.)*
I want to write poetry about men marching to freedom,
roads like great arrows of stone, steel towers humming and
crackling with vast electrical power, tractors ploughing and

harvesting the land for the people, express night mailplanes
rushing through space like rockets.

ANN: *(After pause, wistfully.)* And love doesn't come into it at all.

PETER: Romantic love's had more than its share of attention.
Nine-tenths of it is illusion, anyhow. It's only the sexual
instinct playing tricks on you.

ANN: And that's only a lot of words, Peter – and pretty silly
ones, if you ask me.

PETER: We believe that men and women can be comrades
together –

ANN: *(Sharply cutting in.)* Do you? I don't. Comrades my foot!

PETER: *(Rather sharply.)* All right, I don't want to give you a
lecture. Or quarrel, Ann. But this started because, seeing
that I didn't feel romantic about you, you felt sure that must
mean I was feeling romantic about some other member of
your attractive sex –

ANN: Don't be pompous! What is it that makes men pompous
as soon as they get rather cross?

PETER: *(With the air of being very patient.)* What I'm trying to
make you understand – and this is for your own good.

ANN: *(Sharply.)* Damn my own good! *(Pauses.)* Sorry, Peter, go
on.

PETER: *(Slowly, rather priggishly.)* The business of the poet in this
age isn't to maunder about his own idiotic sick fancies – in
fact, he'd better not have any – but to act as a mouthpiece –
a trumpet – for the dispossessed and downtrodden masses.
When they're set free, there might be time to have the
sort of fine feelings and write the kind of poetry you like,
although I doubt if by that time anybody will want to. In a
classless society –

ANN: *(Cutting in with cheerful rudeness.)* I know, you'll all march
round in shorts, waving flags, and being comrades.

PETER: *(Annoyed.)* Will you listen to what I'm –

ANN: *(Stopping him, loudly.)* And everybody'll sleep with
anybody and nobody'll care and it won't matter – just like
one big farmyard. *(She stops. He looks annoyed, turns away. She*

looks at him a moment, then gently.) I'm not trying to annoy
you, Peter. I'm not paying you out because – you don't
feel about me what I do about you. I see now that really
I'm older than you. And what I feel deep-down inside me
makes me wiser too. You're just a boy, who doesn't really
understand yet, talking big. Sooner or later, you'll learn. I
won't talk to you like this again – but – I shan't change. And
if you ever want me – just – let me know Peter…

*She looks at him a moment, smiles rather uncertainly, then goes
straight back to her seat and resumes listening attitude. PETER, still
in front, moves restlessly.*

PETER: *(As if to himself.)* All that I told her was true. And it's
not only the party line on the question and the opinion of
my group of Marxian neo-realists but also my own genuine
conviction – *(As if suddenly doubtful.)* I suppose – *(As if
convincing himself.)* Certainly it is. For a new age, you need a
new kind of poetry and a new kind of poet. Fortunately, I
happen to be that new kind of poet. No effort at all. Came
quite naturally to me. Sex? That's all right. Nor harm in sex
at all, or in general sexual themes. But let's treat it as the
plain straight-forward business it is – *(Here MRS. A., KATH.,
LADY S. and ANN give a little sneering snigger together. PETER stops
and regards them with suspicion.)* All this Romance – what was
it? The amusement of parasitic women of the leisure class.
An escape from reality. *(Now as if delivering a lecture to an
audience of which the four women are the only visible members.)*
The more tender-minded members of the ruling class
have always wanted to avoid the facts, why? Because the
facts have never been very pleasant to contemplate. They
didn't want to think about the world in which they were
the exploiters. So they escaped into an unreal hot-house
world of Romance, deliberately confusing the elementary
and necessary matter of the sexual instinct with all kinds of
clotted idealistic nonsense.

LADY S.: *(Calmly, clearly.)* My God, what a bore you are!

KATH.: He know this isn't true.

MRS. A.: Of course he does. There's *somebody*.

ANN: Somebody – somewhere. And why couldn't it have been me?

PETER: *(Changing his manner altogether.)*

Yet – once again – hollowness, emptiness,
Desolation inside, just as if here

(Hand on chest.)

The desert began and stretched to infinity
Sand and old bones under a brassy sky,
And the skull that grins at the vulture…

(With sharper tempo.)

Before me are houses, streets, buses, trams:
Stop, Go; Stop, Go; and Keep to the Left,
Cross Here, Tickets Please, No Smoking, All Change.
Try It Now, All The Winners, Why Pay More?
A mush of faces and a mush of minds,
A jelly of dead eyes. All magic gone.
From this bargain basement called the world.

(With great force and passion.)

Where is the garden where my lost love walks?

(Here the whole lighting should change, as if the room had vanished. Possibly the cyclorama could be lighted and one of the windows brightly lit from below. He could run back to this window and sit in it, looking down, as if from a great height. We should see nothing and nobody but him.)

We do not understand the men we are;
Our eyes are not our eyes; there is a heart
Feeding the imagination with strange blood
That's not the heart our mothers heard at night
Wondering what names to give us. Births and deaths
We celebrate in other modes of being.
Because a queen walked in a garden once,
A nameless face these eyes have never seen
Turns all the faces in the world to stone…
It might be Nefertiti the Sun queen

Before the temple where the seven-stringed harp
Could never match the music of her glance;
Or Argive Helen who set Troy on fire
And kept it burning through the long day-dream
Of eighty generations. Or Semiramis,
The golden dove, who conjured Babylon
Out of her loosened hair. It might be Deirdre
Of the white shoulders and the honey-mouth,
Or red-gold Guinevere with the April eyes,
Or Mary of Scots, the delicate witch of love,
A sweetness spilled like wine in the grey North,
Bringing poets out of the heather. O heart
That does not beat this side of the moon yet draws
The very red out of the rose, leave me in peace!

(He should come forward again now and the lights be as they were before. He speaks rather quieter now, though still as a poet reciting.)

Perhaps I still pretend. I am a child,
Wandering, lost, in a vast mansion of dreams –

Enters from L. a middle-aged woman dressed in the style of about twenty years ago, rather shabby, a woman of the provincial lower middle-class. This is MRS. CHILHAM. She comes forward timidly, hesitantly.

MRS. C.: Please, sir – could I speak to Mr. Philip Chilham –?

PETER: *(Who obviously does not see her.)*

…in a vast mansion of dreams,
And in one small room I call the facts, and think
When I'm in there that's all there is to know

MRS. C.: Begging your pardon, sir, but I wonder if I could have a word with Mr. Philip Chilham –

PETER: *(Looking right through her.)*

And wonder why my heart seems haunted there…

MRS. C.: *(Looking at him, helplessly.)* Oh – dear!

PETER: I see the paper on that room's drab wall
And I think the fading patterns are our lives…

MRS. C.: *(Earnestly.)* You see, sir, I'm his mother, Mrs. Chilham...

PETER: Music and laughter sound from the great hall
To haunt us in that room. We stop our ears...

(He breaks off to stare, as if through a mist, at MRS. C.)
Yes?

MRS. C.: *(Confidentially.)* Yes, sir. Mrs. Chilham's the name. I'd just like to have a word or two with my boy, Philip, if it could be managed without upsetting anybody.

PETER: I'll tell him. *(Makes a slight move, then stares at her curiously.)* But – aren't you –?

MRS. C.: *(Breaking in, easily, apologetically.)* Yes, sir. In Nineteen Twenty. It's a lot past that now, isn't it?

PETER: *(Wonderingly.)* Yes. I'll – tell him.

He goes back to his seat, touching CHILHAM before sitting down. CHILHAM comes forward slowly, as PETER resumes listening attitude.

CHILHAM: Mother?

MRS. C.: *(Looking at him eagerly.)* Yes, Phil. It's your mother. Are you all right, boy?

She touches him, and looks him over. After this they can sit down.

CHILHAM: I should think I am! I'm doing fine, Mother!

MRS. C.: Now, are you sure? You're not just telling me that, are you?

CHILHAM: No, why should I?

MRS. C.: Well, that used to be one of your little tricks, y'know, Phil, when you were in that frame of mind. Come home from school or from your work and tell us you were doing fine, when all the time you were getting into trouble and miserable.

CHILHAM: *(With the air of a rather boastful boy.)* Now listen, Mother. I make five thousand – *five thousand pounds* – a year. That's more than twenty times as much as Dad ever made.

MRS. C.: What do they pay you all that for?

CHILHAM: *(Same tone, with touch of defiance.)* Because my column in the *Daily Gazette* is one of the best-known features in English journalism. Everybody reads it and everybody wants to be mentioned in it. They come after me in droves, Mother, famous people – just wanting me to say something nice about them.

MRS C.: Well, I never did!

CHILHAM: *(Increasing the pace.)* I go where I like – theatres, night clubs, restaurants – all for nothing. They offer me free holidays at big hotels. Free cigars and cigarettes and cases of whisky and clothes. I've six beautiful silk dressing gowns, all brand new.

MRS. C.: You've no wife yet, Philip?

CHILHAM: *(Quickly, nervously.)* No, I got engaged, once – but we chucked it. That doesn't worry me, though. Too busy. Having too good a time. Everybody tries to get hold of me.

MRS. C.: *(Eyeing him steadily.)* You're not just telling me this, are you?

CHILHAM: *(Same tone.)* Of course I'm not. It's true every word. I've got one of the best flats in London, right in Park Lane. All the latest electric things – and you ought to see the bathroom! Just think if we'd known what was going to happen back in dirty old Dunley!

MRS. C.: *(Same steady sceptical manner.)* Is this *good* work you do, Philip?

PHILIP: *(With more irritation.)* Of course it is. Why shouldn't it be? There are thousands of fellows who'd leap at it tomorrow if they'd half a chance and knew how to handle the job. It's a lot harder than it looks, keeping going all the time, and nosing things out, and being in the know, smart and yet keeping the ordinary human interest going. I'll tell you, I may make a packet, because with all the things I get given, it's worth a lot more than five thousand a year, but I earn it all right.

MRS. C.: Is it *decent good* work?

CHILHAM: *(Faster and more nervous.)* I'm telling you it is, aren't I? And didn't I say everybody came running after me? Asking me to lunches, cocktail parties, dinners, supper parties, weekends – yes, big swells too – you'd be surprised. And it's not just actresses and society women and the film crowd who want me to mention them, I'll tell you, because some of these politicians and these big city men are just as bad. I was a week on a yacht last autumn. I went down to the South of France – Cannes, Monte Carlo, this Spring. I've got the biggest wireless set you ever saw.

MRS. C.: *(Steadily.)* I'm still asking you.

CHILHAM: *(Almost angrily now.)* And I'm telling you! I've cupboards full of clothes, dozens of silk shirts, six new dressing gowns. I've a valet – never do anything for myself. I've a big car and a chauffeur – you wouldn't recognise me if you saw me rolling round in it. Bit different from that back street in Dunley, isn't it? But, mind you, it's not just luck, I'm clever and I work hard – I tell you, Mother, you have to be on your toes to keep a contract that size with the *Gazette* and with everybody in the same game hoping to see you take a tumble – but that's all right, I can do it. I'm smart. I'm on the top and I'm staying there. I've got everything.

MRS. C.: *(Sadly.)* What's the matter with you, lad?

CHILHAM: *(Almost shouting now, hysterically.)* For God's sake – don't keep on at me like that – I'm telling you I'm right bang at the top – I've got everything – everything – *everything* –

His voice having risen almost to a shriek, he suddenly breaks down, not crying aloud, but burying his face in his hands and shaking violently. His mother looks at him pityingly now.

MRS. C.: *(Sympathetically.)* Now, lad, I could see it was no good and you were up to your old trick – but it can't be as bad as all that. If it is, just have done with it, and try to get something that makes you feel and look more like a man and less like a nervous wreck. Go back to where you came from – Dunley.

CHILHAM: *(Looking up, quietly, tragically.)* I couldn't. You don't understand, Mother.

MRS. C.: Well, it isn't the first time you've said that. But why couldn't you?

CHILHAM: *(Same tone as before.)* I'm like a man driving a racing car round and round a track. I daren't stop or make a turn – I'd crash. All I can do is to go round faster – faster – faster. And I'm sick of it. And I'm frightened.

She gives him a reassuring pat or two, while he looks at her in despair. A stalwart youngish fellow in mechanic's overalls now enters slowly L. His name is TOM, and he should speak a broader version of whatever provincial accent is suggested in DIRNIE's speech.

TOM: *(Stands, just inside.)* I'm looking for Jim Dirnie.

MRS. C.: *(Whispering.)* I'd better be going, Philip. Now you try to do better and don't be just a silly lad.

She goes off L., giving a nod and smile to TOM, who returns them. TOM now comes nearer.

TOM: I'm looking for Jim Dirnie.

CHILHAM: *(As if reciting one of his own paragraphs.)* Sir James Dirnie is seen everywhere these days, and even more – these nights. Usually with Lady Sybil – Snoops – Linchester. Sir James, I'm told, suddenly emerged as a potential big man about ten years ago in the grim engineering world up North. He was appointed general manager of Matson Jones while still in his thirties, an easy record. Since then he's gone up like a rocket, appoints two or three general managers in a morning, juggles with half a dozen big engineering firms, and is often consulted by the Minister of Defence. Has one of the prettiest yachts we know, but only sees it about twice a year.

Goes back to chair, saying in ordinary tones:

TOM: Come on, Jim.

SIR J.: *(Coming forward slowly, hesitantly.)* Oh – it's you, Tom.

TOM: Yes.

SIR J.: Well?

TOM: *(Looking hard at him.)* Can we trust you, Jim Dirnie?

SIR J.: *(With suspicion of awkwardness.)* You ought to know that.

TOM: *(Hesitating.)* Ay – but this is a big thing. And if they so much as thought I told you – it 'ud finish me.

SIR J.: *(Who talks with more accent now, as if a younger man.)* Nay – damn it, Tom – you talk as if I wasn't one of you. It's only a year since I left the Union – and then only because I had to – you can't blame be 'cos I got a bit o' promotion. Somebody's got to look after the shed, and better me than a stranger.

TOM: *(Uneasily.)* I know, Jim, I know.

SIR J.: We've been pals, haven't we?

TOM: Yes. But you know what some o' the chaps feel. If they knew I was letting you in –

SIR J.: I've told you, Tom, why I want to know. It isn't because o' the firm. To hell with the firm! But, as I told you, I want a few days off badly – I've got to see that girl again – and if I knew in advance what's going to happen, it 'ud make it a lot easier for me. Now, Tom –

TOM: All right, Jim, I didn't say I wasn't going to tell you. Only – for God's sake – be careful –

SIR J.: Of course, of course! Well, Tom?

TOM: *(Coming very close to him, lowering his voice.)* It's all settled. We're coming out a week on Monday, the whole bloody lot of us.

SIR J.: *(Earnestly.)* Is that certain?

TOM: Yes.

SIR J.: *(Slowly but with note of excitement.)* Everybody out a week on Monday! Thanks, Tom.

There is something about him, a tone, a look, that TOM suddenly dislikes, and now he puts a hand on DIRNIE's shoulder and looks closely at him.

TOM: You've got a funny look, Jim. You wouldn't rat on us, would you?

SIR J.: *(Uneasily.)* Talk sense, Tom! Here, I've got to go.

TOM: *(Not letting him go.)* I don't like that look. Something wrong with it. If a feller was going to rat on his old mates, he might have a look like that.

SIR J.: *(More uneasily.)* Oh – come off it –

TOM: *(With growing force.)* If you told the bosses what I've just told you, Jim Dirnie, you might make yourself and break the union – and – finish me. You might. You could. *(Looks strangely at him, holding him now with both hands, then with a terrible shout.)* Why – you bloody Judas Iscariot! – that's what you did!

TOM lets him go, staring at him in horror. There is horror and guilt on DIRNIE's face as he returns this stare. This is a long pause.

SIR J.: *(Very quietly, almost amusingly.)* You've been dead fifteen years, Tom. I'd have got you something, after they threw you out of the union, but of course you had to be tragic and go on a blind drunk and end up in Foley's mill pond. Fifteen years ago. I'd almost forgotten you.

TOM: *(Very quietly.)* That's a lie, and one of your poorest.

SIR J.: *(Slowly.)* You don't understand, you poor drowned ignorant big-mouth – you always talked too much, Tom, and it finished you – but you see all these fifteen years I've been alive, very much alive, with the sun shining on me, going up in the world, making money, knowing the big pots, getting into bed with some of their women, *enjoying myself* – so naturally I'd almost forgotten you.

TOM: Not you. There's a bit of you – and a damned important bit – that hasn't been alive these fifteen years no felt the sun shining nor got into bed with a nice piece nor enjoyed itself – and I'll tell you why. That bit of you isn't here.

SIR J.: Where is it then?

TOM: *(Harshly triumphant.)* At the bottom of Foley's stinking mill pond. *(Goes close to him, with sombre face.)* And now, Jim Dirnie, keep on enjoying yourself, just keep on enjoying yourself – *if you can.*

Turns and contemptuously makes noise as if spitting out, then goes off L. without a single look back. DIRNIE. stands rigid, as if he heard a terrible sentence pronounced on him. Then after considerable pause, he mutters.

SIR J.: *(Very slowly.)* Is that why? Is that why?

LADY S.: Why what, darling?

SIR J.: *(Slowly.)* Why it doesn't matter?

LADY S.: *What* doesn't matter?

SIR J.: *(Quickly now.)* Everything. You – amongst it.

LADY S.: *(Sharply.)* Don't be such a lout. Have I ever even pretended to be sentimental with you? I've been quite honest. As for you, I've always imagined that somewhere in the background there was some adventure you once had with a waitress or a barmaid or something that had left you wondering ever since why you never seemed to have all the fun you'd paid for.

Before DIRNIE. can reply there is heard off L. the sound of a girl calling 'Snoo–oops! Snoo–oops!' LADY S. hears it and starts.

SIR J.: Well, you're all wrong – there hasn't been –

LADY S.: *(Fiercely.)* Be quiet!

SIR J.: *(Annoyed.)* What the devil do you –

LADY S.: *(Passionately.)* Oh – shut up! *(She is listening again and she and we hear the voice nearer: 'Snoo–oops! Snoo–oops!'.)* Quick – get out!

In her impatience she pushes him nearer chairs. After giving her a wondering look, he shrugs his shoulders and returns to his chair, at once resuming listening attitude. LADY S's sister, DEBORAH, now enters from L. She is a girl about seventeen dresses as a school-girl on holiday would be dressed about twenty years ago – hair 'not up', etc. She is a tallish slender girl, obviously fond of outdoors.

DEBORAH: *(Rather excitedly.)* Snoops, I've been looking for you all over the place. The extraordinary thing about you is that when you're not wanted nobody can move you and that when you *are* wanted it takes everybody *hours* to find you. And that, of course, is because you're just a young fathead.

LADY S.: *(Now a youngster again.)* I like that, Deb! You're only two years older than I am – and you talk as if you were about *ninety*. What's happened?

They get into a schoolgirlish huddle now.

DEBORAH: It's not half as bad as they said it would be.

LADY S.: How many will there be left?

DEBORAH: What a foul way of asking, Snoops! As if you just *counted* horses, like sheep. You mean, *who'll* be left?

LADY S.: Well – who – which – whatever you like – only *tell me*, hurry up!

DEBORAH: Whitefoot's not going to be sold.

LADY S.: *(Quickly.)* He's no good to us.

DEBORAH: Don't be such a selfish little chump, Snoops. The point is, he's not going and I adore him. Next – we're keeping Brownie and Mack –

LADY S.: *(Quickly.)* Bags I Brownie!

DEBORAH: Don't *snatch.* *(Laughs.)* I'd like to *see* anybody snatching Brownie – I suppose he must weigh about a ton –

LADY S.: I know. He's beastly fat, but we'll soon set about him.

DEBORAH: *(Pleasantly lofty.)* We? As a matter of fact, Snoops, you'll do jolly little riding with me these next two years. I'm definitely going to Madame Marcier's.

LADY S.: *(Promptly.)* You can *have* Madame Marcier's. It'll be beastly. June Franklin's sister went, and June said she loathed it the whole time – no fun and open air – and the most awful French girls – and a general atmosphere of frightful stuffiness –

DEBORAH: *(Pleasantly if proudly.)* I know. I've heard lots about it. But as soon as that's over, I'll be out – really grown-up, going to dances and everywhere, while you're still in the schoolroom, whacking into stew and sago pudding and hiding out of everybody's way. They'll let you stay up just to have a look at me in my new ball dress –

LADY S.: *(Disgustedly.)* Oh – rot! Why, you always get sleepier than I do.

DEBORAH: I shan't then. Different sort of life you see. We've got nothing to do now, once the day's over, but to fall asleep. But then – when I'm out – it'll be *entirely* different. Fun! Loads of it! Mind you, Snoops, although you're such an idiot *and* the most terrible grabber, I wish you were coming out too at the same time. Then we could go round together and have a lot of private jokes. Only two years, though, I'll have to wait for you – and then we'll *really* start – *(Breaks off, looking curiously at LADY S's face, turned away from the audience.)* What's the matter? *(LADY S. shakes her head and DEBORAH stares curiously at her as if she is slowly taking in the fact that something has changed her young sister.)* Snoops – there's – something wrong about this – isn't there? *(Still staring.)* You *are* Snoops, aren't you, darling? *(LADY S. nods assent.)* I didn't really think you weren't – I mean, you must be *you* just as I'm *me* – so that's all right – but you're all changed – and we're not... *(Bewildered, slowly.)* You see, we were in our corner of the garden at Brankleford – and it was the time when Father began selling so many things – and I hadn't gone then to Madame Marcier's – and I was looking forward to coming out afterwards – growing up – the fun we'd have but – we never did, did we? – at least, I didn't – you seem –

LADY S.: *(Sharply, tragically.)* No. No, no. Deborah, it hasn't been like – like you thought it would be – after we'd grown up. It went all wrong somewhere. Perhaps because *you* weren't there, after all, Deb. You just slipped away. You went back to our corner of the garden at Brankleford – for ever. And I've been going further and further away. And less and less things have really *mattered.* That time, that place – they were solidly real to me and could make me feel content. Everything since then has just wobbled and slipped about. I've burned up each day in the hope that tomorrow would be better. It never was. I seem to have been travelling in the wrong direction. I ought to have run back – to you at Brankleford. I know now. Underneath I never grew up, I never faced life properly. It's all wrong, I suppose, but there it is – and – Deborah – what shall I do? *(In tears now, seizing*

DEBORAH by the arm, staring hopelessly at her.) Tell me, tell me
– what shall I do?

*DEBORAH is sympathetic but can only stare helplessly at her. While
they are still silent, RUPERT AMESBURY enters slowly from L. LADY
S. does not see him, but DEBORAH does.*

DEBORAH: *(Quietly.)* Rupert, I don't know what's the matter
with Snoops.

RUPERT: *(Quietly.)* I shouldn't worry if I were you.

DEBORAH: No, but you see, I know she's unhappy – I've felt it
for a long time – but it's all so puzzling – and I don't know
what to do.

RUPERT: *(Quietly.)* I don't think there's anything you can do,
Deb.

DEBORAH: There must be *something.* Did she fall in love with
somebody – and it went all wrong?

RUPERT: No. I doubt if she's every really been in love with
anybody.

DEBORAH: She says being grown-up isn't like what we thought
it was going to be.

RUPERT: *(Gently.)* No, I don't suppose it is.

DEBORAH: She wants to be back with me at Brankleford now,
but when we were there she was always wishing to be out of
it and grown-up.

*They stand together looking down at LADY S., who now rises slowly,
hopelessly as if oblivious even of DEB's presence now. As she turns to
go back to her place, DEB. put out a hand to stop her, but is promptly
checked by RUPERT. So they watch LADY S. go back and resume
former listening attitude.*

RUPERT: You'll just not have to worry about her, Deb.

DEBORAH: I must, you know. She's Snoops. Nothing changes
that.

RUPERT: No, but there isn't anything you can do for her – yet.

*The concluding music of this slow movement now comes through very
softly. Off R. SHIEL's voice is heard calling, not loudly but clearly.*

SHIEL: *(Off R.)* Dr. Ebenthal. Doctor Ebenthal

SHIEL now appears on platform – or if he can do it easily he can come down from platform – but must remain towards R. He is now as we saw him first. There emerges from the L. DR. EBENTHAL, an elderly Austrian-Jewish musician, who should be dressed in a foreign style of twenty or thirty years ago. He speaks with a marked foreign accent.

DR. E.: *(Smilingly.)* Yes – David – I am here. I have been listening.

SHIEL: *(A pupil again, nervously.)* Will it – do?

DR. E.: Yes, David – it will do. It is not perfect. You are not Mozart. But now – you are a good musician. You have something to say in your music and you are beginning to understand how it can be said. Yes, I am pleased.

SHIEL: Hooray! But that first movement's not right yet, is it?

DR. E.: No, I think you announce your second subject too early, before you have properly developed the first. And it will not, that second subject, I think, bear the weight you put on it – it is too small a thing.

SHIEL: *(Humbly.)* I know. I ought to rewrite that first movement. This second's better, don't you think?

DR. E.: Much, much better. It is not easy to get the – the true colour – of it just with the piano. I hope you have scored it lightly – especially that middle section – mostly wood wind, eh? I thought I heard some good passages for oboes and clarinets, eh?

SHIEL: *(Pleased.)* Yes, maestro. But the last movement's the best. I hope you'll agree.

Makes a move as if to return to recess, but is halted on way by DR. EBENTHAL's next remark.

DR. E.: *(Wistfully.)* Ach, David, we should be in Vienna again – and when you had finished we would take that score into my corner at Schwiegler's.

SHIEL: *(Shortly.)* No, doctor.

DR. E.: *(Surprised.)* But, David, you were happy once going to Schwiegler's – and you loved our Vienna. Have you changed then?

SHIEL: *(Gently.)* No, I haven't changed. But Vienna has.

DR. E.: *(Making allowances.)* Well, a little, I suppose – everything does –

SHIEL: *(Quietly but bitterly.)* No, a lot. Vienna's quite different. If you were there now, they'd make you – *(Checks himself.)* No, you couldn't begin to understand how much it's changed. Or the things they do there now. I can't tell you what I feel about it – but the music might tell you.

He has said this, turning, just before going back into recess. DR. E. looking bewildered backs out L. The music comes out stronger and is terribly sad. Just before final notes are sounded, the room looks exactly as it did when the movement began. Music ends. There is the same stir as before, though now rather more subdued.

MRS. A.: *(Quietly, but firmly.)* Yes, I liked that – very much indeed. *(She can do lights again here.)*

LADY S.: *(Coolly.)* M'yes. Drags a little, doesn't it?

PETER: *(To ANN rather than the rest.)* Too romantic and soft.

ANN: *(Whispering.)* I think I like being romantic and soft.

LENGEL: *(Appearing from recess, sarcastically.)* Everybody still awake?

SIR J.: *(Rather heavily.)* Oh – yes – nothing to send me to sleep here. Played it very well too.

KATH.: Thank you, Nick.

MRS. A.: *(To BENDREX, as SHIEL appears.)* Charles – are you all right.

BENDREX: *(Slowly opening his eyes.)* Yes, my dear. Just thinking, remembering.

Closes his eyes again. As MRS. A. looks at him again, KATH. puts a finger to her mouth and shakes her head.

MRS. A.: Is everybody quite comfortable?

SIR J.: *(Bluntly.)* No, I'm not.

ACT THREE

Scene same as Act Two.

LADY S.: Now, Jimmy, don't be a nuisance.

MRS. A.: *(Rises.)* I'm so sorry, Sir James, can I –

SIR J.: I wasn't talking about the seat I'm in – or the temperature of the room. They're all right. But I'm not comfortable. *(To LADY S.)* And neither are you. *(Indicating CHILHAM.)* And neither is he.

LADY S.: Nothing wrong with me – except, if I must confess, I feel a trifle sleepy.

SHIEL: *(Easily.)* My fault. These long slow movements can be a bit of a bore.

CHILHAM: Rather agree with you there, Shiel.

SHIEL: I was afraid you would. Well, we must try and wake you up. The next movement's much brighter.

LENGEL: *(With sarcasm.)* At the beginning you would almost think you were in the Savoy Hotel.

LADY S.: Mr. Lengel, you don't seem to like us very much.

SIR J.: Why should he?

LENGEL: Oh – I'm rapidly becoming just a nasty old fiddler – don't mind me –

KATH.: Nick, don't be silly.

MRS. A.: We're ready, David.

SHIEL: *(Cheerfully.)* All right. Well – now – the third and last movement. Not very long but a bit complicated. *Allegro–agitato–maestoso nobile*, which means that it starts in a nice brisk cheerful style, to wake you up, then it becomes very agitated – y'know, worrying about life, and then it turns all grand and noble, just to end up with.

ANN: *(Impulsively, sincerely.)* Good!

SHIEL: Ah – you approve of it turning all grand and noble in the end – then?

ANN: Yes, of course.

SHIEL: So do I. *(SHIEL and LENGEL go into recess. All settle down a before and music begins. BENDREX remains motionless throughout these scenes, with eyes closed. Once mood of music is established, it begins to fade as dialogue starts. SHIEL just off, very loud.)* Wake up!

LENGEL: *(Just off, very loud.)* Come on, wake up!

SHIEL: *(Coming in, with tremendous zest and spirits.)* Come on, come on, wake up, wake up!

LENGEL: *(Entering in the same manner.)* It's reveille. Rise and shine, my little soldiers, rise and shine. Wake up, wake up!

ANN, PETER, LADY S. and CHILHAM rise at once. MRS. A. and KATH. and DIRNIE first sit up sharply, then can rise afterwards.

LISTENERS: *(Indignantly.)* We haven't been asleep. We haven't been asleep.

SHIEL: *(In ringing tones.)* You've been asleep for year and years.

Presents a large revolver at CHILHAM's head. He starts ludicrously.

LENGEL: *(Extravagantly kissing MRS. A's hand.)* My dear, dear lady – can't I persuade you – as a favour – to wake up?

MRS. A.: *(With surprise, perhaps pleasure.)* Well, yes, you can.

SHIEL: *(Roaring to KATH.)* My love, my love, wake up!

Kisses swiftly but passionately.

KATH.: *(Melting at once.)* Oh – David!

LENGEL: *(Sternly to DIRNIE.)* Now you – see this, eh? *(Produces from his coat a very large stiff folded document tied with red ribbon and holds it out.)* This makes you chairman of both British Thomson-Houston and General Electric –

SIR J.: *(Astonished and delighted.)* Good God!

LENGEL: *(Cheerfully.)* That's better. Wake up! *(Promptly bangs him over the head with the document, then turns to LADY S.)* What about you? Come here.

LADY S.: *(Enjoying herself.)* Darling – certainly.

They kiss and embrace with enthusiasm. SHIEL is now tackling ANN, smilingly.

SHIEL: Still asleep?

ANN: No – really not. *(Runs and nestles against him enthusiastically, then looks at him meltingly.)* I think *you're* sweet.

PETER: *(Coming down to face SHIEL, rather harshly.)* Wait a minute, Shiel. Don't forget I'm a poet. You needn't tell me to wake up. I'm never asleep.

SHIEL: And you couldn't be wider awake?

PETER: No.

SHIEL: I wonder.

Takes out revolver and coolly fires at him.

PETER: *(Startled and angry.)* Why, you fool –

SHIEL: *(Cutting in, masterfully.)* That's all right. You're still alive. And awake. *(Taking them all in.)* You're *all* alive and awake. That's better.

LENGEL: Much better.

As these two hurry back to recess, the four women form a little excited intimate group in front, with the men forming a similar group behind and talking in dumb show.

ANN: *(With happy intimacy.)* I used to think I'd like to be a boy, but now I wouldn't be anything but a girl. It's lovely to be a girl.

MRS. A.: Of course it is, darling –

KATH.: Lovely, lovely –

LADY S.: To be a girl.

ANN: I simply can't describe what I feel some mornings – not special mornings – and yet everything's marvellous – as if you were going through a wood after a long long winter – and all the trees were budding and there were primroses and violets and the birds were beginning to sing again – and all *that* can be going on just with me myself…

As her voice dies away, LADY S. comes in.

LADY S.: But that's only the beginning. After Spring comes Summer, and after buds and pale early flowers the hushed green shade of the woods and in the gardens great crimson roses. And in the nights of summer, made magical by men's

desire of us, we are ourselves great crimson roses, and our
very blood has sweetness and perfume…

KATH.: But the joy can go deeper still, down and down to
the very roots, the strange sweet tangled roots. To feel the
unborn child stirring, the peace that follows the pains, the
groping little mouth reaching for life, the sudden lovely
weight of a sleepy child…

MRS. A.: I've known a woman's spring, summer, autumn – and
now in my winter at least I live again in memory – and
safely, safely now, for what was sure and happy cannot
be spoilt now but must remain sure and happy. And any
evening when I'm tired of friends and music and books I
can go down one of these magical corridors of memory, and
everything is waiting for me, asking to come to life again…

CHILHAM: *(Very happy and excited.)* Ladies, ladies! *(They now
make a general group, very intimate.)* I want to include you all
in an invitation. Y'know, after I've been dining out or after a
first night and supper somewhere, I like nothing better than
to go back to my flat, get into one of my dressing-gowns,
give myself a last whisky-and-soda – and then, turning over
in my mind the day's experiences, the people I've met, the
fun and talk we've had, to write a leisurely paragraph or two,
usually in my best vein. In fact, that's when I'm at my best.
Now why shouldn't you all join me, and see me at my best.

SIR J.: Any time I'm free. But you know what I'd like to do –
and by God I will – is to take you all in my yacht –

ANN: } *(Very quickly.)* South Seas!
LADY S.:} Why not, Jimmy, let's go! And Jamaica and
Martinique and Trinidad.

CHILHAM: } Bali – mustn't miss that – Bali.
PETER: } Cocos and Galapagos –

KATH.: Hawaii and Samoa and Tahiti –

ANN: } Gosh!
MRS. A.:} And the Great Barrier Reef, off Queensland. All my
life I've wanted to have a look at the Great Barrier Reef.

SIR J.: *(Happily.)* Good! Don't care what it costs. What you people don't understand is what a chap like me gets out of it all. It isn't just making money. There's a whole world of adventure in finance that you don't understand. Plans, campaigns, strategies, hair-breadth, escapes, battles, wounds, victories. I've had ten times the fun out of work that I've ever had out of anything else. Once I'd got my start – and that wasn't so easy or pleasant, I'll admit – but once I was off, I enjoyed every damned minute of it.

PETER: *(Happily.)* You've never climbed a good mountain, have you? That's a living. Three or four of you – fellows you can trust – starting in the queer green dawn – the peaks rising like a parade of friends and enemies – the chancy tactics – the thrill of each new bit of conquest – the halts on the ledges – the cold pure air of the heights – the last desperate push to the summits – *(Breaks off to cry, loudly.)* I don't know what life's about – but – by heaven! – it's good.

SEVERAL OF THE OTHERS: It's *good!*

PETER: *(Triumphantly.)* Yes, and soon it's going to be much better. Look what man's done in his short space of time.

CHILHAM: He's almost conquered the world.

SIR J.: Science, engineering, industry!

PETER: Man's discovered how to travel like an arrow – on the ground, underneath the sea, in the air.

CHILHAM: He's surveyed all the continents, charted all the seas, and made his own lakes and rivers.

SIR J.: He produces substances that never existed before. He creates new variations in plant and animal life.

PETER: He observes and calculates the movements of vast galaxies of stars and the tiniest changes of electricity within the atom. Soon it'll be he who will be the God, giving his commands to nature.

ANN: *(With enthusiasm.)* Hooray! And then we'll have more and more and more fun.

LADY S.: We needn't wait until then. We'll have some now.

SIR J.: *(Very heartily.)* Do you know, I *like* you all, I do. *(Laughs heartily.)*

KATH.: And we like you.

CHILHAM: Of course we do.

He laughs too. There must now work up a definite suggestion of a very intimate group being merry together. The atmosphere is more important than the speeches. Everybody must relax.

PETER: I'm such a chump, but I don't mean it really.

SIR J.: I don't believe you do. *(Laughs, and PETER laughs, and the women laugh.)*

MRS. A.: *(Laughing.)* Of course when you think of it all – it's really very funny, isn't it?

LADY S.: *(Laughing.)* It's just divinely idiotic. *(Laughs.)*

CHILHAM: You've just got to laugh! *(Laughs.)*

SIR J.: One minute we're all moping – about nothing – and then – *(Laughs.)*

ANN: *(Laughing.)* Oh – look at Peter! *(Laughs still harder.)*

MRS. A.: *(Laughing.)* Really – you are absurd, Ann – really.

ANN: *(Laughing.)* But – I begin to think – of all the silly things – I've ever known –

SIR J.: *(Exploding.)* So do I.

This sets them all over and its works up to a crescendo of laughter, all rocking and gasping in a compact group. Just as this is beginning to subside, in waves of gurgles and gasps, eye-wipings, etc., there is a terrible cry – which must suggest an agony of fear and pain – from BENDREX. This breaks up their group at once, and they all look at BENDREX who rises slowly and rather unsteadily to his feet, and looks ghastly.

BENDREX: *(More to himself than to them.)* I used to think – privately – that nothing was very real or very important. I was wrong. Now I know better. Pain is very real. Fear is very important. Pain and fear – *(He groans as if shaken by another heart spasm.)* Fear and pain. Sometimes I suspected them. I'd wake up in the middle of the night and then wonder if fear and pain might be waiting for us in the end.

They are. They catch you alone in the dark. The empty dark, because nothing stays with you, not one of the things you've made such a fuss about. The houses and streets, the clubs and theatres, the gardens of your friends, cities and whole countrysides, they all go streaming away; and then there's just you left behind in the empty dark, and then suddenly you find fear and pain there. They need plenty of space – perhaps the whole universe... *(In small far-away tones.)* Everything streaming away...cascades of darkness... not only streets and houses – and people – but the faces and voices of friends – going away...going away...going.

He collapses into his chair and remains motionless until his next speech comes. The others, who have been looking at him with wonder and fear, are now terribly uneasy and are beginning to be very much afraid too.

CHILHAM: *(Nervously.)* I'm afraid. I always have been. You see, a germ – the tiniest thing you could imagine – what can it do? I'll tell you. That tiny germ can destroy everything you've got that makes life worth living. It can eat your clothes and pictures and books and houses, and your profession and your friends, eating and eating away, until there's nothing left. Just the tiniest germ can do that.

PETER: *(Uneasy tone.)* We used to live near a lunatic asylum in the country. The lunatics used to come out in a shambling sort of procession, muttering and giggling and gibbering. I used to think – I do so still – what if everything went blank for me and then when I was properly conscious again I found myself in that procession, shambling and muttering and gibbering like the rest of them?

SIR J.: People laugh at the idea of D.T.s – (delirium tremens). Nothing to laugh at, let me tell you. I had a brother who went down with D.T.s, and I'll never forget it. He said things – things like big crabs – came out of the wall to get at him – they made a dry scuttling sort of noise, he said – and – by God! – I began to hear that noise myself. I tell you. There's something inside us – might be some peculiar cells in the brain – that's got whole lashings of fear to play with. Let one of those cells – or whatever they are – set to work on you and – by thunder – you're not just afraid, you're lost in a damned nightmare jungle of fear.

ANN: Cats! They terrify me. I can't help it. They *terrify* me. I once went out to tea and there were four or five of them – and – was nearly sick and had to run out. I've always been afraid that one day I'd find myself in a *roomful* of them and not be able to get out – and then they'd *turn* on me – ugh! – horrible!

KATH.: About two months before my first baby was born, I saw a woman in the park with a child – and this poor little thing had a veil over its face – but just as I passed the wind blew this veil aside – and I saw this – this – creature – had a face – And I couldn't forget it, and night after night I couldn't sleep and I prayed and prayed that my baby shouldn't be like that. And even now, just talking about it, I feel afraid again.

LADY S.: Dreams! I loathe them. I'm not frightened of ordinary things at all. I've taken the craziest risks and not given a damn. But dreams get me down. These queer shifting sorts of rooms and places you find yourself in, and the strange people, like people you know and yet not like them – devils – who come up and stare and mutter at you…horrible…

SIR J.: *(Grimly.)* If you go on dreaming after you're dead –

LADY S.: *(Almost screaming.)* Shut up, you damn fool! Do you think I haven't thought of that?

MRS. A.: *(Beginning quietly.)* I was once staying in an old house in the country. It was supposed to be haunted, and though nobody saw any ghosts, it certainly had an unpleasant atmosphere. As if somebody, who'd lived in it a long time, had been terribly unhappy there. Well, one night in this house I woke up in an *agony* of fear. It was just as if in a mad dream I'd reached a place, a world perhaps, where there was *nothing* but fear – and that I'd pulled myself out of this dream, deliberately awakened myself up, only to find it was still true. Fear – pure fear – like an enormous blackness, a weight of horror, was pressing down –

BENDREX: *(Cutting through with a terrible cry.)* Aie! Aie! *(They look at him, then slowly he sits up in a ghastly parody of a chairman at a meeting and speaks now very clearly with a kind of horrible irony.)* The giant ringmaster of our circus is Pain. You must have wondered why things are for ever in a flux, why all the living never rest but hurry and scurry and keep changing their shape. Pain is cracking his whip in the ring. Behind the scene is Pain. And waiting at all the exit doors is Pain. There is no escape; there is nothing else; and all the roads lead one way. *(Nods with final irony.)* Ladies and gentlemen, I wish you a pleasant journey.

He relaxes, closes his eyes, and now remains motionless.

SIR J.: *(After a pause.)* I think I've known it all along. Yes, all along! That's why I've said, 'Come on, let's make a night of it! Hello! Sit at my table. Bring some champagne. Tell the band to put some life in it. Whoopee!' *(With cutting scorn.)* Whoopee, my foot! D'you think I'd spend my money on the God-damn fools if there hadn't been something I wanted drowning inside – *(Checks himself, remembering.)* Drowning! That's it. *(Faces them, like prisoner confessor in low miserable tone.)* Listen, I'm guilty, see? Guilty, that's what I am. Years ago I got myself a job by ratting on a pal. It gave me my start but it finished him. He drowned himself. Yes, he drowned *himself* – but *(With tremendous intensity.)* Christ! – I can't drown him. I'm guilty, see? Guilty.

CHILHAM: *(In frightened tone.)* You're not the only one. My mother was a working woman – but she saved some money – and I said I'd invest it for her – I had to get to London – daren't ask her for it – so I took it. Of course I'd have paid her back, but she died – quite suddenly she died – before I could pay her back. And now all the time she watches me. And won't believe a word I tell her.

LADY S.: *(Same tone.)* After my sister Deborah died, I didn't care a damn – or thought I didn't – but I was nearly caught with a man in a bedroom at home – and my maid got me out of it by taking the blame herself. She was turned out, but I promised to look after her. But I didn't. She wrote and tried to see me. I dodged her. I've always dodged things but that was the worst. I know I'm a swine.

ANN: *(Wonderingly.)* What is it that falls like a great lead weight and crushes all our happiness?

PETER: Why do I feel now as if I too had betrayed my friends and he had drowned himself?

KATH.: Why should the maid that was turned out and never helped begin to haunt me too?

SIR J.: I couldn't have taken that money from my mother – I always have her plenty – and yet I feel guilty of that too. Guilty, guilty, guilty!

MRS. A.: We are all guilty creatures. But we can beg forgiveness.

ANN: Yes, we can beg forgiveness.

KATH.: We can beg forgiveness.

LADY S.: *(Distressed.)* Oh, no, we can't. There's nobody to forgive. *(She sobs quietly.)*

SIR J.: *(Harshly.)* We can't beg forgiveness from an empty throne. Heaven's to let, but we seem to have a longer lease of Hell.

CHILHAM: *(Miserably.)* It's true. There is a Hell and we are in it.

As they seem to sink into misery, the music plays a triumphant cord or two, then SHIEL appear, looking impersonal, strange, majestic.

SIR J.: *(Harshly.)* This is James Dirnie, Shiel, and I tell you we are all guilty and are in Hell.

SHIEL: *(In calm impersonal tone.)* James Dirnie may be in Hell, but what is James Dirnie? Nothing. And what is David Shiel? Nothing. In this world of appearances, yes, something – but only one faulty nervous system among billions, a name, a date or two, a few addresses, some remarks in the reference books, an ill-assorted bundle of habits, a rotting bag of tricks. In the real and great world, David Shiel is a mere appearance, a part, a mask, a shadow. So I tell you – sink deeper, deeper. Forget and then remember. Go down and down and discover what you are.

He raises a hand and as they group themselves, closely together, the music announces a final majestic theme, and now the lights change so that the room seems to have vanished and we see a wide sky behind and in front of it two columns that might be part of some dateless temple. The whole effect should suggest humanity itself outside time.

At the same time the dead should be grouped at one side, in such way to as to suggest there are countless numbers of them, that we are only seeing the beginning of a vast crowd.

PARKS: We are those that you call the dead.

They begin to drift away.

MRS. A.: *(Urgently.)* Rupert – my son – the child I bore –

RUPERT: *(Far away.)* Your son even yet – but something more.

CHILHAM: *(Appealingly.)* But you came and spoke to me, you, my mother.

MRS. C.: *(Far away tone.)* Yes, my son – yet already, another.

SIR J.: *(Agitatedly.)* I had a friend once – he was drowned.

TOM: *(Cool, far away.)* A fool in a dream was all I found.

SHIEL: *(Calling.)* Master, this music we seem to make. How does it come our way?

DR. E.: *(The last of the dead.)* The spirit stirs the depth of the lake, and we are the fountains that play.

The dead have faded out now, and the living make a close group as if they were one creature.

ANN: *(In wondering tone.)* I have gone down, down, and I am alive and awake, but I do not know who I am, and it does not seem to matter, for I am alive, awake, and have no sorrow.

PETER: I am remembering… To crouch in the cave and see the great deer in the knobs and hollows of the stone and then to paint the great deer and the other creatures on the walls of the cave…

KATH.: It was hard at first to come down from the bare hills into the thick forests, with the children afraid of the shadows… but afterwards it was better…

LADY S.: When the men with dark faces who came for the metal went back to their ship we went with them, and afterwards when it was calm on a blue sea we sat and combed our yellow hair which the dark men loved…

MRS. A.: Across the desert came the soldiers with their great shining helmets and the faces of gods and goddesses upon their shields and they burned our cities…

PETER: *(Ecstatically.)* I remember from the time when the world grew cold and the ice came…

KATH.: *(Ecstatically.)* I remember from the time of the great flood…

MRS. A.: *(Same.)* I remember from the time of the baking of bricks and the shaping of pottery…

CHILHAM: *(Same.)* I remember from the time of the first canal…

SIR J.: *(Same.)* I remember from the time of the first forging…

ANN: *(Same.)* Remembering and remembering, not in any one time or place…

LADY S.: *(Same.)* But in all times and places since there were men and women…

KATH.: *(Same.)* Always going on and on, young then growing old, finding love or losing it…

SIR J.: And the guilt of one is the guilt of all and one cannot suffer without all suffering…

MRS. A.: And sorrow and expiation and forgiveness are themselves a kind of deep remembering…

PETER: *(With great joy.)* And now there cannot be you and I, or any separate selves, and we are walled in no longer but are free, free!

The music plays a few majestic chords and a blaze of light can come from the recess.

SHIEL: *(Just off, very impressively.)* Hail to the one great heart and mind!

THE FOUR WOMEN: *(Together or split up.)*

Now can we salute,
The heart beating through our hearts,
The earth's great heart
That is love itself.

THE THREE MEN: *(Together or split up.)* Now can we salute
the one mind that is ours yet infinitely greater than ours
unresting until the whole world is aware of itself and wise.

ALL: *(In a tremendous shout.)* Hail!

ONE VOICE: *(Quietly and slowly.)*
Forgetting much, remembering more, we find
The one great heart, the ever-enduring mind,
All love, all wisdom. So let nothing sever
This light, this blinding vision. Keep us for ever.

ALL: *(Strongly rhythmical.)* Keep us for ever. Keep us for ever,
ever and ever. Ever and ever.

*The are saying this to the final chords of the music, and now they are
back in their places as their voices fade and the music grows louder,
and the room looks as before and they are in their listening attitudes.
BENDREX, who should be turned away from the audience, keeps
perfectly still. Now when the music stops, they all stir and make the
usual vague appreciative noises.*

MRS. A.: *(Who has had a glance at BENDREX, softly.)* Just a
moment, please, everybody. I know we all want to talk
about this really great work, but I can see that poor Charles
Bendrex is asleep and I don't feel we ought to wake him.
He needs all the rest he can get. So will you be very quiet
please, until we get into the other room, where there are
drinks and sandwiches. *(They murmur agreement. She calls
softly into recess.)* Thank you so much, David. And you, Mr.
Lengel. We'll all tell you what we think about it in the other
room. We don't want to wake Mr. Bendrex. *(She turns and
sees CHILHAM looking curiously at the place in the set where the
dead entered.)* No, Mr. Chilham, there's nothing there, we go
this way, you know.

She indicates to him, now that he's turned, then exit.

CHILHAM: *(Strangely confused.)* Yes – of course – I was forgetting.

CHILHAM takes another puzzled glance at the wall.

MRS. A.: *(Gravely regarding him.)* What is it, Mr. Chilham?

CHILHAM: *(Exchanging bewildered glance.)* Oh – nothing – really.
I'm sorry – it must have been the music.

MRS. A.: I hope you enjoyed it.

CHILHAM: *(Confused.)* Oh – yes – fine! But I'm afraid I've got into a bad habit – instead of listening properly – of thinking about all sorts of things – you know –

MRS. A.: Yes, I do that too.

CHILHAM: *(In a sudden rush of confidence.)* I came originally from a place called Dunley, y'know, Mrs. Amesbury. Just working people. My mother – *(Suddenly checks himself, giving short laugh.)* here – I don't know why I should bore you will all that stuff.

MRS. A.: You're not, Mr. Chilham. You were saying – you mother –?

CHILHAM: *(Rather uneasily.)* My mother? Oh – I've forgotten – some bit of nonsense – *(Turns to KATH. who has come down near exit with them.)* Quite an interesting work, I though it, Mrs. Shiel.

KATH.: You didn't find it dull? I was afraid you might.

CHILHAM: No, not at all – slow movement a bit long, perhaps – but the rest of it first-class.

MRS. A.: I'm sure everybody enjoyed it *enormously*, Katherine my dear, and you ought to be very proud. Come along.

She leads the way out, followed by KATH. We now hear what PETER and ANN are saying, as they move slowly down.

ANN: You don't mind, Peter, if we don't stay long now?

PETER: No. One drink and a word with Shiel – and I'm through, if that suits you.

ANN: *(Hesitatingly, with sincere charm.)* Yes, rather. And – Peter – would you be awfully bored – if you didn't' just drop me at home – but came in – and talked to me a bit? –

PETER: No, I'd like that, Ann. But what do you want me to talk about?

ANN: Anything you like that's really *serious*.

PETER: Oh – if that's how you feel. I'll probably talk your head off.

ANN: My head *wants* to be talked off. Though I'd like to say a few things too.

PETER: *(Amused.)* What things?

ANN: I don't know – yet. But when I'm listening to music, like that, I get the *queerest* ideas sometimes –

They go out. Now DIRNIE and LADY S. who have been whispering move down. LADY S. has watched PETER and ANN. DIRNIE has watched her.

SIR J.: You needn't look so bitterly at those two kids. They can't help being young.

LADY S.: I wasn't thinking about them. I was wondering why you'd suddenly decided to go north tomorrow.

SIR J.: *(Rather awkwardly.)* Well – I dunno – suddenly thought I'd like to have a look round. Haven't been up there for some time. There was a fellow I knew years ago – *(Checks himself suddenly.)*

LADY S.: *(Looking at him curiously.)* Well?

SIR J.: Nothing. I'd finished. Better go in, hadn't we?

LADY S.: Just a minute. We can't talk in there.

SIR J.: We can do all the talking we want to do afterwards.

LADY S.: No, you see that's what I was going to say. There won't be any afterwards. I'm going to slip away very soon and I want to go home – alone.

SIR J.: *(Quietly.)* I see.

LADY S.: I'm not angry or anything, my dear.

SIR J.: I didn't think you were.

LADY S.: I'm – just – well, that's how I feel.

SIR J.: And that's why you'd better not go home – alone.

LADY S.: What do you mean?

SIR J.: Because you're not angry. You're unhappy. Aren't you? I know.

LADY S.: All right, Jimmy, I'll admit it. Came over me just after that music stopped – nothing to do with the music – in fact,

I didn't care for it much – but suddenly I felt quite bloodily unhappy.

SHIEL and LENGEL appear out of the recess.

SIR J.: *(Impressively.)* What we both need are a few drinks. *(Sees SHIEL and LENGEL.)* Thanks very much. Enjoyed your piece.

LADY S.: *(Smiling at them as she goes.)* Divine.

They go out. SHIEL and LENGEL looking rather tired, come down a bit.

LENGEL: We'll try it again some afternoon next week, I need a lot more practice on it, David.

SHIEL: I wish you'd mark those three phrases that you say are so hard to finger.

LENGEL: I will. And I'll show you where you want to give your soloist a longer rest in the third movement. But what I want now is a very large whisky and soda.

SHIEL: So do I. *(Glances at the motionless BENDREX and indicates him.)* Not very complimentary to us, is it, even at his age?

LENGEL: *(Going nearer.)* No, I could understand him dozing off for a few minutes – but – *(He has looked at him now.)* Hello!

SHIEL realises what his sharp glance means and joins him, looking down on BENDREX.

SHIEL: He's not asleep, Nick.

If necessary, one of them can turn BENDREX's chair now, so that he is in full view of audience.

LENGEL: He's dead.

SHIEL: *(Bringing LENGEL down, urgently.)* A doctor's useless now, but there'll have to be one. You go straight through to the hall and telephone for one, and I'll take Mrs. Amesbury on one side and tell her what's happened. No good frightening everybody.

LENGEL: *(As they go.)* All right. Poor old Bendrex.

When they have gone, there should be a subtle change of the light. If practicable, the second act music should be heard far away, a ghost of a sound. After a moment or two, PARKS comes in – from dead entrance – carrying the straw hat – and looks about him a little and then goes over to BENDREX.

PARKS: Mr. Bendrex, sir! Mr. Bendrex!

A ghostly suggestion of the sunshine light of their previous scene should now come in. A BENDREX does not wake, PARKS touches him on the shoulder. BENDREX slowly opens his eyes. PARKS steps back a little, respectfully. BENDREX frowns a little, then recognises PARKS.

BENDREX: *(Slowly, still an old man.)* What? Ah – Parks – I must have dropped off.

PARKS: Yes, sir, took the liberty of waking you, sir, as it's nearly luncheon time.

BENDREX: *(Slowly rising.)* Thank you, Parks. *(Puts a hand to his head.)* Touch of headache.

PARKS: It's the sun, sir. I thought you might like this. *(Gives him the straw hat.)*

BENDREX: *(Half wonderingly.)* Thank you, Parks.

PARKS: This is the nearest way, sir.

He indicates the entrance he came in, and then moves towards it. BENDREX puts on the hat and suddenly become a smiling middle-aged man and strolls off just as curtain is coming down.

Curtain.

THE LONG MIRROR
A Play in Three Acts.

Author's Preface

The Long Mirror was written and first produced in Oxford, where I spent a term in the early part of 1940. I had promised the repertory company at the Playhouse there a new play to do, and then, finding that the play I had in mind was not suitable, I wrote *The Long Mirror*. The producer Andre van Gysegham and leading lady Jean Forbes Robertson took the play for a provincial tour that lasted many months.

The play, I know, was written too quickly, and it suffers from the defect of having a central and all-important situation that seems to many people wildly unreal. The fact is, however, that although the setting and the characters of this drama are imaginary, its theme, based on an extra-sensory or second-sight relationship between a girl and a man, was not imaginary but was taken from life, one of the two persons concerned being very well known to me. Nor did I heighten the real story but, if anything, tended to modify some of its more fantastic features.

One day I hope to see the play revived under easier conditions of production, with far more time for careful rehearsal than we had at Oxford. So far it remains the Cinderella of my more serious plays; nevertheless, it pleased and excited some people for whose opinion I have respect.

J.B. Priestley, 1943

Characters

in order of appearance

MRS. TENBURY

THOMAS WILLIAMS

BRANWEN ELDER

MICHAEL CAMBER

VALERIE CAMBER

SCENES

The action, which is continuous, takes place in the sitting-room of a small private hotel in North Wales.

First produced at the Oxford Playhouse, in March 1940, with the following cast:

MRS. TENBURY, Betty Hardy (afterwards Barbara Everest)

THOMAS WILLIAMS, Julian D'Albie

BRANWEN ELDER, Jean Forbes Robertson

MICHAEL CAMBER, Bernard Lee

VALERIE CAMBER, Rosemary Scott

ACT ONE

The scene is a sitting-room of a small private hotel, once a country house, on the shore of a lake in the mountains of North Wales. The room suggests a private house rather than an hotel. It is pleasantly furnished in an early Victorian style. On the right (actors') wall are large french windows opening on to a path with lawn and trees beyond, and it must be possible for an actor to stand outside these windows and be clearly seen by the audience. On the back wall, R. not centre, is a door leading to dining-room, etc. (a) If possible this should be built about three feet above stage level with small staircases leading to it. Obliquely between back wall and Left wall is another (b) on stage level, leading to front entrance of hotel, kitchen, etc. The fireplace is downstage in L. wall. Between fireplace and door to front entrance is a large mirror. A few small tables, for afternoon tea, etc., some comfortable but not very large chairs, a bookcase or two long back wall.

At rise, the time is just after four on an October afternoon. The light not too bright, and warm, is coming through french windows and fourth wall. MRS. TENBURY, a woman in her sixties, pleasant, shrewd, is sitting with a book, ready for tea. THOMAS WILLIAMS, in his fifties, a friendly little Welshman, who acts as waiter in the hotel but looks more like a parlourman in a private house, wearing striped jacket and dark trousers, now enters with tea things. His manner is freer than that of the usual hotel waiter. He begins putting out the tea things on a small table near MRS. TENBURY. She regards him quizzically.

MRS. TENBURY: Thomas, if your respected employer, Mrs. Saxon, were here, do you know what she'd say?

THOMAS: Oh – I don't know where she'd start or where she'd finish, but I can imagine some of the things she'd say in between. But it's the first time she's left me an' Mrs. Williams to look after the hotel all by ourselves, so I don't think we're doing so bad, are we?

MRS. T.: No, you're not. But what she'd tell you this minute is that that coat absolutely *reeks* of tobacco.

THOMAS: Ah – I dare say she would now. It's a great fault of mine, I know. I'll tell you the truth of the matter now. You see, of an afternoon, which is the only time I get my bit of rest, as you might say, I go into that little back place of mine to have a look at the paper and smoke my pipe. And then out I come, I dare say, smelling terrible.

MRS. T.: What you ought to do is at least change your coast. I don't know why you men don't do that any more. I remember my father always kept a special coat for smoking. It was blue velvet with black frogs or facing of whatever they are. When I was a little girl I used to think it a wonderful coat.

THOMAS: And your father a very grand gentleman, I'll be bound.

MRS. T.: Yes. And in some ways he was.

THOMAS has now finished laying the small table.

You'd better wait for Miss Elder. She said she'd be back for tea.

THOMAS: I'll wait till she's in before I make the tea. Unless you're in a great hurry for yours.

MRS. T.: No, no. Please wait, I've only been dozing and dreaming, and I can doze and dream a little longer.

THOMAS: I'm a great one for dreaming myself. Only this afternoon, after I'd washed up the lunch things and made everything tidy, I hadn't been sat down ten minutes with my paper before I was away altogether. Everything here clean gone.

MRS. T.: *(Amused.)* Where were you?

THOMAS: Back in the army – Royal Welch – and in India, up on one of the hill stations, playing Crown and Anchor again with the sun outside as hot and bright as ever, and all the noises I haven't heard for thirty years. Then it all gave a sort of shiver, as you might say, and there I am – back in the pantry. India and back in half a second. That's magic for you!

MRS. T.: I often dream of places I've never seen before, and they seem quite real and sensible. I don't see how I could invent them. So much convincing detail too. I don't believe I'm as clever as all that. And all the people too, where do *they* come from?

THOMAS: *(Confidentially.)* The wife now – Mrs. Williams – is a wonderful dreamer. Has she told you?

MRS. T.: No, she hasn't.

THOMAS: *(Impressively.)* Oh – well, she can dream of trouble coming. It's always the same dream. She's wandering about in a great wood – miles and miles of ash and beech, as you might say, and there she is, all by herself, and the wood is thicker and thicker and darker and darker, until she's lost – and crying maybe. Lost and crying in this thick dark wood.

MRS. T.: Horrid! And that means trouble?

THOMAS: Always some trouble is on the way. She'll say to me, 'Thomas,' she'll say, 'I was lost in the wood again last night. There's trouble coming for somebody here,' she'll say. And she's always right.

MRS T.: Dear me! I hope she hasn't dreamed about her wood since I've been her.

THOMAS: *(Solemnly.)* Not till last night.

MRS. T.: *(Half amused, half worried.)* Oh dear! Oh dear! Not that I mind, because I don't really believe in such things, but I know you do.

THOMAS: I don't want to, but I can't help it. There it is.

MRS. T.: Oh, I'd better look out, eh?

THOMAS: *(Very confidentially.)* No, not you, Mrs. Tenbury. My wife was sure of that. 'Nor Mrs. Tenbury,' she said, when we were talking about it this morning. *(Dropping his voice still lower.)* Might I ask a question?

MRS. T.: Not like that, please, Thomas. Terrifying!

THOMAS: *(Apologetically.)* Oh no – I just wanted to ask a question, that's all. But I didn't want you to think I was being – well – nosey.

MRS. T.: *(Laughing at him.)* I know very well you're nosey – as you call it – Thomas. But go on. Ask your question.

THOMAS: *(Very confidentially.)* Do you happen to know why Miss Elder is staying her?

MRS. T.: *(Not much liking this.)* I must say I think that's a very *odd* question.

THOMAS: I know. That's why, you see, I was – well, I hesitated. And indeed I wouldn't have asked at all if my wife hadn't been so troubled, as you might say.

MRS. T.: About Miss Elder?

THOMAS: I think this dream of the wood, you see, upset her. And then I'd noticed Miss Elder – well, not looking very happy, as if she was on a holiday, but worried in her mind, I should say she is, and – and – waiting – waiting...

MRS. T.: *(Serious now.)* I know what you mean, Thomas. She does rather give one that impression, but it's probably just her rather taut strained manner. I imagine she's a highly-strung girl – and an artist too – and that she came down here to be quiet.

THOMAS: *(Hastily.)* Yes, yes, indeed. It was my wife who was asking. I said to her, 'Woman,' I said, 'it's no business of ours,' I said, straight out – 'no business of ours.' But, mind you, she meant to harm at all. It was because of the dream and something she saw in Miss Elder's face.

WOMAN'S VOICE off.

WOMAN'S V.: 'Thomas has taken the tea in, Miss Elder.'

He breaks off because he hears a noise outside door B. He moves away from MRS. TENBURY a little, then waits. BRANWEN ELDER enters B. She is a quick, sensitive woman, twenty-eight to thirty-two, and should be wearing clothes that suggest she has been walking. She looks rather pale and drawn. She does not come in at first but stands just inside door.

MRS. T.: Just in time for tea, Miss Elder. What's the matter? You look as if you'd seen a ghost.

BRANWEN: I have seen a ghost.

Comes forward now.

I just saw her on the drive again.

THOMAS: Would that be the little old woman in grey?

BRANWEN: Yes.

MRS. T.: What's this about?

BRANWEN: Several times, I've seen an angry little old woman in grey. She flits about the drive, staring and muttering. I told Thomas about her yesterday. And he knew about her.

MRS. T.: *(Turning.)* What – have you seen her too?

THOMAS: No, ma'am, I never saw a ghost in my life. Not to know he *was* a ghost. But my wife's sister from Ffestiniog came here and saw her – a little old woman in grey, she said, just the same as Miss Elder. I'll bring you the tea now.

He goes out B.

MRS. T.: *(Slowly.)* That's very curious.

BRANWEN: This is the kind of place one does see them in. I've seen others here too, just dimly. The little old woman in grey is the clearest. Perhaps because she's so miserably angry. Like a rebellious prisoner.

MRS. T.: I think they were angry and rebellious prisoners, many of the women in houses like this, in the old days.

BRANWEN: Their lives were often narrow but – deep. If a lover or husband, a favourite son or daughter, went away and was lost to them, there was nothing but grief or a jealous anger left them. That's why they can so often still be seen. I mean – the intensity of their feeling explains it.

MRS. T.: But it's such a horrible idea!

BRANWEN: What is?

MRS. T.: The idea of these earth-bound spirits…poor creatures… who go on haunting the places they once lived in….who can't get clear of their miserable lives in this world. It's horrible. I simply don't want to believe it.

BRANWEN: But why should you? I don't.

MRS. T.: *(Surprised.)* But – you, you *see* these people – this little old woman here, for instance –

BRANWEN: NO, the people themselves aren't there. It's only an impression they've left on their old surroundings, like footprints in sand, or the marks of one's finger on a glass. That's why I said the intensity of their feeling explains it. They make a deeper impression. So those are the ones you see the clearest...except now and again...when...

MRS. T.: When what?

BRANWEN: *(Slowly.)* When you see – or you experience – I don't know what to cal lit – somebody who's wonderfully happy, a flash of somebody's ecstasy, nearly as quick as lightning...and as terrible.

MRS. T.: Is it the Past you're seeing?

BRANWEN: No, that's something different. It doesn't happen often – at least it doesn't to me. But those impressions that people have left behind on their houses and gardens and walks, these hollow ghosts, they're quite frequent, and I believe everybody has some sense of them, even if it only seems a kind of uneasiness. But when you go into the Past, there's nothing – well, spectral about it – nothing thin and ghostly – it all seems solid and real, at least it does for the few moments you're there.

MRS. T.: *(Regarding her curiously.)* You're a most unusual kind of girl, Miss Elder.

BRANWEN: *(Rather embarrassed.)* No – not really.

MRS. T.: And are not *trying* to be, as so many young women are these days.

THOMAS enters with teapot and hot water jug.

THOMAS: There you are, ladies. And there ought to be everything here you want.

MRS. T.: And more than is good for us, thank you, Thomas. *(As he is about to go.)* By the way, I meant to ask you before, have you heard from Mrs. Saxon?

THOMAS: Yes, ma'am, this morning. She wrote to say we must expect another visitor – perhaps two – this evening.

He goes out.

MRS. T.: *(Staring, quietly.)* Is there anything wrong, Miss Elder?

BRANWEN: *(Trying to hide her agitation.)* No. Nothing.

MRS. T.: I thought for a moment you were ill.

BRANWEN: *(Confused.)* No. As I told you, when I came here I was rather – tired – run down…although I oughtn't to have been, after the voyage from Cape Town.

MRS. T.: *(Now handing tea, etc.)* Perhaps it was the change of climate.

BRANWEN: Yes. And everything seems so – so heavy here now, after two years of South Africa.

MRS. T.: I've often meant to go, but never have gone.

BRANWEN: There, it's light and clear. The air is thin. You see mountains a hundred miles away. No wonder they find diamonds there. The country itself is like a diamond.

MRS. T.: And you liked that?

BRANWEN: At first I loved it. And being a painter I was excited by the new strange quality of light in the crystal-clear air. *(Pauses, then slowly.)* There seemed to be nothing between you and the sun. I don't mean merely no clouds or haziness, but no history, none of that thickness of atmosphere which you get when people, hordes and hordes of people, have lived a long time in a place. The air had no weight of memory. And I liked that too, at first…

MRS. T.: I went to Australia once. You have it all there too. I didn't like it. Too empty. The country – not the people but the country itself – seemed unfriendly. It had done without people for so long it didn't want to start bothering them now. Did you find that afterwards in South Africa?

BRANWEN: Yes, to some extent. I wasn't sorry to leave. Suddenly I felt quite homesick. I felt I wanted a cosy country again. But this afternoon it seemed so melancholy here, with everything decaying in a little closed valley, and no light and space.

MRS. T.: It's beautiful near the lake.

BRANWEN: It wasn't, somehow, this afternoon. There was mist everywhere. The woods didn't begin or end. They just hung there, half smothering in cotton wool. Yet there were some lovely little things to see – ghostly silver birches; a tree all alive with starlings, enormous beaded spiders' webs and crimson fungus, all out of the fairy tale world. But it was a dying world.

A moment's silence while they continue eating and drinking.

MRS. T.: *(Very seriously.)* I can never make out what this cake of Mrs. Williams' is supposed to taste of. Reminds me of a medicine cupboard.

BRANWEN: *(Idly.)* I know. Something I was given as a child for the early stages of toothache.

MRS. T.: Another cup of tea?

BRANWEN: No, thank you. I think I'll have a cigarette if you don't mind.

MRS. T.: No, why should I? I can't smoke myself because of my wretched throat, but it doesn't worry me if other people smoke. Is that why you haven't smoked here for the last two days, because I told you about my throat?

BRANWEN: Well – I thought – perhaps –

MRS. T.: Very thoughtful of you, my dear, and a very nice change to find somebody so thoughtful. But it doesn't matter in the least. Smoke away. It may soothe your nerves, and I believe they need soothing – um?

BRANWEN: I'm sorry.

MRS. T.: Sorry? Why?

BRANWEN: I'm sure you've found my restlessness a nuisance.

MRS. T.: Oh – no. Shall we ring so that Thomas can clear these things?

BRANWEN: *(Going to bell.)* I'll ring.

She does. Then lights her cigarette, smokes, and moves restlessly.

MRS. T.: *(Easily, not pointedly.)* You haven't done any painting here yet, have you?

BRANWEN: No. I tell myself it's because I must get used to the different light. But really I think it's because I'm lazy.

MRS. T.: No, you're not lazy. I'm certain of that.

BRANWEN: *(Smiling.)* Are you? Why?

MRS. T.: Because I am lazy, and always was. We born lazybones can always recognize one another. And you're not one of us. No, if you're not working it's for some other reason.

She looks rather hard and enquiringly as and after she says this. BRANWEN meets her look a moment, then looks away. THOMAS enters and comes for things.

THOMAS: Oh – have you finished?

MRS. T.: Yes.

THOMAS: *(Looking at table.)* It's a terrible poor tea you both make.

MRS. T.: I haven't been out so I don't deserve any at all.

THOMAS: Oh – don't start talking like that, ma'am, because if it's a case of only getting what we deserve, the Lord help us all!

He gathers things together and begins to move.

BRANWEN: *(Who has not been at ease, suddenly.)* Thomas!

THOMAS: *(Stopping.)* Yes, miss?

BRANWEN: *(After an effort.)* Did you say – somebody was coming here this evening?

THOMAS: *(Rather importantly.)* Yes, miss. We have to expect another visitor – and perhaps two. That was the message I had this morning.

He waits, as if expecting a further question.

BRANWEN: *(After a further effort.)* Did – you – I mean, were you told – who it was?

THOMAS: No. No names were given to me.

He still waits, looking at her curiously. There is a feeling of tension.

BRANWEN: *(After a pause.)* That's all, Thomas, thank you.

THOMAS: I'm sorry I can't tell you any more, Miss Elder.

After he goes out, there is a moment's silence. MRS. TENBURY has been watching BRANWEN steadily and curiously. We still feel the tension.

MRS. T.: *(After a pause.)* I might as well tell you that you've aroused the curiosity of Thomas and his wife. He was asking me about you, just before you came in for tea. Quite nicely, you know.

BRANWEN: *(Nervously.)* Yes, of course. I like Thomas.

MRS. T.: I couldn't satisfy his curiosity. And hinted that I didn't think it quite necessary. What I *didn't* add was that I'm equally curious – and puzzled – myself.

BRANWEN: *(Smiling slightly.)* I'm worried. – don't fancy myself as a mysterious figure, you know.

MRS. T.: I know that. And – well, I feel that during these few days we've shared this hotel together we've become something rather better than hotel acquaintances – um?

BRANWEN: Yes. I feel we're friends.

MRS. T.: I'm glad you do. Well –

Some mutual embarrassment here. Both women give a short laugh.

BRANWEN: *(Still smiling.)* Well?

MRS. T.: *(Plunging in.)* My dear, call me an inquisitive old woman, if you like, but I'll confess – frankly – that I'm curious. *And* – rather worried.

BRANWEN: About me?

MRS. T.: Worried about you. And, of course, curious.

BRANWEN: Why?

MRS. T.: *(Smiling.)* You're a suspicious character.

BRANWEN: What – just because I came straight here the moment I returned from South Africa!

MRS. T.: Well, I think that's odd, after all. To come straight here – to this out-of the-way place. And you didn't come to work because you're not working. Nor to rest, because you're obviously not resting.

BRANWEN: *(Lightly.)* It's those detective stories you read. You win!

MRS. T.: *(More seriously.)* Now, my dear, admit it – you're nervous, restless, on edge. If you weren't, this curiosity of mine would be inexcusable. But as it is, and being a much older woman who's had all kinds of troubles of her own, I can't help wondering whether – perhaps – I couldn't help.

BRANWEN: *(Earnestly.)* I wish you could.

MRS. T.: Well then – tell me, and I'll do my best.

BRANWEN: *(Hastily.)* No, I don't mean that. I mean that I don't really need any help. There's no way in which you could help me. There's never been any way in which anybody could help me. That's what has always made it so difficult. Even to talk about it – has been impossible. I can't –

She breaks off sharply.

MRS. T.: *(After waiting a moment.)* Yes?

BRANWEN: No, that's all. I was just rambling on. Stupid of me. What I really wanted to say way – that if I were in any difficulty in which I thought you could help me, I wouldn't hesitate to explain it to you. I'm not really a secretive sort of person. And I know you'd be friendly – sensible – wise. But, you see, it isn't like that.

MRS. T.: *(After a short pause.)* Shall I tell you what I believe?

BRANWEN: *(Looking at her gravely.)* Yes, please do.

MRS. T.: *(Carefully.)* I believe you expected to meet somebody here – and yet were afraid of that meeting.

BRANWEN: *(Surprised.)* I didn't know I'd given myself away so completely.

MRS. T.: Then it's true.

BRANWEN: Yes, it's true.

MRS. T.: Well, it's happened to most of us in our time. Only, of course, instead of being kept waiting minutes or hours, you've been waiting two or three days, which must be a tremendous strain.

BRANWEN: Yes, it has been. Still is.

MRS. T.: And I'll confess that I've been wondering – in spite of what you told me when we first met – whether you're not married after all and are really waiting to meet a husband from whom you've been separated.

Hastily, with relief.

There! That's out.

BRANWEN: *(Smiling a little.)* I'm afraid it's out to no purpose, Mrs. Tenbury. I was telling the truth when I said I wasn't married.

MRS. T.: *(Taken aback.)* Oh dear!

BRANWEN: *(Firmly.)* I'm not married. I've never been married. And as far as I know there isn't the remotest chance that I ever shall be married. And there! That's out.

MRS. T.: *(Looking at her sympathetically.)* But it was – or is – a man you were expecting to meet here?

BRANWEN: Yes.

MRS. T.: It always is, of course. And *he's* married.

BRANWEN: Yes, this man is married.

MRS. T.: *(Sighing a little.)* I'm sorry, my dear. I wondered whether that was it. Please don't feel that you need say any more.

BRANWEN: But now I think I'd better say a little more. You see, to begin with, I've never exchanged a word with this man in my life.

MRS. T.: *(Astonished.)* Oh – but I assumed –

BRANWEN: I know you did. But it's not like that at all. This man isn't coming here to meet *me*. I don't think he's even aware of my existence.

MRS. T.: *(Bewildered.)* You don't know him?

BRANWEN: *(Gravely.)* No, I can't say that.

MRS. T.: But you just said –

BRANWEN: *(Cutting in.)* That I didn't think he's even aware of my existence. But – I know him. I know him better than I know anybody else in the world. I think I know more about him than anybody else does.

MRS. TENBURY now rises, in her bewilderment, and puts a hand on each of BRANWEN's arms, staring at her. BRANWEN laughs nervously.

It's all right, Mrs. Tenbury. I'm quite real. I'm also quite sane.

MRS. T.: But are you *serious*?

BRANWEN: *(Very quietly.)* I'm desperately serious. This is the most serious thing that's ever happened to me or ever will happen to me. I'm certain of that.

MRS. T.: Did this man *tell* you he was coming here? But no, you said you'd never exchanged a word with him. But he could have written, of course –

BRANWEN: No, he didn't. I told you. He's not even aware of my existence. At least I don't think so.

MRS. T.: But you learned somehow that he intended to come and stay here?

BRANWEN: Yes. Just as I was reaching England. And I knew he was unhappy, unable to work or even to think properly. And I felt – *(Breaks off.)*

MRS. T.: *(After a pause.)* I can't pretend to understand. But – tell me – you say he's married. Where does his wife come into all this?

BRANWEN: They weren't happy together. They'd separated – how or when I don't know. But I gathered they were both coming here probably – to see if they could make it up. I think that's why they chose this place. Some friend had told him about it. And they felt if they were away from people for a few days, in some quiet remote place, they might come to some understanding. I believe the people all round them all the time have helped to make the barrier between them. He has to be in constant touch with a lot of people. He can't help that because of his work.

MRS. T.: This isn't more curiosity but just common sense, seeing that *somebody* is apparently arriving here quite soon, according to Thomas. I mean, hasn't you better tell who this man is?

BRANWEN: Yes, I see what you mean. Well, his name is Michael Camber. He's a composer.

MRS. T.: *(Slowly.)* Yes, I know his name, though I don't seem to have heard it much lately.

BRANWEN: No. He's been in America.

MRS. T.: I think I've heard one or two things of his, though I
don't pretend to know very much about modern music.
Rather nervous, strident sort of things they were, I seem to
remember.

BRANWEN: *(Eagerly.)* Yes, nearly all his work is. Technically it's
very brilliant, as everybody admits, but the trouble is that
none of his work yet, except perhaps one or two tiny things,
really represents him. Only half of him – and the worried,
rebellious despairing half – gets through in the bigger things.
He's like a man who wants to speak quietly and tenderly
to somebody he loves but somehow, can never find the
occasion and the right words. He's a difficult complicated
person who's always quarrelling with other people and with
life itself, often when he doesn't want to, but simply because
he becomes dominated by terrible, bitter, black moods.
Over and over again I've seen – *(She breaks off.)*

MRS. T.: *(After waiting a moment, quietly.)* Yes?

BRANWEN: *(With an effort.)* I'm sorry. I oughtn't to have gone
on like that.

MRS. T.: *(Wonderingly.)* And yet this is the man who probably
doesn't know you exist, the man you've never exchanged a
word with… I'm – well – I'm completely bewildered, you
know –

BRANWEN: I realised that. I've told you more than I intended.

MRS. T.: But not enough to make me understand.

BRANWEN: I know. And I don't feel I can tell you any more,
certainly not now.

MRS. T.: You're a very strange young woman. I knew that from
the first.

BRANWEN: *(Smiling a little.)* Not really. I'm old enough now
to feel that I'm not very different from other people and to
be glad of it. What is really strange, so much stranger, so
infinitely more complicated, than people imagine now, is
our life. We pretend that it's so much simpler than it really is.

MRS. T.: I agree. But on the whole, I think that's one of our
better pretences. It enables us to live with a greater feeling

of security. For instance. We're told, by all the people who know about such things, that the earth is really a vast spinning globe rushing through space. Now if we were conscious of that all the time, it would be dreadful. But as it is, for all ordinary practical purposes the earth is still the flat unmoving surface our ancestors imagined it to be, and so we still feel fairly comfortable on it. Eh?

BRANWEN: No. It doesn't matter about the earth, of course, and anyhow, one day we may discover it isn't a spinning globe any more than it's a flat unmoving surface. But I think it's terribly dangerous to over-simplify life and always to mistake the appearance for the reality. It's like being wilfully blind. Groping with your eyes closed when you could be walking with your eyes open. People are made desperately unhappy by things they are told don't exist, and go to see doctors when it isn't doctors they need at all but a truer conception. Of what life really is. In the same way, they refuse happiness – just because they have been told that the doorway into it is nothing but a blank wall.

MRS. T.: But what is this doorway or this blank wall? I don't –

She is checked by a sudden movement of BRANWEN's.

What's the matter?

BRANWEN: *(Very quietly but urgently.)* He's here. I know he is.

MRS. T.: What – your Michael Camber?

BRANWEN: *(Stifling.)* Yes, I know he's here.

She is now sitting with head bent, turned away from the windows.

MRS. T.: *(After a moment.)* I'll see.

Goes out C. MICHAEL CAMBER, a dark figure against the light behind him, now appears outside windows, and after staring about him a moment begins to peer through the windows. MRS. TENBURY returns.

There's nobody there.

She now sees the figure of CAMBER and gives a little cry. BRANWEN turns now and also sees him, and gives a short checked scream, and then turns her head way again, as if overcome by deep emotion. CAMBER now enters. He is a virile, masterful, but highly nervous man in his late thirties or early forties, with more personal charm than his actual speeches might suggest. His manner is quick, abrupt, his speech staccato, but he should also suggest between speeches and movements a deeply brooding quality.

MICHAEL C.: *(Approaching BRANWEN.)* Valerie! You here already! I didn't expect –

Here he breaks off because he has reached BRANWEN, and she has turned her head so that he sees her face clearly now. He is astounded.

I beg you pardon! I thought you were my wife.

Stares in bewilderment at her. Taut, she looks searchingly at him. He frowns in bewilderment.

You must think me very stupid…staring at you like this… but…we've met somewhere, haven't we?

BRANWEN now rises, still looking at him.

BRANWEN: *(Shaking her head.)* No.

Now she hurries out of the room through door A. He watches her go, still amazed. When she has gone, he looks at MRS. TENBURY who is looking at him, with a little smile on her face.

MRS. T.: Mr. Michael Camber?

MICHAEL: *(Still puzzled.)* Yes.

MRS. T.: I'm Mrs. Tenbury.

MICHAEL: *(His mind still elsewhere.)* Oh – yes. Most extraordinary thing!

Now giving her his attention.

What's the name of that girl?

MRS. T.: *(Rather deliberately.)* Miss Elder. Branwen Elder.

MICHAEL: *(Chewing it over.)* Branwen Elder. No. I'd have remembered that. Perhaps I met her somewhere without catching her name. Often happens, doesn't it?

MRS. T.: You – er – feel you know her, um?

MICHAEL: *(Almost irritably.)* No, I can't say that exactly. When I was standing out there –

MRS. T.: *(With a hint of reproach.)* Frightening us.

MICHAEL: Did I? Sorry! Though I can't imagine why it should have frightened you. The fact is, I've just arrived. Never been to this place before, only heard of it from a friend. And it looked so completely unlike an hotel that I began prowling round to try and make head or tail of it. Also, I thought if there was a crowd here, I wouldn't stay. Want to be quiet, you see.

MRS. T.: You'll find it very quiet her. But you were saying – when you were outside – ?

MICHAEL: I'm hoping to meet my wife here. She's been staying with friends and I've just come back from Paris. And I could have sworn that was Valerie – my wife. Then there didn't seem any resemblance. And then I felt I recognised her. But I don't know her. Sorry to go blathering on like this, but these little things can be so disturbing. I suppose the fact is I've met her at some crush or other, perhaps years ago, and can't remember.

MRS. T.: *(Calmly.)* No, I don't think so. You haven't met her before.

MICHAEL: How do you know?

MRS. T.: Because she told me you'd never met. And I'm quite sure she was telling me the truth.

MICHAEL: *(Astonished.)* She told you? When?

MRS. T.: Just before you came.

MICHAEL: *(Grimly.)* I see. Excuse me a moment. Where's the bell?

MRS. T.: *(Indicating.)* There. Is there – anything wrong?

MICHAEL: *(Ringing.)* Yes. I hate people who can't keep their word, who make a promise and then instantly break it.

MRS. T.: *(Surprised.)* Well, so do I, but I don't quite see –

MICHAEL: *(Cutting in.)* No, no. Nothing to do with you, of course. It's these confounded people here.

MRS. T.: Really, Mr. Camber, if you mean Mrs. Saxon, who owns the hotel, or Thomas, the man here, I assure you – and I know them very well – that they're quite exceptionally nice people.

MICHAEL: Then they should keep their promises.

THOMAS appears at B.

THOMAS: Oh – you're here, Sir. And you've changed your mind about having a cup of tea, eh?

MICHAEL: *(Rather savagely.)* No, I haven't. But I've probably changed my mind about staying here at all.

THOMAS: *(Shocked.)* Oh – I'm very sorry to hear that, Sir. Why, is there anything –

MICHAEL: *(Cutting in, sharply.)* There's a good deal wrong, if that's what you're asking. When I wrote to the woman who runs this place – Mrs. – Mrs. –

THOMAS: Mrs. Saxon?

MICHAEL: Mrs. Saxon. When I wrote to Mrs. Saxon, I made it a condition of my staying here at all that she should keep my name to herself. I'm not a film star and so may not be very important to the gutter press, but even so it's showing an unwelcome interest in my private affairs, and I wanted to come down here and be safe from any impertinent interference. She promised faithfully to keep my name to herself. Now I find that not only she passed it on to you, but that you've instantly passed it on to these ladies who are staying her! Now what do you say to that?

MRS. T.: Mr. Camber, I –

MICHAEL: *(Cutting in sharply.)* Please. This is between me and these people. Now what do you say?

THOMAS: *(Blankly.)* Sir – all I can say is – I haven't the smallest notion of what you might be talking about.

MICHAEL: *(Flaring up.)* Now that's just damned impudence!

MRS. T.: *(Rising, with great authority.)* Mr. Camber!

MICHAEL: Well?

MRS. T.: You're making a great mistake and behaving very foolishly. Thomas, Mrs. Saxon told you that another guest – and perhaps two – might be coming here this evening, but she didn't mention any names to you, did she?

THOMAS: No, she didn't. I was just going to ask this gentleman his name, for he didn't register when he came a few minutes since, and so indeed I hadn't a name for him.

MICHAEL: *(To MRS. TENBURY.)* But he told you I was coming here?

MRS. T.: He didn't. He merely said *somebody* was coming, that's all.

THOMAS: *(To MICHAEL CAMBER gravely.)* Mrs. Saxon is a good employer and this is a nice place, but even to please her and to stay working here, I can't allow anybody to call me to my face a liar.

Looks steadily at MICHAEL CAMBER.

MRS. T.: *(Soothing him.)* All right, Thomas.

MICHAEL: I didn't call you a liar. Apparently it's all a misunderstanding, and though I don't pretend to know what's happened, obviously it's nothing to do with you. Forget I spoke.

THOMAS: *(With dignity.)* Very well, sir. And now, if you don't wish to register just now but you are staying here –

MICHAEL: Yes, I'm staying, though I don't know for how long.

THOMAS: Then what is your name, sir, please?

MICHAEL: Well, seeing that everybody else here seems to know it, you might as well know it too. It's Camber, Michael Camber.

THOMAS: Very good, Mr. Camber. I've taken your luggage to you room. It's number six. *(Points to door A.)* Through here, along the corridor. Thank you, sir.

He retires through B with dignity. There is a moment's silence.

MRS. T.: *(With hint of reproach.)* Thomas is not quite the ordinary hotel servant, just as this isn't quite the ordinary country hotel.

MICHAEL: *(Not unpleasantly.)* In other words, stop shouting at him and making a nuisance of yourself – eh? You won't believe it, but it was really my modesty that was at the back of that mistake I made.

MRS. T.: Your modesty? I'm afraid I don't follow.

MICHAEL: And don't believe a word of it. But look at it from my point of view. I'm a composer, a composer of serious modern music. How many people in this film-and-football-ridden country take the last glimmer of interest in serious modern music? Perhaps one person out of every fifty thousand. Well, knowing that's the ratio of interest, naturally I don't expect to be the subject of discussion in an hotel sitting-room only a few minutes before I arrive there. Unless, of course, you knew I was coming. And now, it seems, you didn't.

MRS. T.: *(Calmly.)* But we did.

MICHAEL: But – but – you said –

MRS. T.: That Thomas didn't know. Quite so. But you see, Miss Elder knew. She expected you.

MICHAEL: How could she? Ah – but wait a minute. It's Valerie – my wife. That's what it is, of course.

MRS. T.: No, Mr. Camber, I don't think Miss Elder knows your wife.

MICHAEL: *(Rather savagely.)* You know – Mrs. – er –

MRS. T.: Tenbury.

MICHAEL: Mrs. Tenbury, you're having a glorious time, aren't you?

MRS. T.: *(Demurely.)* No, not a glorious time, but I *am* rather enjoying myself.

MICHAEL: Mystifying the loud-voiced stranger, eh?

MRS. T.: Partly that, of course. But also passing on my own mystification. There's always a pleasure in that, isn't there?

MICHAEL: Possibly. Well, at any rate you won't say I've been making a lot of fuss about nothing.

MRS. T.: Certainly not. In your place I should want to know a great deal more before I'd done.

MICHAEL: Then you can tell me some more. For instance, how on earth could Miss Elder know I was coming here is nobody told her?

MRS. T.: *(Rising.)* That's what I've been wondering. But – as you'll probably discover – she's rather an extraordinary young woman.

MICHAEL: I'm afraid I dislike young women who think they're extraordinary.

MRS. T.: I didn't say she *thinks* she is. She doesn't, as a matter of fact. I said she *is* rather extraordinary.

MICHAEL: *(Almost muttering.)* It'll probably amount to the same thing.

MRS. T.: *(Preparing to go.)* You'll find some beautiful walking country round here.

MICHAEL: *(Not too rudely.)* I shan't. I hate walking.

MRS. T.: *(Calmly.)* Oh – what a pity! What do you like?

MICHAEL: I like working. And occasionally taking violent exercise. And often just doing nothing.

MRS. T.: You'll find this a very good place to do nothing in. I know I do.

BRANWEN now appears through door A. and should remain just inside, up the stairs if there are any. MRS TENBURY, who is not just going, sees her.

Miss Elder, I think you'd better tell Mr. Camber what he'll enjoy doing here.

She goes out B. BRANWEN stays where she is. MICHAEL CAMBER goes and rings bell.

MICHAEL: I propose to have a drink. Will you join me?

BRANWEN: *(In low voice.)* No, thank you.

MICHAEL: Well, I hope you'll watch me having one. I want to talk to you.

THOMAS appears A.

Bring me a whisky-and-soda, will you?

THOMAS: *(Hesitating.)* Oh – well now – we have no proper bar here, you understand –

MICHAEL: *(Suddenly flaring up.)* Have you a licence?

THOMAS: Yes.

MICHAEL: *(Getting angrier.)* And perhaps there's such a thing as a little whisky and a little soda in the place, you –

BRANWEN: *(Sharply.)* No, don't!

MICHAEL: *(Suddenly cooling.)* Are you asking me not to have a drink?

BRANWEN: *(Hurriedly.)* No, of course not. Something else.

MICHAEL: *(To THOMAS.)* A whisky-and-soda, if you please.

THOMAS: Oh – certainly sir, certainly. I was only going to tell you I could get it for you all the same although we have no proper bar here.

He goes. BRANWEN comes into room slowly. MICHAEL CAMBER watches her curiously.

MICHAEL: *(With a strained politeness.)* I thought you said 'No, don't!' to me, a moment ago.

BRANWEN: I did.

MICHAEL: What did you mean?

BRANWEN: *(Looking at him steadily.)* I knew that in another second you were going to boil over in a foaming black rage with that harmless little man. I wanted if possible to check you, both for Thomas's sake and you own sake.

MICHAEL: All right. I'll admit I was about to fly into quite an unnecessary rage. That fellow irritates me. But do you usually check people – people you don't really know – like that?

BRANWEN: No.

MICHAEL: *(Abruptly, after a pause.)* You told that woman – Mrs. – er – Tenbury – that we'd never met.

BRANWEN: Yes.

MICHAEL: Why?

BRANWEN: Because it's true.

MICHAEL: Haven't we met, don't you think, at some party – just for a minute or two perhaps – years ago?

BRANWEN: No.

MICHAEL: Then you know my wife – Valerie?

BRANWEN: I've never set eyes on her.

MICHAEL: Some friend of hers then?

BRANWEN: No. I neither know her nor anybody she knows nor anything about her.

MICHAEL: But you told Mrs. Tenbury I was coming to stay here?

BRANWEN: I'm sorry she told you that.

MICHAEL: Which means that you did tell her?

BRANWEN: Yes.

MICHAEL: How did you know I was coming here?

BRANWEN: What does that matter?

MICHAEL: Because the two or three people who knew had promised to say nothing about it, and one of them must have let me down.

BRANWEN: No. Nobody's let you down.

MICHAEL: Then how did you find out?

BRANWEN: I – *(Breaks off.)*

MICHAEL: Well?

BRANWEN: Oh, why do you go on?

MICHAEL: *(Masterfully, looking hard at her.)* I'm sorry but I insist upon knowing. If somebody's been chattering –

BRANWEN: *(Cutting in sharply.)* Oh – nobody's been chattering. I've told you that already.

MICHAEL: *(Very emphatically.)* All right then. But how did you come to know? *(She is silent.)* Well?

BRANWEN: *(As is mastered.)* I – I heard you say you were coming here –

MICHAEL: Heard me? When? Where?

BRANWEN: You were talking on a telephone – a long-distance call – I think you were in Paris…

MICHAEL: *(Staring at her, amazed.)* You think I was in Paris! But – but –

BRANWEN: *(Forgetting herself.)* Oh – Michael, please – don't' drive me so hard!

MICHAEL: *(Astonished.) Michael!*

BRANWEN: *(Confused.)* I'm sorry. I don't know how I came to use your name like that. I suppose because I used to hear a good deal of you music and sometimes talked about it, and your name being so familiar to me, I suppose it slipped out like that. Sorry!

MICHAEL: No, that's all right. But – well, I suppose it could happen like that.

BRANWEN: Yes, of course it could.

MICHAEL: *(Deliberately.)* It could but I don't believe it *did.* The way you said it was – well curious – I don't understand all this.

THOMAS enters with a whisky-and-soda, which he hands to MICHAEL CAMBER. The light has been fading during this last scene.

Thanks!

THOMAS: I was wondering it you could do with a bit of light on the subject now.

MICHAEL: *(Pointedly.)* Yes, I could do with plenty of light on the subject.

So THOMAS begins drawing curtains at window and tidying a little round there, and afterwards turning on the lights – which should be so arranged as to permit of some variety in them during the next two acts. He should time his business to last throughout the following dialogue.

THOMAS: A terrible weight there was in one of you bags, Mr. Camber, now. Books maybe.

MICHAEL: Some books and a lot of music manuscript. I write music, and full scores are heavy and bulky.

BRANWEN: Have you some work to do here?

MICHAEL: I've just resurrected a symphonic rhapsody I started about four years ago and then dropped, and lately I've been working on it pretty hard.

BRANWEN: *(Forgetting herself, eager, delighted.)* No, *The Seabirds?*

MICHAEL: Yes.

BRANWEN: Oh – I'm so glad.

MICHAEL: It's queer, but when I first began it the thing swept me along for a time and then suddenly I couldn't make any headway at all like a man trying to walk through glue. I was in despair, a bit frightened too. For the first time – there was the target, but I couldn't even take aim at it…

BRANWEN: *(Eagerly.)* I know, I know!

MICHAEL: *(Surprised.) You* know?

BRANWEN: *(Confused.)* Well – I mean –

THOMAS: *(Calmly.)* Miss Elder is an artist too – a painter, so they tell me.

MICHAEL: Oh – I see. Then you'll understand what I felt.

BRANWEN: *(Eagerly.)* Of course. And now it's come to life again?

MICHAEL: Yes. Not with the same first rush and swing, but stronger now and more solid, though actually I'm not using such a massive orchestration. But of course I've learnt something during these last four years. I wouldn't be much use if I hadn't. So there it is, in my bag, just waiting for a little peace and quiet, inside and outside my head – *The Seabirds.*

BRANWEN: *(With enthusiasm.)* Oh grand! You know I always felt –

Breaks off, realising she has said too much.

MICHAEL: *(Who is staring at her.)* Yes, you felt –?

BRANWEN: No, nothing…

MICHAEL: *(With sudden impatience, to THOMAS.)* Oh – that'll do. Stop fiddling about, man!

Drains his glass quickly, then holds it out.

Here!

THOMAS: *(With hint of gentle reproach.)* Thank you, Mr. Camber, sir.

Takes glass and goes.

BRANWEN: *(Who is afraid now.)* We dine rather early here. I think I must go and –

MICHAEL: *(Stopping her, imperatively.)* No, please, never mind about that. This is really important. I've remembered something. Now it was you who first actually mentioned the name *The Seabirds*, wasn't it?

BRANWEN: *(Nervously.)* Was it?

MICHAEL: Yes, it was. And only one other person in the world knew that four years ago I began a symphonic rhapsody called *The Seabirds* and that was Hugo Stander. And he's dead.

BRANWEN: *(Calmly.)* He isn't.

MICHAEL: Of course he is. He was my best friend. I watched the life go out of him and scattered his ashes.

BRANWEN: How can Hugo Stander ever be ashes?

MICHAEL: All right, we won't discuss immortality now – I didn't see what you were driving at when you said he wasn't dead. But he's dead to us, out of our world.

BRANWEN: He's out of our time.

MICHAEL: And we're still in it, so it amount to the same thing.

BRANWEN: No, it doesn't because a good part of us is out of our time too.

MICHAEL: I don't know what you mean, but I'm willing to let you explain it all afterwards if you'll explain a few things I want to know first. And I say that nobody but Hugo Stander knew about *The Seabirds*. Yet when I said I'd resurrected a work I began and then dropped four years ago, you said at once *The Seabirds*. Now how did you know?

He waits for her reply, but she is silent. He shrugs his shoulders, brings out a cigarette case, which should be of an odd pattern, and is about to take one, when he offers it to her, and speaks with marked change of tone.

Sorry! I seem to have dropped all the poor rags and tatters of manners I ever had since arriving here.

BRANWEN: *(Who is staring at the case.)* Thank you!

Takes a cigarette mechanically.

MICHAEL: *(Still in a light style.)* Rum-looking case, isn't it? Had it for years.

BRANWEN: *(In low toneless voice.)* Yes.

Suddenly she turns away, as if overcome by sudden emotion. Then she moves, rather blindly towards window. He puts case in his pocket, brings out matches or lighter, and goes towards her. All this should be slow but tense.

MICHAEL: A light?

BRANWEN: *(With an effort.)* Thank you.

She turns, obviously controlling herself, and accepts the light. Then he lights his own.

MICHAEL: *(In deliberately light easy manner.)* You been staying here long?

BRANWEN: *(Trying to recover.)* Three days.

MICHAEL: Did you come down from London?

BRANWEN: Yes. Well – I just called there. I'd just come back from South Africa, only landed four days ago.

MICHAEL: So five days ago you were still at sea?

BRANWEN: Yes. Why?

MICHAEL: *(With return to earlier manner now.)* Because it was five days ago when I telephoned from Paris – to my wife – to say that we'd better meet here. So that when you say you heard me talking on the telephone – and you said yourself you thought I was in Paris then – you were actually out at sea?

BRANWEN: *(Beaten down.)* Yes.

MICHAEL: *(Going up to her.)* Now, Miss Elder. If you haven't been merely amusing yourself, talking a lot of nonsense –

BRANWEN: *(Faintly.)* I have no been talking a lot of nonsense.

MICHAEL: *(Close to her now.)* Then I think you'll admit you owe me an explanation.

BRANWEN: I was a fool to come here at all.

MICHAEL: *(Ignoring her remark.)* And a pretty elaborate explanation at that.

BRANWEN: How can I give you an explanation when you are in this mood.

Suddenly appealing to him, urgently.

Let me go! Please! Let me go!

Her hand is on his arm and it stays there. He stares at her in bewilderment.

MICHAEL: But – all I'm asking for is an explanation. I can't force you to stay and give it to me.

BRANWEN: I know. I don't mean that.

MICHAEL: Then why do you ask me to let you go?

As they stand there, with BRANWEN still looking her appeal at him and MICHAEL staring in bewilderment, door A opens and VALERIE CAMBER enters. To stand looking down on them. She is wearing a travelling coat but no hat, and is a girl in her middle twenties, with some resemblance to BRANWEN but rather younger, more obviously good-looking and a weaker character.

VALERIE: *(After a moment.)* Michael!

MICHAEL: *(Turning to see her.)* Valerie!

He and BRANWEN open stage and VALERIE comes down, staring now with hostility at BRANWEN, VALERIE stands between the other tow.

VALERIE: Hadn't you better introduce me.

MICHAEL: Oh – er – Miss Elder – my wife.

BRANWEN: How d'you do.

VALERIE: How d'you do.

BRANWEN goes towards door A, then turns just outside it.

BRANWEN: I had wondered whether to leave here at once. But now – for all our sakes – I'd better stay.

She goes out, and as they stand staring after her, the Curtain falls.

ACT TWO

Exactly as at end of Act One. The door A has just closed behind BRANWEN, and MICHAEL and VALERIE are still turned to watch her go. A moment's pause, then VALERIE turns to look at MICHAEL, who returns her look. They hold it a moment before she speaks.

VALERIE: *(Shaky but doing her best.)* Well, Michael? Whatever we are going to decide about the future I do think this is rather unforgivable.

MICHAEL: What do you mean?

VALERIE: To be here with her.

MICHAEL: I'm not here with her. I came to meet you as arranged.

VALERIE: *(Rather defiantly.)* Then who is that girl?

MICHAEL: *(With ironic care.)* Her name is Miss Elder. She's a painter.

VALERIE: *(After short wait.)* Go on.

MICHAEL: That's all.

VALERIE: You mean – all that it's necessary for me to know?

MICHAEL: My dear Val, I haven't the least idea how much it's necessary for you to know. But that's all I can tell you.

VALERIE: That's silly, of course. But – shall I tell you something?

MICHAEL: I wish you would. You seem to know more about all this than anybody else.

VALERIE: Give me a cigarette – and stop being so irritating. You seem to be nearly at your worst tonight.

She takes a cigarette and accepts his light.

MICHAEL: Go on, then. Tell me.

VALERIE: *(Earnestly.)* I won't unless you promise not to be deliberately stupid about it, Michael. I can't be real if you're just pretending and trying to talk like somebody in some clever-silly novel you've read. We must both be natural and sensible.

She sits, and he also sits, not too close.

MICHAEL: Carry on.

VALERIE: *(Deliberately.)* You haven't seen that girl for some time
now. But you used to see a very great deal of her – she was
very close to you – about the time we first met and even
right up to the time we were married. She was the one you
wouldn't even mention to me. The others didn't matter, they
were half a joke. But not this girl. She was the closest one
and therefore the secret one.

MICHAEL: When did you discover all this?

VALERIE: *(Deliberately.)* The moment I saw you standing
together here, I knew. In a flash! But before we were
married, I knew somehow that she – or at least somebody
like her – existed, somebody to whom you went and told
things, all the things you liked to hide from everybody else.
Then when we were married, she – well, she disappeared.
That's why I was so happy at first. I realize that now. I felt
I was beginning to share everything with you. At last I had
you to myself. And now she's back. I suppose you sent for
her. An S.O.S. Or to make me feel a fool, rushing here to try
and make it up.

MICHAEL: *(Who means it.)* I find this absolutely fascinating.

VALERIE: *(Sharply.)* Stop that! You promised to –

MICHAEL: *(Cutting in quickly.)* I meant that. I'm as curious as
you are. *(Rises, takes a stride or two, then turns, with change
of tone.)* Valerie, I've been working hard on a symphonic
rhapsody called *The Seabirds.* I started it four years ago then
suddenly dropped it. Did *you* know I'd ever begun such a
work?

VALERIE: No. Why?

MICHAEL: That girl did. She knew all about *The Seabirds.*

VALERIE: *(Bitterly.)* Thank you for that.

MICHAEL: You've missed the point.

VALERIE: Oh – no. Don't worry. The point's got home all right.
I wonder why you have to be such a cruel devil sometimes,
Michael.

MICHAEL: You know, you don't understand me at all.

VALERIE: Naturally. I'm your wife. But *she* understands you perfectly.

MICHAEL: *(Wondering, half-humorous.)* And I wouldn't swear she doesn't. By God, what if she really knew all about me!

VALERIE: *(Half hysterically.)* Michael, stop it!

MICHAEL: What?

VALERIE: *(Quieter now.)* If you won't talk sensibly and naturally and be frank with me, I'm going. I wish I'd never come here –

Suddenly begins crying quietly. Rather shocked, he tries to put a comforting arm round her but she pushes him away.

No. Leave me alone. Go away.

She pushes him away but holds on to him, then allows him to come nearer again, and buries her face in his coat or sleeve a moment. When she has recovered a little –

Oh – why can't we just be cosy and happy again together?

MICHAEL: *(Seriously.)* I don't know, my dear. We seem to have lost the secret.

VALERIE: *You've* lost it.

MICHAEL: But I like to be cosy and happy just as much as you do. Perhaps even more than you do. And now you'd better understand at once that you've been telling yourself and me an unpleasant little fairy-tale.

VALERIE: You mean – about that girl?

MICHAEL: Yes. Do you know when and where I first met her?

VALERIE: No, and I don't want to know. I've told you what I think.

MICHAEL: *(Angrily.)* You've told me a lot of rubbish. *(Is grimly silent.)*

VALERIE: *(Wearily.)* Well, go on. When and where did you first meet her?

MICHAEL: In this room about half an hour ago.

VALERIE: *(Sitting up.)* Michael, that's impossible. Why, you said yourself she knew about your rhapsody –

MICHAEL: *(Irritably.)* I know I did. And she also knew I was coming here today, and told another woman who's staying here. And she also heard me telephoning in Paris when she was somewhere out at sea. And when I first looked into this room I mistook her for you – God knows why – and then I was certain I'd met her somewhere. But I haven't. I don't know the girl. And can't make head or tail of her. And just as I was demanding an explanation from her, you walked in and told us we'd been living together for years. And there doesn't seem to be any damned sense or reason in anything she says, or the other woman says, or you say, and whether it's all the fault of you women or I'm going quietly off my head, I don't know.

VALERIE: *(Staring at him.)* But Michael, if this is true –

MICHAEL: *(Irritably.)* Of course it's true. The girl's a complete stranger to me. I don't know how old she is, where she lives when she's at home, don't even know her Christian name – no, that's not true. That other woman – Mrs. Tenbury – told me. It's some fantastic old Welsh name. I know – Branwen. That's it – Branwen. She's probably a Welsh witch. The whole country's a bit unreal. There's a lake outside where at any moment an arm clothed in white samite may be seen waving the Sword Excalibur.

VALERIE: But why should I have felt at once that she'd known you for years? As soon as I came in I –

MICHAEL: *(Cutting in.)* And if you hadn't come in then, I'd have had some explanation out of her.

VALERIE: *(Bitterly.)* Everything I do is wrong, isn't it?

MICHAEL: *(Impatiently.)* No, I don't mean that. And let's stick to the point.

VALERIE: *(After a slight pause, remembering.)* Why did she say – that she'd decided to try and leave here at once – but now, for all our sakes, she'd better stay?

MICHAEL: A minute before, she'd been imploring me to let her go.

VALERIE: *(With a touch of suspicion.)* But how were you keeping her here?

MICHAEL: *(Impatiently.)* How the deuce do I know! *(Meets the suspicious look in her eye.)* For God's sake don't look at me like that! I'm in no mood to start explaining all over again that I don't know the girl –

He breaks off because MRS. TENBURY enters A carrying a coat. MRS. TENBURY looks curiously at VALERIE as she comes down.

MRS. T.: *(To VALERIE.)* Good evening!

VALERIE: Good evening!

MICHAEL: Oh – Mrs. – er – Tenbury, this is my wife.

MRS. T.: How d'you do? *(Going to sit down.)* This is my gambling night. Twice a week I gamble with an old friend who lives no far away, Mrs. Trebarron Jones. We play six-pack bezique – and most ferociously too, reaching out and grabbing the cards until our arms ache. Last time she came here – and jumped well ahead with a triple bezique – and now tonight I go to her – to try and catch up. Do you ever play bezique?

VALERIE: I do. But my husband doesn't like it.

MICHAEL: It's such a snatching, accounting sort of game. You sit there like a couple of miserly competing drapers.

MRS. T.: *(Demurely.)* No doubt that is what Mrs. Trebarron Jones and I enjoy.

VALERIE: *(After a short pause, impulsively.)* Mrs. Tenbury – *(Breaks off.)*

MRS. T.: *(Smiling encouragement.)* Yes?

But VALERIE is looking for support to MICHAEL who is merely raising his eyebrows. MRS. TENBURY looks quizzically from one to the other.

About Miss Elder – um?

VALERIE: *(Surprised at being found out.)* Well – yes.

MICHAEL: Mrs. Tenbury, are you Welsh too?

MRS. T.: I'm half Welsh.

MICHAEL: It's witchcraft.

MRS. T.: *(Coolly.)* There might be a little about. I've often wondered if we're quite fair to the witch-hunters of the sixteenth and seventeenth centuries. My brother, who's an historian and has read many of the old documents, always says that the trials seem quite fair and reasonable and that there was an astonishing amount of really solid evidence. *(Pause.)* What about Miss Elder, Mrs. Camber? I don't know her really well, of course, but we've had three days here alone together.

VALERIE: *(Hesitatingly.)* It's just that – from what Michael has just told me – it's hard to believe she's telling the truth.

MRS. T.: *(Blandly.)* I consider myself a good judge of character, and I am quite certain that Miss Elder is an exceptionally truthful person.

VALERIE: I see – it seems very queer.

MRS. T.: No doubt that like the rest of us she's capable of self-deception. This afternoon we were discussing the people she says she sees here – and elsewhere. I never see any of these people myself – though sometimes I've had the feeling that they've just whisked round an invisible corner, so to speak – but she obviously believes she sees them, and she doesn't hesitate to describe them in detail.

MICHAEL: I don't understand. What people?

MRS. T.: *(Blandly.)* People who are commonly supposed to be dead and gone.

VALERIE: *(Rather awed.)* Oh – you mean ghosts.

MRS. T.: She says they're merely the impressions – a kind of footprint or finger-print – that people have left behind them. But sometimes, apparently, she goes clean into the Past, and then, she says, there's nothing thin and ghostly – but it all seems solid and real. She's certainly told me some extraordinary things. A most interesting and unusual girl.

MICHAEL: *(Dryly.)* I don't doubt that. *(With change to sincere tone, rather muttering.)* But I don't see what all that's got to do with me.

MRS. T.: No, I don't either. And, frankly, I'm very curious. I gather she knows a good deal about you.

VALERIE: *(Impetuously.)* I think this is – *hateful!*

MRS. T.: *(Regarding her seriously now.)* No. Disturbing perhaps, but not hateful.

VALERIE: *(Muttering, rather childishly.)* That's how it seems to me.

MRS. T.: *(Gravely.)* I think you should try and see it in another and better light.

THOMAS enters B.

THOMAS: Oh – Mrs. Tenbury – I told Morgan Evans on the telephone his car was wanted again, and he's coming in five minutes – or ten minutes.

MRS. T.: All right, Thomas. I'll wait here.

THOMAS: *(To the CAMBERS.)* My wife says would you like your dinner now. It's ready if you are, she says.

MICHAEL: Thanks. Can't say I feel very hungry yet, though.

VALERIE: Yes, Michael, come on.

MICHAEL: All right.

THOMAS: *(Indicating door A.)* Along to the end of the passage there, please. Will you be wanting anything to drink with your dinner now, please?

VALERIE: *(As she goes.)* Not for me, thank you. Michael?

MICHAEL: *(Going.)* No, I don't think so.

They go out A. THOMAS watches them go, and if there is room at door can hold it open for them.

MRS. T.: Thomas, where is Miss Elder?

THOMAS: Oh – I don't know at all. She wasn't in the dining-room. Perhaps she's gone to her room. Do you want to see her?

MRS. T.: No, no. Don't disturb her.

THOMAS: *(Confidentially.)* When I saw her last she seemed quite upset about something, Miss Elder did. I met her in the passage, Mrs. Tenbury, and she was like a ghost herself, her face as white as a sheet. *(Dropping his voice.)* And afterwards I thought I hear her crying. Some trouble, you see, it came at once, didn't it?

MRS. T.: Now, Thomas, you're not to talk like that.

THOMAS: No, no, I've finished. I won't say another word about her except she is a young lady of a very fine nature. But this Mr. Camber. I think he is a very troublesome man.

MRS. T.: He's obviously not very good-tempered, Thomas, and just now he seems to be on edge. So you'll have to be careful, that's all.

THOMAS: Oh – I will. You heard me now, asking specially if he wanted something to drink with his dinner – not to keep him waiting a single minute, you see? But he calls me a liar. As soon as he comes here, before he has set a foot in his room, he calls me to my face a liar.

MRS. T.: Now, Thomas, that's all over.

THOMAS: *(Broodingly.)* I try to make myself useful and agreeable to all kinds of people. There was a woman came here once to stay, with four little dogs – *four* – all of them petted and spoilt to death – and I still made myself agreeable. But – I tell you frankly, Mrs. Tenbury, because I know you are a friend to us all here – I tell you, I don't like this Mr. Camber. And if he goes as suddenly as he came, I won't be the one to grumble.

BRANWEN appears at door A looking pale and strained.

MRS. T.: *(Calling, cheerfully.)* Come along, Miss Elder. I'm just waiting for that horrible old car to take me over to Mrs. Trebarron Jones, but it may be another ten minutes yet. I know Morgan Evans of old.

THOMAS: *(Preparing to go.)* Shall I hurry him up on the telephone?

MRS. T.: No, just let me know when it's here. I have an idea it's going to rain hard.

THOMAS: Yes, it is. *(He goes. BRANWEN comes forward.)*

MRS. T.: Come and sit her, and be cosy.

BRANWEN: No, thank you. I feel…rather restless.

MRS. T.: *(Looking hard at her.)* As an evening's amusement, watching two old women play bezique very definitely has its limitations, I know, but if you'd like to come with me tonight, my dear, you've very welcome to.

BRANWEN: *(Smiling slightly.)* That's very nice of you…but… *(Shakes her head.)*

MRS. T.: I thought you might like to – escape for an hour or two, that's all.

BRANWEN: *(In almost a whisper.)* This is one of the times and there are an awful lot of them, when there really isn't any escape. I thought earlier of running away from here, at once, tonight. But now I can't do that.

MRS. T.: I've just met Mrs. Camber. Poor little thing! Doesn't know where she is, and I don't blame her.

BRANWEN: Neither do I. I'm sorry for her.

MRS. T.: *(After hesitating.)* I've got to say it. So please don't be angry, but think of me as a friend. Are you in love with him?

BRANWEN: *(With a slight smile.)* In love? When I was eighteen I was terribly in love with a dashing youth who owned a bright red sports car. Two years after that I was even more terribly in love with a golden-haired young giant at the Art School…

MRS. T.: Is that your answer?

BRANWEN: Yes. Because it seems to me that being *in love* belongs to that atmosphere of youth and bright foolishness and ignorance. You are fascinated by somebody who's attractive and quite strange. But supposing you know somebody as nobody, not even his best and oldest friend, knows him? You've lived with his heart and mind. You've suffered when he's suffered, and been glad when he's been glad. Surely that's a whole world beyond being in love. It's a different sort of relation altogether. And we haven't a set of words for it.

MRS. T.: But – a man you don't know –

BRANWEN: A man I don't know! I was held a prisoner in the very centre of his life. I had to share every mood, every impulse, every secret thought. I knew him so well that I no longer had any real life of my own.

MRS. T.: *(Hesitatingly.)* I know you've felt all this deeply, my dear. I'm not doubting that. But are you sure you've not imagined most of this – what shall I call it – clairvoyant relationship?

BRANWEN: Didn't I ask myself that over and over again? I didn't *want* all this to happen. I struggled against it. But it was no use my pretending, as I often tried to do, that I was simply making it up. It was all too strong, too sharp, and I had too many proofs. Didn't I know he was coming here, didn't I see and hear him telephoning in Paris five days again, when I still was out at sea? Could I have made *that* up? I *knew* then he was coming here, miserably unhappy, to try and patch up his marriage. And you've seen them for yourself. Was I wrong?

MRS. T.: From the little I've seen and heard, I should say you were only too right. By why did you feel that you had to come here too? Because he needed you?

BRANWEN: Yes. He was desperate.

MRS. T.: Then you love him.

BRANWEN: *(Rather distressed.)* How can I help loving him… when I've shared so much…know him as…he hardly knows himself…?

THOMAS enters B.

THOMAS: Morgan Evans is here. Says the old engine's behaving terrible tonight.

MRS. T.: All right. *(To BRANWEN.)* He can wait a few minutes if you –

BRANWEN: *(Cutting in.)* No please. You must go. And don't worry about me.

MRS. T.: I shan't be late.

She goes, THOMAS holding door B open for her. Just as THOMAS is about to follow, BRANWEN speaks to him.

BRANWEN: Oh – Thomas!

THOMAS: *(Remaining at door.)* Yes, miss?

BRANWEN: I suppose I couldn't get a train to London late tonight, could I?

THOMAS: Oh – no, you couldn't.

BRANWEN: Nothing before morning now?

THOMAS: That's right. Eight-thirty-five, that's really the first one now. But you're not thinking of leaving us, are you, Miss Elder?

BRANWEN: *(Vaguely.)* I don't want to, Thomas. It isn't that I don't like this place. But – well – I may have to go.

THOMAS: *(Who has been observing her shrewdly, now coming forward a little.)* Now I'll tell you. If these new people are worrying you at all, don't you mind about that, because, I'll tell you, they won't stay. I always know whether people are going to stay or not. I don't know how I know, but I do. You ask my wife. She'll tell you. Over and over again, I've said to her, 'These people won't stay, you'll see.' Or I've said, 'They will stay.' Just as the case may be, as you might say. So don't you worry about that at all. For I tell you, they'll be gone very soon. I know.

BRANWEN: I believe you're right, Thomas. But –

She stops because she hears – and we hear – the sound of voices – MICHAEL and VALERIE's raised angrily – coming through door A. THOMAS hears them too.

THOMAS: *(Whispering.)* There you are, you see. Angry! Quarrelling!

BRANWEN: *(Hastily.)* I'm going out.

THOMAS: It's raining.

BRANWEN: I don't care.

She slips past him through door B. He remains a moment at door, looking from her up to door A, then goes out B as we hear MICHAEL's voice nearer. MICHAEL enters, looking angry, through A, followed by VALERIE, who can be still wearing her coat.

VALERIE: You might at least have let me eat my dinner in peace.

MICHAEL: *(Angrily.)* I'm not stopping you. Stay there and eat a dozen dinners. Only don't expect me to sit looking at you, trying to make damn silly conversation for the sake of that old Welsh waitress. I can't do it. Either I'm too old or not old enough. But don't mind me. Go back and eat away in peace.

VALERIE: I didn't come here to eat but to talk to you.

MICHAEL: Then don't blame me if you're not still eating. We seem to have this place to ourselves. So talk, talk!

He goes to the windows and pulls back a curtain and opens the window. We catch a glimpse of black night, and hear the patter of rain.

Black rain among the mountains like lumps of slate! Wet Wales!

Muttering as he stares out moodily.

That old waitress hated the sight of us. You could almost hear her muttering spells! Tomorrow we'll be lost in a fog. We've probably said goodbye to the sun for weeks. What a country! Why did I leave California?

VALERIE: *(Who knows very well.)* What did you say?

MICHAEL: *(Half-turning.)* I said, 'Why did I leave California?'

VALERIE: I can tell you that. Because just when you'd persuaded me I wasn't really homesick and that the Pacific Coast was perfect, and I'd refurnished the bungalow for you and found a couple of servants who weren't thieves and robbers, you said you couldn't stand California a week longer and that you never wanted to see its damned empty meaningless sunshine again.

MICHAEL: *(With a sudden unexpected grin.)* I know. And I meant it too. There's something profoundly wrong with that country. It's got everything and it amounts to nothing. Probably because it's fallen out of the hands of God. He doesn't know it's there any longer.

VALERIE: *(Rather bitterly.)* That's where you're lucky. You've always got a grand reason for all your whims and fancies.

MICHAEL: That's because they're not really whims and fancies. They come from deep down inside. The promptings of the spirit.

VALERIE: *(Courageously.)* Because you're spoilt and have always had too much of your own way.

MICHAEL: *(Shocked.)* My own way! You don't begin to understand what my life's like. For twenty years I've been like a man with an urgent message who has to invent every damned syllable he speaks before he can get a word of it out.

VALERIE: *(Rather brokenly.)* All right, Michael. I don't understand. You've told me so a thousand times. But please remember before you go on cursing this place and me and everything, it was your idea that we should meet here and talk.

MICHAEL: Which means, I suppose – though God knows why – that now I have to pretend that everything here is perfect, that I enjoyed my dinner, that it isn't raining, that –

VALERIE: *(Sharply.)* Michael – please!

MICHAEL: Well?

VALERIE: We have a chance to talk properly. And I can't stand much of this. So let's try and talk sensibly.

MICHAEL: All right. Sorry! Go ahead.

VALERIE: When you arrived here, Michael, you weren't already in this mood were you? I mean, all disturbed…and… bitter….angry…?

MICHAEL: *(Quietly.)* No I wasn't. I haven't had any better time the last two months than you have. And I can't stand much of this either. I can't work properly. And I came here hoping that we'd find some way – talking quietly about ourselves – away from people and the usual fuss – to come together again so that you wouldn't be perpetually feeling hurt – and I wouldn't be forever shouting and storming. And that's the truth. I wanted either to mend it – or end it.

VALERIE: So do I. And that's what I feel now, though… I'd hoped… I suppose I was silly…but I'd hoped.

She looks like breaking down.

MICHAEL: I know….but – well, you must admit that anything's better than what we'd been making of it.

VALERIE: *(In low voice.)* I tell myself so. Over and over again, I tell myself so… I hope it's true.

MICHAEL: *(After pause.)* Well? What about my coming here and the mood I was in?

VALERIE: If you felt like that, when you arrived, what's changed you so quickly?

MICHAEL: *(In a hard voice.)* We're getting back to that girl now, aren't we?

VALERIE: Probably.

MICHAEL: You're not going to start telling me all over again that I must have known her for years, are you?

VALERIE: No. I believe now you haven't. And I'm sorry I thought you had, though anybody else would have thought the same. But – you can't pretend it hasn't made any difference. And – what does it mean?

MICHAEL: As far as I'm concerned it only means that I'm naturally determined to get to the bottom of it, because either something very queer – has been happening or what's more likely, some people I thought I could trust have let me down. Either way, I want to know. And of course the thing's put me on edge a bit. It would you or anybody else. You can't blame me.

VALERIE: *(Uncertainly.)* I'm not. But you see…well, I feel there's something between you…that she –

MICHAEL: *(Warning her.)* Now then! We've already had that out.

VALERIE: *(Hastily.)* I'm sorry, Michael, but I must say it. It may not be sensible, but it's what I feel deep down – I can't help it – that she…she's the one I always knew somehow was there…the one I'm really frightened of…

MICHAEL: Frightened – of what?

VALERIE: *(In low voice, uncertainly.)* I don't know. Perhaps… because at first I always felt there was somebody…

watching…knowing about you…more than I knew…or could know…and that in the end she might come and take you away…for ever…

She puts a hand to her heart.

She cries quietly. After watching her, bewildered, a moment, he strides up and down the room.

MICHAEL: *(After pause, brusquely.)* I'm sorry, Valerie, but this isn't fair.

VALERIE: *(Controlling herself.)* What isn't? *(Hastily adding.)* Not that anything is, anyhow.

MICHAEL: *(Impatiently.)* Well, how can we settle anything, how can we find any sort of common sensible ground, in this monstrous atmosphere?

VALERIE: *(With more spirit.)* Is it my fault?

MICHAEL: Of course it is. You've taken a few odd guesses or coincidences or whatever they are – which the girl herself can probably explain in five minutes once I can get at her – and you've magnified them and blown them out and coloured them until we're moving about in a tragic mystical haze and you're worrying about something that wouldn't stand two minutes examination. And then you ask me to talk quietly and sensibly.

VALERIE: But you feel it yourself.

MICHAEL: *(Storming.)* I don't. I'm my usual self. I admit that's nothing to boast of. I'm probably half barmy and I'm certain the world's rapidly because a vast madhouse. But you knew all that or if you don't it's time you did.

VALERIE: *(Afraid, brokenly.)* Don't, please, Michael!… I can't bear it when you glare and shout at me…it's not so much what you say…

MICHAEL: *(Angrily.)* You don't listen to what I say. I don't believe you ever did. That's why as soon as we came to our senses we've always been at cross-purposes…

VALERIE: *(Almost moaning.)* You're only trying to hurt me… saying anything just to hurt me…

MICHAEL: *(Angrily contemptuous.)* Oh – for God's sake –

135

VALERIE: *(Bursting out in tears now.)* Oh!

Bursts into sobbing.

THOMAS now enters B and comes in a little, taking in situation. MICHAEL has turned away from this door.

THOMAS: Mr. Camber!

MICHAEL: *(Angrily.)* Can't you leave us alone in this damned place? Clear out, you fool!

THOMAS: *(Standing up to him.)* I came in to ask you about the morning. Only doing my duty.

MICHAEL: *(Angrily, going nearer.)* I'd like to know who told you your duty was to come peeping and prying –

THOMAS: *(Cutting in, firmly.)* I'm not peeping and prying. And let me tell you, Mr. Camber, that I won't be sworn at and called a fool by you or anybody else. I was a man – yes, and a soldier – when you were still a boy at school. And I won't have it, see. And if you can't behave properly here, then go somewhere else.

MICHAEL: *(In a blind fury, advancing as if to hit him.)* You have the damned impudence to talk to me like that – I'll – I'll

THOMAS: *(Bravely.)* Go on. What will you do?

MICHAEL: *(Hardly knowing what he is saying or doing.)* Wring your neck, you –

Talking through his clenched teeth, he has seized THOMAS by each upper arm and is glaring into his face. Now BRANWEN, wearing no hat but a raincoat that is rather wet, has appeared at window.

BRANWEN: *(Sharply.)* Michael! *(Comes in a pace.)* Remember the Admiral!

MICHAEL turns and regards her, thunderstruck, and the anger dies out of him.

MICHAEL: The Admiral? How can you know that?

BRANWEN: *(Ignoring this.)* Thomas, please go now.

THOMAS: *(Hesitating.)* Well – I don't know – he's –

BRANWEN: *(Sharply.)* Please! It's all right now.

THOMAS nods and goes out B. VALERIE and MICHAEL are staring at BRANWEN.

VALERIE: *(In low voice.)* What does she mean?

MICHAEL: *(Slowly.)* When I was a boy I suddenly lost my temper with another boy, and might have killed him if an old naval commander – we used to call him the Admiral – hadn't interfered… *(Suddenly to BRANWEN.)* And then? What then? You pretend to know all about it.

BRANWEN: *(Quietly.)* He was a big man, though getting old, and he shook you and shook you until all the anger had left you and you were just a frightened little boy…

MICHAEL: *(Slowly.)* And he said, 'There's a black mad dog inside you, young Camber, and one day he may rush out and drag you to the hangman. Never forget that black mad dog.' *(Challengingly to BRANWEN.)* He told you. You know him.

BRANWEN: *(Quietly.)* No. But I saw him once – shaking you.

MICHAEL: *(Impatiently.)* How could you?

BRANWEN: Because, I think, you were remembering it. You'd just lost your temper badly, and then suddenly you remembered the Admiral and the black mad dog. It was when you were sitting in your room at an hotel – just after a competition – in Brussels.

MICHAEL: Three years ago?

BRANWEN: Yes.

MICHAEL: *(Staring at her in wonder.)* My God! *(Still staring at her.)* Now we have to talk. I'll take no excuses. You've got to tell me.

VALERIE: *(Starting up.)* No, no, Michael. Let's go away *now,* and never mind about all this.

He completely ignores her, still staring at BRANWEN. VALERIE clutches him to try and attract his attention. He waves her aside. She is crying in desperation.

BRANWEN: *(Sorry for her.)* Mrs. Camber –

VALERIE: *(Desperately.)* It's always been you, hasn't it – all the time?

BRANWEN: *(Shaking her head slowly.)* No.

VALERIE: *(In despair.)* Yes it has. Michael, it's always been her, hasn't it?

She moves almost blindly towards door B, then stops and turns. The other two are still staring at each other. She makes a last appeal.

MICHAEL: Valerie, please, I want to understand all this. *(Without looking at her.)* Either be quiet – or go away.

Exit VALERIE.

BRANWEN: *(Uncertainly.)* I ought to have gone away.

MICHAEL: And if you had gone, I'd have followed you.

Here he can go and switch off lights back R. to change lighting, if necessary.

I must be told now. There are things about me that you know that no other living person knows. Why? How? *(As she hesitates.)* Don't be afraid. No more rages. I'll listen quietly. Only – tell me the truth.

BRANWEN: It's very difficult. And I never meant you to know – never.

MICHAEL: Better sit down.

She does so. He can too, if necessary.

And I'll do my best to help you. Now either you've collected – a lot of information about me from all over the place –

BRANWEN: No.

MICHAEL: Or there's something supernormal in all this. Clairvoyance? Telepathy? What do you call it?

BRANWEN: I just call it *seeing*, though of course there's much more than mere ordinary seeing in it. Sounds. Feelings. Thoughts.

MICHAEL: Seeing at a distance?

BRANWEN: Yes. Sometimes at a very great distance. And then again, at certain moments, quite clearly back into the past.

MICHAEL: You mean – the past generally – or my past.

BRANWEN: I've seen both. But now we're talking about your past.

MICHAEL: But why me at all?

BRANWEN: I don't know. At first I was always asking myself that. Perhaps it began as a mere accident – like – like telephone wires getting crossed. Or perhaps there's some link that we can't understand, outside this world, outside time. I know enough now to be sure of one thing – that there's a great part of us that is outside this world and outside its time.

MICHAEL: Possibly. But tell me how it all began.

BRANWEN: Five years ago, just when I was recovering from a bad attack of flu, and I went to a concert at the Queen's Hall –

MICHAEL: *(Eagerly.)* Are you a musician?

BRANWEN: No. And then I knew very little about music. I know more now. Through you.

MICHAEL: *(With a touch of complacency.)* Well, that's something.

BRANWEN: *(Half laughing.)* Oh – Michael – that's so like you!

MICHAEL: *(Catching her easy familiar tone.)* Why, what's wrong with it? *(Breaks off, realizing.)* Good Lord, I'm beginning to behave as if I'd known you for years.

BRANWEN: *(Gravely.)* I think you have.

MICHAEL: *(Slowly.)* I wonder. *(Hastily.)* No, no, no. Go on. At this concert –?

BRANWEN: You were conducting a new work for the orchestra.

MICHAEL: *(Eagerly.)* Which was it?

BRANWEN: The *Night Riders*.

MICHAEL: I remember. Yes, that would be five years ago. Well?

BRANWEN: *(Carefully.)* This isn't easy to explain. But while I was listening to you work, I began to drift away from myself. But my mind wasn't merely wandering, as people's often do when they're listening – or half listening – to music. I began to feel almost as if I were conducting the orchestra. I felt that I knew what was coming next in the score. Then, when they were all applauding, I was my ordinary self again, only feeling very shaky and wondering if I'd been a fool to go out so soon after flu. But when I got back home, and I was sitting in front of the fire, thinking about the concert, quite suddenly I wasn't in my flat at all. I was in a restaurant – I think it was Manzoni's but I was never sure – looking down on a little supper party. It was being given by a heavily-built, oldish man with a sallow tired face, and you were there, with Rachel Flower, the pianist.

MICHAEL: Yes, I remember. And it *was* at Manzoni's. Old Beckerman gave the party. Still, somebody might have seen us there, and told you afterwards –

BRANWEN: No, no, I saw you and heard you that very night, while the rest of me was still sitting staring at the fire in my flat. And now I'll prove it. Can you remember that night clearly? Can you remember how you were behaving and what you were really feeling. Please try.

MICHAEL: Don't worry. I've a good memory. That supper party comes back to me quite clearly. Well, what's your proof?

BRANWEN: Not only did I see and hear you, just as if I was really hovering above the table, but I knew at once, as I always did afterwards, exactly what you were feeling. You were pretending to be very gay. But actually you were rather miserable. You were disappointed. The orchestra needed at least another rehearsal. You knew the work had been badly played. You tried to persuade yourself that was all that was wrong. But underneath you were still disappointed because you couldn't help feeling that the *Night Riders* was probably not good enough, too diffuse, violent without being really strong – *(He is about to speak, but she checks him hurriedly.)* No, let me give you this final bit of proof. While you were pretending to be gay, and underneath were wrestling with this feeling of disappointment, you stopped yourself dropping into a black depression by making a plan, deciding to spend the next year at least working at small things – especially at a quintet for strings and oboe –

MICHAEL: *(Staring at her in amazement.)* But it's true. Every word. And nobody could have told you, because nobody knew.

BRANWEN: *(Calmly.)* And that's how it began, you see, Michael. I'm sorry if it worries you – my calling you Michael – but I've got into the habit.

MICHAEL: *(Hastily.)* What does it matter what you call me, after this? You know more about me than anybody else. And – my God! – it's – it's not only uncanny – but it's terrifying. But go on, go on, what happened after that?

BRANWEN: I can't begin to tell you all that happened, of course. It would take me hours.

MICHAEL: *(Hastily.)* You're going to tell me one day. I've a right to know.

BRANWEN: For the next three years, there was hardly a day when I didn't *see* you. Working or amusing yourself. Alone or with friends. In England. Abroad – France, Germany, Switzerland, Belgium, America. I proved to myself over and over again that I wasn't merely making this up –

MICHAEL: I was going to ask that. You could check this seeing of yours?

BRANWEN: Easily, at least when you were in London. Often I wrote down in advance where you said you were going to be – attending a concert, a play, and so on – and then discovered, either by going there myself or sometimes through other people or the newspaper, that you were there.

MICHAEL: I believe you, though I don't think those things are important.

BRANWEN: Neither did I. What was important to me was – first – the way I came to see you not only in the present but also in the past –

MICHAEL: Like the episode of the Admiral?

BRANWEN: Yes, and dozens and dozens of others. I could never decide if I saw them because you were remembering them yourself. Once I saw you as a little boy, spending a foggy Christmas at a farmhouse.

MICHAEL: Good Lord – yes!

BRANWEN: Going to a Cathedral Choir School. Having a terrible quarrel with an uncle –

MICHAEL: He brought me up. In Filchester. He was a lawyer there.

BRANWEN: I know it. I've seen the dark house, with its front of blackened stone, and the monkey tree, and in the hall was a grandfather clock with a moon face painted on it –

MICHAEL: *(Eagerly.)* Yes, yes, yes!

BRANWEN: And as a boy you used to play in a little room at the top and back of the house. There was a toy railway line leading up to an old fort. And there was your cousin, the boy who stammered, and once you cut his head open with a toy sword…

MICHAEL: *(Seizing her by the shoulders and staring at her.)* For God's sake – girl! You don't know what you're doing to me – telling me all this. My own past, so far away, suddenly coming to life again in somebody else's mind! It's enough to turn a man's heart right over.

BRANWEN: Do you believe me, now, Michael?

MICHAEL: Yes, of course I do. And it's – it's horribly disturbing. It's frightening.

BRANWEN: I had three years of it. More and more compelling all the time. Sometimes I felt that if it lasted much longer I'd go mad. When I was seeing you clearly, I had to share your moods. There was a terrible heavy black mood of yours – when you'd feel as if there was nothing left but yourself and the dark chasm you peering into –

MICHAEL: Yes, yes. Over and over again. I still feel it, when things seem unbearable.

BRANWEN: After a time I knew you were lost in one of those black moods even before I saw you again. Suddenly, behind everything that was going on round me – I'd know that chasm was there, and I'd know that the first moment I could be quiet I'd be with you, peering down, sick with horror, alone…

MICHAEL: You make me feel ashamed.

BRANWEN: No, I knew quite early that it wasn't your fault. You had these moods of complete despair just as you had your sudden flashes of rage.

MICHAEL: But to have your life eaten away by some damned idiotic, half-cracked stranger –

BRANWEN: You weren't a stranger by that time. How could you be?

MICHAEL: Good Lord – no. People have lived side by side for fifty years and known less about one another.

BRANWEN: Besides – with us – there had to be understanding or nothing. Misunderstanding was impossible.

MICHAEL: *(Wonderingly.)* With us?

BRANWEN: I'm sorry. It's so difficult to believe you knew nothing about it. In fact, I don't believe it.

MICHAEL: Neither do I now. Why, when I first saw you here, didn't I insist that we'd met before? That is, I did after first mistaking you for Valerie. Why did I mistake you for Valerie? Was it just some trick of light?

BRANWEN: It might have been.

MICHAEL: You don't believe it. All right then, why did I mistake you for Valerie?

BRANWEN: Perhaps because you'd already mistaken Valerie for me.

MICHAEL: *(Startled.)* How could I? What do you mean? Now wait –

BRANWEN: *(Firmly interrupting.)* I didn't mean to say that. Please forget it. But I thought – certainly during the last year – there were breaks, you know – and sometimes I deliberately refused to see – but during the last year, I thought often you knew I was with you. Sometimes I felt – when things were very bad for you – that you called to me.

MICHAEL: Is that how you came to be here?

BRANWEN: Yes. Two years ago, when you met Valerie, I made a tremendous effort to close my mind to you. That's why I went to South Africa. I felt that unless I changed everything, went off a long way, made my ordinary existence new and rather difficult for myself, I'd never be able to shut you out… At first there seemed so little left of my own…a thin ghost of a life…

MICHAEL: But it was better afterwards?

BRANWEN: Yes, it was – better. And then, feeling – shall I say? – cured, or in an advanced stage of convalescence, I thought I could safely come back home. As we were coming up the Channel, I was so confident that I even allowed myself to think about you – and then –

MICHAEL: It started all over again.

BRANWEN: I was there, close to you, when you were telephoning in Paris – about coming here – and I knew you were desperately unhappy again – and – I knew why.

MICHAEL: But why didn't I feel that you were there? Why have I never felt anything?

BRANWEN: *(Puzzled.)* Haven't you?

MICHAEL: *(Slowly.)* No, I don't think so. I admit – there was something about you – that seemed…

BRANWEN: Are you *sure* you never have?

MICHAEL: *(Sharply.)* Tell me.

BRANWEN: What do you mean, Michael?

MICHAEL: I don't mean that I'm disbelieving you again, Branwen. But this is the supreme test. You see, if I tell you one or two things that have happened – possibly nothing more than odd fancies of mine – you're an imaginative creative, and without the least notion of being untruthful you might claim them as part –

BRANWEN: Yes, I see what you mean.

MICHAEL: But if *you* tell *me*, and then I'm the judge, that's very different.

BRANWEN: I'm not afraid. I don't know that it's fair – but then I don't think you are a very fair-minded person, are you, Michael?

MICHAEL: No, I'm not. I'm a rather unscrupulous devil in some ways. Not in others, though. I'm fair from now on. And I challenge you. Now then! Your instances.

BRANWEN: Once…nearly three years ago…in the winter. You were in America, and you were staying, only for one day and night, in a city near a great lake…

MICHAEL: Chicago?

BRANWEN: No, and don't interrupt and prompt me, or you'll say afterwards you said it all for me. It wasn't Chicago because you'd just come from there. You were staying, high up, in a huge hotel near the railway station. To get to the hall where they were playing your music, you had to go down a long, long street, miles of it…

MICHAEL: *(With growing interest.)* I know now. Have you ever been to America?

BRANWEN: No. And I've remembered the name of the city. It was Cleveland, Ohio.

MICHAEL: *(As before.)* Yes, it was. Well, what happened there?

BRANWEN: *(Slowly, carefully.)* I saw you sitting in your room. Some people had been, had a few drinks, and had gone. You were terribly tired, almost nervously exhausted, all the travelling and rehearsing and arguing and fuss. And you'd been sleeping badly. Once you went to the window and opened it, and an icy wind with rattling particles of ice in it, swept into the stuffy room, and it was too cold, you had to shut the window again. And you felt like death. You tried to read and couldn't. You hated everything, that room, that hotel, the whole city, the whole continent, and you felt like blotting everything out. And you stared out at nothing. I watched you eyes… *(She hesitates.)*

MICHAEL: *(Suppressing his excitement.)* Yes, go on.

BRANWEN: I was standing in front of you. But you didn't see me. You saw nothing but your own disgust and misery. And then, because I was watching your eyes, I thought – quite suddenly – just in a flash – *you saw me.*

MICHAEL: *(With growing excitement.)* Now – for God's sake – be careful and try to remember exactly – what did you mean then, what did you do then?

BRANWEN: *(With some agitation.)* I put my hand, very lightly on your forehead, and you leaned your head back. And them, after a moment or two, I closed your eyes and told you to try and rest…and you fell asleep…

MICHAEL: I fell asleep and slept for an hour or two, and then when I awoke I remembered and thought it had been a dream…

BRANWEN: It was a kind of dream.

MICHAEL: *(Wonderingly.)* And that was you. It's all true, every bit of it. I remember the particles of ice – everything, everything. And it was in the middle of December, three years ago, in Cleveland – *(Breaks off, looks searchingly at her, then cries.)* There should be something else, not long afterwards – something else. Can you remember?

BRANWEN: And what if I can?

MICHAEL: *(Vehemently.)* If you can tell me, if you can explain, when I'm remembering now – I must begin my life all over again. And so must you. We must start living – from the moment you tell me – if you can. So I warn you. Don't say I didn't warn you, Branwen.

BRANWEN: I've been warning myself, for the last hour. I never meant this to happen. I thought – in some vague silly way – I might be able to help without your ever knowing, perhaps say something to your wife –

MICHAEL: *(Eagerly.)* Never mind about all that now. I want to know if you can remember – or ever know – something that happened not very long after that night in Cleveland – something that I remember and will never forget. If you do, tell me.

BRANWEN: You were in the Far West. It was very early in the morning, hardly light. I saw you just waking up, after only a few hours restless sleep. The night before, you'd quarrelled with some people – a musician, his wife and her brother –

that you'd thought would turn out to be good friends. You remembered this – and other things – you hated yourself more than you hated them – and you wondered if you could just disappear into a nameless stupid animal life, perhaps somewhere in the South Seas. And then you saw me again, but this time not just for a second, but you saw me truly as I saw you. And I said, 'Let's get out.' And you said 'Yes,' and then you were quite different, simple and easy and happy, like a boy. And so we went out – and it was just dawn – there was a smoky gold all over the desert – and because we'd really found one another at last, and knew we had, and our hearts were at peace, there was a magic in everything, and a magical sun rose upon a magical world, and there was a light on the hills we had never seen before… *(She breaks off because she is now crying silently.)*

MICHAEL: *(Bending over her.)* And I thought it was a dream. And it was you.

BRANWEN: It was a kind of dream. But we were real in it.

MICHAEL: I know now why you said that I'd already mistaken Valerie for you. It's true. That's what I did. I met her not long afterwards, when I was still like a man haunted by a glimpse of paradise, and there must have been something – some little trick of looks or speech – that reminded me of you, and I thought she must have cast a long shadow, so I hurled myself in love with her, swept her off her feet, married her – *(Breaks off.)* It was then, I suppose, I lost you!

BRANWEN: Yes. I couldn't go on – dreaming…

MICHAEL: And I've been looking for you ever since m–

BRANWEN: But you didn't realise –

MICHAEL: *(Masterfully.)* I waited for something – a dream on the other side of the dark, a light on the hills of the morning – that never returned. That was you. For years because I was unhappy, you were unhappy. Now – for years and years – my happiness shall light up yours. Everything you've said proves that we belong to each other and only have a shadow of a life when we're apart. I belong to you. You belong to me. I didn't know before so I couldn't do anything about it. But now I do know, I must claim you. I've no alternative.

BRANWEN: No, Michael, that's not true. I can go away now –

MICHAEL: Yes, but not alone. Only with me. How can I let you go now? You're my life. I don't say anything about love. This is something stronger and more fundamental than what generally passes for love. It's our life. So – *(Rings the bell.)*

BRANWEN: Why are you ringing?

MICHAEL: To tell what's-his-name I shall want my car at once. You see, Branwen, you and I must go – it doesn't matter where, so long as we're together – but we must go tonight, at once. It's our only chance, to keep straight on as we are now, not even to stop talking about ourselves. No recriminations, compromises, arrangements.

BRANWEN: Are you sure you don't want to hurry in order to stop yourself thinking?

MICHAEL: No, I'm not sure. I don't particularly want to think. I'm beginning my life. That's not the time to think. But it's the time to hurry. Don't forget. I've a lot of good work I want to do, and now I believe I can do it.

BRANWEN: *(With great tenderness.)* Michael! I know now so terribly well – and I love you so dearly.

MICHAEL: And I tell you – you're my hope, my morning, my life! *(Dominating her.)* And you'll come with me, for the remainder of our time on earth, tonight, now?

BRANWEN: Yes, Michael, I'll come with you.

MICHAEL: For ever?

BRANWEN: For as long as you want me.

MICHAEL: It's the same thing.

Goes towards the bell again.

Why doesn't that fellow answer the bell?

As he rings again, and BRANWEN has her eyes fixed on him, the Curtain falls.

ACT THREE

Exactly as at end of Act Two. MICHAEL is just ringing the bell. We wait a moment after the bell has been rung.

MICHAEL: *(Impatiently.)* What's the matter with the fellow?

BRANWEN: There are only two of them – Thomas and his wife – to run the whole place, and perhaps he's been called away to do something.

MICHAEL: Don't see why he should be. Struck me as an inattentive chap, who's probably been spoilt.

BRANWEN: *(With spirit.)* You don't know anything about poor Thomas, and I know you don't. And you know I know you don't. So why pretend? Actually, he's a pet. And – Michael – *(She hesitates.)*

MICHAEL: Well?

BRANWEN: If you lose you temper with him again tonight, I shall lose *my* temper – with you.

MICHAEL: *(Rather surprised.)* Do you lose your temper?

BRANWEN: Sometimes.

MICHAEL: That's bad. Two of us losing tempers. One of us ought to be calm.

BRANWEN: Don't worry. Compared with you, I *am* calm. But I can be very angry. *(Looks at him a moment.)* You've made me so angry sometimes.

MICHAEL: I can understand that. When – especially?

BRANWEN: It's stupid to get wildly angry at all –

MICHAEL: I agree. I don't enjoy it.

BRANWEN: One part of you does, I think. It's a kind of release.

MICHAEL: Well, I shan't need any more releases now.

BRANWEN: *(Not too severely.)* I might as well tell you at once Michael – there's one outlet for that deep rage of yours that I think really hateful. And that's why I've just warned you about Thomas. I've always simply hated it when I've seen you losing your temper and yelling and bawling –

MICHAEL: *(Cutting in.)* At waiters, porters, and the rest of 'em, eh?

BRANWEN: Yes. All the people who aren't allowed to defend themselves properly and answer you back as you deserve to be answered.

MICHAEL: I know. I hate it too. Though it usually evens out in the end.

BRANWEN: You mean you're generous with them? I know that. Do you remember that man in Rome – at the hotel – what was it called?

MICHAEL: Do you mean the Excelsior?

BRANWEN: Yes – and you threw a parcel at the man –

MICHAEL: And knocked a tray out of his hand. Oh – there was a stinking row about that – you know what they are in Italy! But – good lord! – you saw that too. It's fantastic.

BRANWEN: There are thousands and thousands of things I can remember.

MICHAEL: You're going to tell me about them. But don't imagine I'll be the idiotic self-torturing fool you're seen so often…and pitied so often, eh?

BRANWEN: Yes, pitied – and tried so hard to comfort.

MICHAEL: *(Taking her hands.)* You won't have to try any more. I'm home at last – and at peace. You don't know what it means.

BRANWEN: I do. I feel it too.

MICHAEL: *(Exultantly.)* I'll be quite different – just as I was that morning when we saw the desert's smoky gold and the mountains like amethysts. That's my real self – that's always struggling to come out into the sunlight.

BRANWEN: As if I didn't know! My dear, I've know it – lived on it – breathed it – oh, in a way you can't understand – for years and years. It's been more to me even than my work. And I'm a real painter, Michael.

MICHAEL: *(Happily.)* I'll bet you are. *(Crosses to table and turns.)* And we're going to work now, you and I, really get down to it. I've been held up, choked up, this last year or two, and you must have been too. Now it'll all be different. To be with somebody who not only understands what's going on in you head, but who's an artist herself with work of her own, why – it'll be like living on a new earth. *(Quickly, like a happy boy, pulling her up C.)* Where shall we go?

BRANWEN: *(Happily, eagerly.)* Anywhere you like, I don't care.

MICHAEL: *(Same tone.)* You're quite right. It's not where but when. And when is now. Cut all the old knots in one clean stroke. Clear straight out. For the first hour we'll take every right-hand turn we come to, then the next hour every left-hand turn –

BRANWEN: *(Laughing.)* And end up in either Warrington or Crewe.

MICHAEL: Well, if we do. I'm like you, I don't care. We'll –

He stops short because VALERIE now enters.

VALERIE: Well, have you now solved the great mystery?

She comes into scene, looking sharply at each of them. It is clear from their attitude and stricken looks that they had forgotten her existence and are now most unpleasantly reminded of it. There is a pause.

MICHAEL: *(Awkwardly.)* Valerie –

VALERIE: *(In small tight voice.)* Well? Go on.

BRANWEN: *(To MICHAEL.)* You'd better let me – *(Up to him.)*

MICHAEL: *(Cutting in.)* No, this is my job.

VALERIE: *(To BRANWEN, cuttingly.)* I do happen to be his wife, you know.

BRANWEN: *(Bitterly.)* I didn't think you'd overlooked the fact.

VALERIE: No, but perhaps you have.

MICHAEL: *(Up to her.)* Wait a minute, Valerie. It would be truer to say that you *were* my wife. We arranged to meet her and decide whether we should continue in that relationship. I've decided that we can't. And I'm leaving tonight – now.

VALERIE: By yourself?

BRANWEN: No, with me.

VALERIE: I thought that was probably the arrangement.

MICHAEL: *(Explosively.)* Arrangement! You talk as if it were some miserable little affair –

VALERIE: *(Sharply.)* Well, what else is it then? Half an hour ago you pretended you didn't know each other –

MICHAEL: *(Angrily.)* Don't try and jeer at something you can't begin to understand.

VALERIE: *(Angrily.)* No, no, of course, I can't understand.

MICHAEL: *(Stormily.)* Oh – for God's sake – try for once to see –

BRANWEN: *(Forcefully cutting in.)* No, Michael – please!

MICHAEL: *(Checked.)* What?

BRANWEN: You want to go soon –?

MICHAEL: Yes. Whatever happens, I'm leaving this place tonight, and as soon as I can. How can I stay here – torn to –

BRANWEN: *(Cutting in, decisively.)* No, then go and get ready to go. Put your things together. Get the car out. And let me talk to Valerie – please!

MICHAEL: *(After giving both women a quick doubtful glance.)* All right.

He goes out. VALERIE stares at BRANWEN resentfully.

VALERIE: *(Crosses to R. arm of sofa, sits and lights cigarette.)* If you think I'm going to give him up, you're quite mistaken. We separated for a little while because he was nervous and on edge and said he couldn't work, but I might as well tell you I didn't come here merely to talk it over, as he thinks, but with the definite intention of carrying on our marriage.

BRANWEN: *(Quietly.)* Why?

VALERIE: Why? Because I'm his wife and he's my husband.

BRANWEN: *(Scornfully.)* You talk as if he were something you'd bought out of a shop. You don't see him a person at all. You don't realize he's a man who has great work to do and can't do it while his life's being frittered away in stupid little quarrels. What have you done for him?

VALERIE: And what right have you to ask me such a question.

BRANWEN: Every right. Because I respect him and admire him and love him.

VALERIE crosses R. to fireplace to put match down.

Yes, I've loved him, in a way you can't begin to understand.

VALERIE: And that's why you came here to take him away from me.

BRANWEN: I didn't come here to take him away from you. I didn't know anything about you. I came here because I knew he was desperately unhappy. For two years while I was out of England, I tried to forget about him and only hoped that he was happy. But when I came back, the other day, I knew at once that he needed help, that he was in danger of being ruined as an artist and miserably unhappy as a man.

VALERIE: How did you know?

BRANWEN: *(Desperately.)* Because I can't help knowing. You don't know what I've had to go through here. It's like being torn to pieces. If you could have done anything for him, I'd have gladly gone away, without ever saying a word. But now I know you're all wrong for him. And you're not willing to let him go, even if it destroys him.

VALERIE is obstinately silent.

BRANWEN now changes her tone to one of pleading.

Valerie, think of him, don't think of me. I'm not thinking about myself.

VALERIE: *(Bitterly.)* Of course you are. You love him and so you want to take him away.

BRANWEN: But even if I do, can't you see that's only the beginning and not the end of it?

VALERIE: *(As before.)* It's the end of it for me.

BRANWEN: Don't go on thinking about yourself – or about me – but about him. Please try to understand, Valerie. For years my mind was linked to his mind. I don't know how or why, but there it was. I had to share some of his life, in the spirit, where I knew every mood. I didn't love him before then. I didn't know anything about him. When it began he was a stranger to me. But *after* it began, when I came to know so much about him, how could I help loving him dearly and deeply? And when I know how great his possibilities are and how to release him from the misery he brings on himself, how can I refuse to go away with him? For his sake, let him go.

VALERIE: *(Unhappily.)* I can't. I can't.

BRANWEN: But you've never been happy together.

VALERIE: That's not true. If it were true, I'd try not to think about him again, just let him go. But you see it isn't true. At first we were very happy. It was wonderful. Michael met me and fell in love with me at once – it was all like – lightning. I felt as if I'd been waiting for him all my life, that there never was and never could be anybody else. Just like that. And I'll swear he felt exactly the same.

BRANWEN: Then why did you say to me, 'It's always been you all the time'?

VALERIE: *(Rather confused.)* I don't know. It's all rather strange. But afterwards I felt as if there'd been a shadow between Michael and me –

BRANWEN moves slowly back to table.

As if somebody you couldn't see was watching – oh, I don't know. But as soon as I saw you here – in a flash – I knew you loved him, and had loved him for a long time. But even so that doesn't make any difference, because I tell you, at first we were wonderfully happy.

BRANWEN: *(Harshly.)* You don't understand.

VALERIE: What don't I understand?

BRANWEN: *(Deliberately.)* When Michael first met you – he –

BRANWEN stops, hesitates, and now VALERIE plunges in, speaking with great warmth.

VALERIE: Whatever you say can't spoil that. And nothing that can happen between Michael and me can spoil it. Because it was perfect. Oh – he was suddenly like a boy who'd been let out of school. So easy and gay and happy. He'd make up the most extravagant stories about us. He pretended I'd once come in through the window of some hotel he'd been staying in – out in America, where he'd just been. And that I'd taken him running out into some desert to see the daybreak. And I was almost ready to believe him. He just swept me along with him. It was heaven. And when you said, so solemnly, 'When Michael first met you', it all came back to me with a rush, that wonderful time, and I had to tell you how perfect it was and how nothing now could spoil it for me.

BRANWEN: *(Slowly.)* Nothing could spoil it for you.

VALERIE: When it all began like that, how could I help loving him and feeling nothing else mattered? Nobody else could make me feel like that. Only Michael. And I'm not telling you this to show you how much I've meant to him or to make you feel jealous. *(Moves sharply towards BRANWEN.)*

BRANWEN: *(Sharply.)* I'm not feeling jealous. *(A pause.)* Go on.

VALERIE: No, it was you. You were going to tell me something about what happened when Michael first met me.

BRANWEN: *(Turned away.)* It doesn't matter now. *(Round table in front of window.)*

VALERIE: But it sounded – as if –

BRANWEN: *(Sharply turning, fiercely.)* I say it doesn't matter now. *(A pause – then quietly.)* I think – I misunderstood you.

VALERIE: *(Crosses to chair above table and sits.)* Michael doesn't understand me either. It's been my own fault. I've never wanted him to know how hopelessly dependent upon him I am. I thought it would be fatal. I've been pretended to be as doubtful about our marriage as he's been. Agreeing to this trial separation – talking it all over – all that horrible rubbish. When all the time I've been aching and crying for him. You see, Branwen, I love him so very much that if he goes for good and I know I've really lost him, I shan't want to go on living. And people who don't really want to go on living, even if they don't commit suicide in the ordinary ways, they die.

BRANWEN: He doesn't know you feel like this.

VALERIE: No. Perhaps I've been wrong all this time, not letting him see it.

BRANWEN: I believe you have.

VALERIE: *(With emotion.)* But how can I make him see it now? He wouldn't believe it. He'd think it was just a kind of horrible possessiveness – and it isn't, it isn't – I love him so much I think I'm going mad – *(She begins sobbing.)*

BRANWEN: Valerie, please try and stop. There isn't much time. *(Round back of table to VALERIE.)*

VALERIE: *(Trying to stop.)* I know. He wants to go away tonight – now.

BRANWEN: Yes, he's very insistent about that.

VALERIE: I believe he's afraid. He doesn't want to think about what he's doing.

BRANWEN: Yes, but you must remember that all this has come so suddenly and so stirred up the depths in him that he feels he must *do* something – something tremendous, final.

VALERIE: *(Sadly.)* You know him much better than I do.

BRANWEN: Yes.

VALERIE: I've tried so hard to understand him and couldn't. He'd change just as the sky changes, black clouds hurrying up from nowhere, and I wouldn't know why. But even then it didn't matter. But without him, life won't be anything. Better to die and be done with it.

BRANWEN: But you can't be done with it until it's ready to be done with you. You talk as if life were some little toy you could play with and then throw away. It's not like that at all.

VALERIE: You're only trying to frighten me. I'm trying to give you some sense and courage – and – *(With a little nervous laugh.)* I haven't very much left for myself.

MICHAEL, wearing an overcoat but no hat, opens the door and stands there.

MICHAEL: The car's out.

VALERIE rises, drying her eyes, and turns to the window.

MICHAEL breaks off, and looks suspiciously at the two women.

What's happening here? *(As if to warn her.)* Branwen!

BRANWEN: No, Michael, please. If you interrupt now I don't know where we'll be or what'll happen – oh, just a ghastly fuss and muddle.

MICHAEL: Well, that's just what – *(Crosses round sofa to R. arm.)*

BRANWEN: *(Urgently – crosses to him.)* Listen, Michael, please! Wait just another ten minutes – even five minutes – and then you can come back.

MICHAEL: I don't want to come back. I want to go. I'm in a hurry to begin my life. I've been waiting to do that for a long time.

BRANWEN: *(Urgently.)* Please, Michael. It's terribly important.

MICHAEL: All right. Remember, Branwen, no weakening now.

He goes out again.

BRANWEN: *(Up to chair.)* There isn't much time, Valerie. He's capable of going blinding off into the night by himself, half crazy with rage, and God knows what might happen to him.

VALERIE: I know. Go on.

BRANWEN: *(Crosses to R. of chair.)* Michael knows a good deal now that he didn't know before. It may change him completely – I don't know – but it'll certainly make some difference. And there are things about you – how really dependent you are upon him, for instance, that he ought to know. But even then I'm wondering how you can expect to make him happy. No, not happy – but at least not unhappy, reasonable contented, able to face life and get on with his work. You see, I'm thinking of him, not thinking about myself at all.

VALERIE: Yes. And I'm thinking of him now, and not about myself. Will you believe that?

BRANWEN: *(After giving her a long look.)* Yes. What is it?

VALERIE: *(Simply, appealingly.)* I'm not an artist, and not clever or wise or mystical or anything. I suppose I'm really a simple person, just a woman in love with a man. I don't understand him as you do. He's always doing and saying things that don't make sense to me. But I love him. I may love him in a very ordinary kind of way – I don't know. But I want a real life with him – and children – *his* children.

BRANWEN: Yes, Valerie, but –

VALERIE: No, please, Branwen, I haven't finished yet. You see, because I feel like this – and now I wouldn't want to hide it any more – he's only to let me love him, just to be friends and not to hate me, to make *me* happy.

BRANWEN: Yes, but what then? What about him?

VALERIE: *(Simply, rather timidly.)* Well, don't you think that – perhaps – after a time – because we're together, sharing things, and I'm happy, and he knows he's making me happy – that he'd become more contented and peaceful and perhaps in the end – happy himself.

BRANWEN: It's possible.

VALERIE: *(Making her final appeal.)* I know I'm asking an awful lot from you, Branwen. But you're stronger and wiser than I am. And you've got things – like your painting – that I haven't got. I don't really understand what there's been between you and Michael – and now I'd rather not know – but you can live alone, without him –

BRANWEN: *(In a low voice.)* Yes, I can live alone, without him.

VALERIE: And if there is something between you, some sort of invisible link or whatever it is – then it's nothing I can ever take away from you?

BRANWEN: No, that's true.

VALERIE: But you can take everything away from me.

BRANWEN looks at her a moment, sombrely, then gives her a nod.

BRANWEN: You'd better go and get your things together. *(Down L.)*

VALERIE: You mean – you won't go with him?

BRANWEN: *(Nods.)* I'll stay here.

VALERIE: *(Crying with relief.)* Oh – Branwen – you're – I don't know what to say – I'm – *(To her.)*

BRANWEN: But if I don't go away with him tonight, then you must. You realize that, don't you? *(Crosses to below L. chair.)*

VALERIE: Yes. Are you – going to talk to him?

BRANWEN: Yes. And it won't be easy. I'll have to –

She stops abruptly, standing quite rigid. VALERIE stares at her in astonishment.

VALERIE: What's the matter?

BRANWEN: Michael –

She makes a move towards door, but now THOMAS enters hastily, then stands looking at the two women.

Yes, Thomas?

THOMAS: *(Looking from one to the other.)* I thought I ought to tell you, now, though maybe you know all about it and will tell me to mind my own business next time.

VALERIE: *(Sharply.)* But what is it? *(Up and kneel on sofa.)*

THOMAS: Mr. Camber. He didn't even ask for a bill, but put two pound notes in my hand and jumped into his motor car and went tearing off like a madman.

VALERIE: *(Turning to BRANWEN.)* That's why you stopped suddenly?

BRANWEN: Yes. I knew then – he'd gone.

VALERIE: But why – *(But she is checked by BRANWEN who now turns to THOMAS.)*

BRANWEN: Thank you for telling us, Thomas.

THOMAS: *(Preparing to go.)* Oh – I wouldn't have done only it was the way he went off, so suddenly – and such a black wet night too. But he's very good with a car, no doubt.

VALERIE: He isn't. He's much too reckless.

THOMAS: *(Really going now.)* Well, if there is anything I can do just ring for me, will you? Though I don't see there is anything we can do. He didn't even say where he was going to. *(Nods at them dubiously and then goes out.)*

VALERIE: *(In agitation.)* But why did he suddenly go off like that?

BRANWEN: Because, perhaps for the first time, our communications worked the opposite way. When I decided a few minutes ago that I wouldn't go away with him, when I *told* him I wasn't going, he got it, in a flash, and too angry even to argue about it, he jumped into his car –

VALERIE: *(Agitated.)* And went blinding off into the night, as you said he might do. Oh Branwen, I'm frightened. Not just because he's gone – but because – driving along – in a fury – on a night like this –

BRANWEN: I know, I know.

VALERIE: *(Almost breaking down.)* And what can we do? We can't do anything. We don't know where he's gone or what –

BRANWEN: *(Sharply.)* Be quiet.

VALERIE: Why – what?

BRANWEN: *(Cutting in.)* Don't interrupt or you'll ruin the only chance we've got. *(She moves towards the window.)* I'm going to try and bring him back.

She stands rigid, staring out of the window, though not too close to it. VALERIE watches her. BRANWEN closes her eyes, obviously concentrating. A pause. Then BRANWEN gives a loud cry of alarm, sways and looks as if about to faint. VALERIE, alarmed, goes over and supports her into a chair below table and takes charge of her, while BRANWEN slowly regains control of herself. The whole scene must be played slowly and for all it's worth.

VALERIE: *(As she fusses over her.)* Branwen – Branwen – are you all right now? – What's the matter? – What happened?

BRANWEN: *(Slowly.)* He's coming back.

VALERIE: *(Wonderingly.)* You – spoke to him?

BRANWEN: If you can call it that. I begged him to come back.

VALERIE: But why did you cry out like that? As if something terrible had happened.

BRANWEN: *(Shudderingly.)* He was nearly killed – it seemed – for a second – as if – oh, it was horrible.

VALERIE: But what happened?

BRANWEN: He tried to turn without stopping – round a space at the side of the road –

VALERIE: Yes, I've know him do that. It's crazy.

BRANWEN: It was a blind corner – and another car came round – and missed him by an inch, and I felt what he felt – saw the face of Death –

VALERIE: *(Shuddering.)* How horrible!

BRANWEN: *(Slowly.)* The face of Death – it's a blinding light – I always imagined it was – and now I know – you suddenly see a blinding light –

VALERIE: *(Very quietly and sincerely, rising.)* Branwen, I wish we'd met – not like this – but a long time ago. So that we could have been friends. You know so much more than I do. About Michael – and everything. And I'm not really silly and proud – I'd have liked you to teach me – perhaps some day – you could –

BRANWEN: *(Now in complete control of herself.)* Yes, Valerie. But he'll be back any moment now, and he mustn't find us both together. I've got to talk to him myself. Get your things together.

VALERIE: I never unpacked properly.

BRANWEN: *(With decision now.)* Get ready. Then wait in the hall. Hurry, but don't let him see you until I've talked to him

VALERIE: *(Happily.)* Yes. And – thank you, Branwen.

She hurries out through upper door. BRANWEN gets up and stares out of the window again, summoning her strength. We hear the pattering of the rain. MICHAEL, wearing an overcoat but no hat, enters, BRANWEN turns and they look at each other.

MICHAEL: When I turned round I was nearly killed.

BRANWEN: I know. I felt that I nearly died too. It was horrible.

MICHAEL: I know you'd suddenly decided not to come away with me.

BRANWEN: Yes. For once it worked the other way, from me to you.

MICHAEL: I rushed off because I didn't want any talk about it. I don't think I want any talk about it now.

BRANWEN: There has to be.

MICHAEL: Why? It's simple enough. You've let me down.

BRANWEN: I couldn't let you down, Michael. And sometimes I've kept you going just when you thought everybody and everything had let you down.

MICHAEL: I don't feel this is the time to remind me of that.

BRANWEN: I do. It's absolutely essential you should remember. Michael, please, please remember it now, or everything may go wrong.

MICHAEL: *(Bitterly.)* Everything *has* gone wrong. You've decided to open a man's life and then shut it again all in one evening. Better to have left it alone.

BRANWEN: You're forgetting that at first I wanted to leave it alone. It was you who forced me to speak.

MICHAEL: All right. But having spoken, having proved to me who you are and what there is between us, how can you expect me to go away and leave you as if nothing had happened?

BRANWEN: *(Crosses to him.)* Oh – Michael, please – help me – help *us* – Resentment and bitterness are never any use and now they're worse than useless. Unless we talk now from deep inside ourselves, we'll regret it for ever.

MICHAEL: I'm trying to be quiet. I'm listening. Go on.

BRANWEN: You knew I'd decided not to come away with you. But you don't know why.

MICHAEL: *(Bitterly.)* I suppose this isn't spectral enough for you. We're man and woman, flesh and blood – not ghosts.

He catches the wounded look on her face, drops his eyes and is ashamed. He sits on the sofa.

BRANWEN: And you ought to be ashamed. It's about the worst thing that's ever been said to me.

MICHAEL: I'm sorry. Please forgive me.

BRANWEN: I will, so long as you admit that it simply isn't true.

MICHAEL: I know it isn't. Whatever your reason for changing your mind, it wasn't that. But what was it? If you suddenly saw that – well, I wasn't worth it, I suppose I can't blame you, though I wish you'd thought of it before.

BRANWEN: *(Tenderly crosses to him and kneels.)* No, my dear, of course it wasn't. I know you as nobody else does. I know a Michael Camber that nobody else has ever seen. And I love you most dearly.

MICHAEL: That's what I believed. Then how could you suddenly change your mind?

BRANWEN: Because there was somebody I didn't know. Valerie.

MICHAEL: *(Surprised.)* Valerie? But Valerie means nothing as between us. You know very well we've tried and failed to make a life together. *(Rises.)* The fact is she's wept and wheedled and you've given in.

BRANWEN: No, Michael, you must listen.

MICHAEL: *(Sweeping her interruption aside.)* She's been telling you how happy we were at first, hasn't she?

BRANWEN: Yes, but not as you think – *(Rises.)*

MICHAEL: *(Driving on, with force.)* I thought so. And you know very well that was because I thought she was you. All our happiness came out of that. But you didn't tell her, did you?

BRANWEN: No, I was going to – then I didn't.

MICHAEL: *(Triumphantly.)* I thought that was it. Then I'll tell her now. *(Moves as if to go.)*

BRANWEN: *(Very urgently, stopping him.)* No, Michael. Please, please! You mustn't. You can't.

MICHAEL: Why? Because it'll hurt her? But it's the truth. Why shouldn't she be hurt by the truth?

BRANWEN: Because now I know Valerie – and you don't.

MICHAEL: What – my own wife?

BRANWEN: Yes. Valerie is a woman who loves you dearly, desperately. She can think of nothing but you.

MICHAEL: No. She may not want to break up her marriage, but she's been as doubtful about it as I've been.

BRANWEN: She hasn't. That's the silly game she's been playing with you. It's been a pathetic attempt to please you, and all part of this new damnable pretence of hiding the deeper feelings.

MICHAEL: But why should she pretend and play a game as you call it? *(Away from her round table.)*

BRANWEN: *(After him.)* Because, loving you so much, she was ready to pretend anything for your sake. She's not really hard and sophisticated and all the other things she's pretended to be. You and I are really ten times harder than she is, just because we have our work, and so we're infinitely more self-contained. You said that I was your life. But I am not your life. You are not even my life, though part of me will always be either watching or wondering about you. But Valerie's different. You are *her* life. All she has or wants to have, until you should have children.

MICHAEL: Children? I don't think Valerie would like to have children.

BRANWEN: Of course she would. All she wants is a real woman's life with you. She's entirely dependent on you.

MICHAEL: I never knew, Branwen. If I had known, there are a lot of things I would never have said or done. If I mean so much to her, I see now why you couldn't tell her that those first months of happiness that she and I had were nothing but a mistake of mine.

BRANWEN: You see, Michael, we don't know anything like the whole truth about ourselves and this life. We're mysterious beings and our life's a mystery. But one thing we do know for certain – and that's the truth of love and happiness. There can't be any argument about that, Michael.

MICHAEL: No, there can't be any argument about that. And you're right. I ought to have known what she felt. I've seen her eyes brighten just remembering little things from those first months. If I tell her it was all a mistake, it's murdering her heart.

BRANWEN: Yes. So you can't do it.

MICHAEL: And you're sure she depends upon me? *(Up round table to chair above.)*

BRANWEN: Yes, Michael, just as you, during that very bad time, seemed to depend upon me.

MICHAEL: As much as that?

BRANWEN: No, more than that. You still had your work. Just as I, when I cut you out of my life, still had my work. Another kind of responsibility, and another kind of happiness.

MICHAEL: I see all that. And it makes an enormous difference. Another Valerie, a different relationship. But even so, Branwen, it's not going to be easy.

BRANWEN: *(Up round table to him.)* No, but it'll be just as much the beginning of a new life as if we'd gone away together. You're not retuning to the old life. And Valerie said a true thing about it. That if you'd only let her love you, if you were only friendly and kind, she'd be happy, and that perhaps – seeing how happy you made her – you might soon be happier too.

MICHAEL: Yes, yes, Branwen, I don't know why I'm whining about its not being easy. If I charged into her life and made her dependent upon me, then I've no right to make her unhappy. Besides, this is a Valerie I thought didn't exist. *(With sudden decision.)* Branwen, I'll take her away tonight. We'll start again.

BRANWEN: I'm glad, Michael. It's the only thing to do. If we'd gone away we'd have taken everything from her. But, as she said herself, there's something between us that she can't take away.

MICHAEL: And she won't mind its being there, for whatever happens it will always be there now?

BRANWEN: No, she won't mind now. It'll all be different. Valerie won't be the same. You won't be the same. We've met here. You know something of what happened between us.

MICHAEL: I know you're right. It will be a new life. And probably it's time I was responsible for somebody. Perhaps I've been missing that. But, having found you at last, I have to lose you again so soon.

BRANWEN: No, not really. And you'll probably feel better than you've done for years. The Admiral's black dog will probably disappear for ever. I shan't have to say to you before I go rising on my broomstick, 'Whistle and I'll come to you, my lad.'

MICHAEL: But – this has all been so sudden and strange. And even now all I know for certain is that when you're here I feel at peace, and I love you very dearly.

BRANWEN: *(In a whisper.)* Oh Michael, I've been waiting – so long – to hear you say that –

MICHAEL: *(After a pause.)* Do some good painting. We've never talked about that.

BRANWEN: We've never really talked about your music. Do some good music.

MICHAEL: I believe I will now. But still I can't understand how – between us – it's got to be – just goodbye –

BRANWEN: It can't. Not really. Look!

She puts a hand on his arm and moves him so that they are facing the large mirror above the window. They do not go near it.

MICHAEL: You pretend to be calm. But your hand's fluttering on my arm like a bird.

BRANWEN: *(In a whisper.)* I'm not calm. I can only just about see this through. *(With change of tone.)* Now look!

MICHAEL: Well, I see us, together, in the mirror.

BRANWEN step to one side so that he can no longer see her reflection.

BRANWEN: Now! You're alone in there, aren't you? I've gone. But does it matter?

MICHAEL: No, because I know you're here, only a yard or two away.

BRANWEN: Yes, and in the place where we're really ourselves and not mere reflections.

MICHAEL: You think life's like that?

BRANWEN: Yes, I think this outward world in time, where you and I are going to say goodbye and then vanish from one another's sight, is only like a long, long mirror, full of twists and cracks and corners, stretching from the cradle to the grace. All you see in it are images. What is real and true –

THE LONG MIRROR: ACT THREE

and *alive* – is here, not in there. We only saw each other for a moment there. But here –

She puts of her hands and he catches and holds them, as she smiles rather uncertainly at him.

MICHAEL: *(Very quietly.)* I see. And I'll try always to remember.

BRANWEN: *(Taking her hands away.)* You'd better go now, Michael. Valerie will be ready now.

MICHAEL: Another minute…

BRANWEN: *(In quick, almost hysterical tones.)* No, now. You'll have to drive for hours in the rain among the black mountains, but you won't mind that – will you? I think I'd like that – sitting behind the lonely searching light – with the rain flashing– and the great black night roaring all round – *(She is very close to tears.)*

MICHAEL: Branwen –

BRANWEN: No, please go, Michael. Hurry, hurry!

MICHAEL: *(Staring at her.)* Goodbye!

BRANWEN: *(In a tiny whisper.)* Goodbye!

He goes out quickly B. She watches the door close, then makes one or two blind movements, then stands crying quietly. There are sounds of voices off through B – MICHAEL's, VALERIE's, MRS. TENBURY's, THOMAS's. Then a silence, and through it BRANWEN's quiet sobbing and perhaps the rain.

MRS. TENBURY enters B, perhaps taking off her heavy coat. She looks curiously at BRANWEN – takes in the situation and then ignores it.

MRS. T.: It's a dark rainy night but not quite as bad as you think it's going to be… As a matter of fact I find hardly anything's as bad as you think it's going to be. I've often wondered whether that makes me a pessimist, because I expect the worst, an optimist, because it's never as bad as I thought, or just a muddler, because I'm all mixed up… *(Settling herself, and ignoring BRANWEN who is now calming down.)*

BRANWEN: *(In very low voice.)* I think I must go to bed.

MRS. T.: No, don't do that, my dear, unless you feel you really must. It's a good idea to have just a bit of cosiness at the end

of the evening. Come and sit by the fire. I've told Thomas to
bring us some tea.

BRANWEN sits, a rather rigid figure, staring into the fire.

BRANWEN: *(Murmuring.)* You're very kind.

MRS. T.: I'm very sensible. I'm nearly a thousand points ahead
of Mrs. Trebarron Jones. She tried for triple *bezique* again
several times and never got it, whereas I was fortunate
enough to have sequence seven or eight times. Somebody
once said: 'Cards are the poetry of old age.' That's over-
stating it, I think, but I do think it's good for us old women
to snatch at aces and tens of trumps, for we have to snatch at
something. Are you all right now, my dear?

BRANWEN: *(Small voice.)* Yes…thank you.

MRS. T.: Thomas says it'll be fine tomorrow –

THOMAS has entered B with tea tray.

Oh – thank you, Thomas. Didn't you say it would be fine
tomorrow?

THOMAS: *(Putting down tray for them.)* Oh – yes, I think all the
rain will come down tonight, and then in the morning,
after a little mist maybe, the sun will come out and it'll be
a beautiful day indeed. You're not leaving us tomorrow, I
hope, Miss Elder?

BRANWEN: No, I think I'll stay on a few more days at least.

THOMAS: Well done! The weather will be better. Beautiful
effects upon the lake, you'll see! And I think you ought to do
some painting, don't you, Mrs. Tenbury?

MRS. T.: *(Pouring out tea.)* it's just what I was going to suggest,
Thomas. *(To BRANWEN.)* Painting – um?

BRANWEN: I think it is about time I did some work.

THOMAS: *(Humorously.)* Work! I don't call that work. Why, you
ought to pay to do it.

MRS. T.: *(Quietly.)* Sometimes they *do* pay.

BRANWEN: *(Quietly.)* Yes, sometimes we pay quite a lot.

*As she stares ahead, THOMAS looks enquiringly at MRS. TENBURY,
who gives a quick nod of reassurance.*

THOMAS: *(Humorously.)* Oh – well, ladies, if you're going to be argumentative, I'll say good night.

MRS. T.: *(After they have said goodnight and THOMAS is going out.)* I don't think I've mentioned my Uncle Frederick, have I? He was an amateur painter – and really the most absurd character I've ever known. He spent a great deal of his life in the East – he was a governor or commissioner or something – and he went and married a most extraordinary Italian woman who'd been left stranded out there by an opera company. She was a gigantic woman with a moustache and she must have weighed at least two hundred and fifty pounds, and she'd two children by her first husband, who was a Portuguese Jew from Brazil…

But now the Curtain is down.

End of Play.

EVER SINCE PARADISE

A Discursive Entertainment,
chiefly referring to Love and Marriage, in Three Acts.

Author's Preface

This experimental comedy was originally written in 1939 and then much re-written at odd intervals. With some extremely adroit music by Dennis Arundel, with Ursula Jeans and Roger Livesey playing Helen and William (and all that involved), in a production I directed myself, with much valuable help from Roger Livesey and Osmund Wilson, *Ever Since Paradise* started on a long and very successful provincial tour in the summer of 1946. At the end of that tour there was no theatre for us in London, so we laid off the production for six months, and then opened at the New in June 1947. I think it is true, as several knowledgeable persons have told me, that we achieved a sparkle and gaiety in the original touring production that we never quite recaptured afterwards. Nevertheless, the reception this play had in London (though it ran for several months and made many friends) was a shock and bitter disappointment to me. Many of the notices were not merely inadequate but downright wilfully stupid. Let me give one example. One critic who, I know from personal observation, was not even in the auditorium during the funniest scenes of the play, condemned me – in this of all plays – for solemn preaching. Being producer as well as author, I often looked in at this play, and always the audiences appeared to be having an uproariously good time (as they have done since with it in many Continental capitals); yet it is a fact that fifty per cent of the Press was sullenly hostile. And why, I cannot imagine, unless it was because I was at least trying to do something new. One final point: although this play, if properly produced and acted, should often have the air of being a gay charade, it was in fact written and re-written with great care and made great demands on such technical knowledge as I possess.

But it was worth the time and trouble, not only because of all the fun we and the audiences had with it, but also because here and there it seemed to me to create a new and valuable relationship between players and audience, and because it might possibly drop a hint or two to younger and more hopeful playwrights.

J.B. Priestley, January, 1949

Characters

The Musicians

The Commentators

The Example

PHILIP

WILLIAM

PAUL

JOYCE

HELEN

ROSEMARY

The Action is in many different places,
and the time is the Present, but between Wars.

First produced at the New Theatre, London, on June 4th, 1947, with the following cast:

PHILIP	Dennis Arundell
JOYCE	Jane Carr
WILLIAM	Roger Livesey
HELEN	Ursula Jeans
ROSEMARY	Joy Shelton
PAUL	Hugh Kelly

ACT ONE

The main curtain may or may not be used, according to the size of the stage. On each side of the stage, as far as possible, is a grand piano, each exactly alike, with the keyboard downstage, at an angle of about sixty degrees to the footlights. Near each piano, a little farther upstage, is a chair for each commentator. These are backed by dark curtaining, hiding the stage behind, and there is an entrance through this curtaining at each side, used only by WILLIAM and HELEN. Set a little farther back, occupying all the centre of the stage, with a small proscenium formed by a continuation of the curtaining behind the platforms, is a separate little stage, which may or may not be raised on small rostrum, and is eight or nine feet high, and it is essential that this can be pulled up or drawn along very easily, apparently at a touch. At the opening this curtain is down, and the inner stage cannot be seen.

House lights do down and both pianos are lit. PHILIP and JOYCE, two youngish people in simple evening dress (PHILIP in dinner jacket.) are seated at the pianos. PHILIP at the right and JOYCE at the left. They begin playing the overture, which goes along splendidly for two or three minutes, both keeping perfect time. Then they begin to sound ragged and look worried. He wants to increase the tempo and she is lagging behind. Finally, with a discordant crash, they stop, glaring at each other.

PHILIP: *(Rising angrily.)* There you are, you see!

JOYCE: *(Rising angrily.)* It's not my fault.

PHILIP: Of course it is.

JOYCE: No it isn't, it's your fault.

PHILIP: No it isn't, you were dragging it again.

JOYCE: I wasn't. You were racing away at a ridiculous pace.

PHILIP: I wasn't.

JOYCE: You were. Always the same! Want to rush everything.

PHILIP: I don't want to rush everything.

JOYCE: Yes, you do. Going and taking the cottage!

PHILIP: *(Very angrily.)* What's my taking that cottage got to do with your dragging the time again – ?

177

Enter WILLIAM in dinner jacket.

WILLIAM: *(Reproachfully.)* I say, I say, this won't do, you know. You two ought to be playing, not shouting at each other. *(To audience.)* I'm so sorry about this. Do excuse us, please! *(To the pianists.)* You were playing so well too. I was just remarking to Helen how well you were playing – and then – no more music but another quarrel.

JOYCE: It's his fault. He began to rush it again.

WILLIAM: Now, Philip, you musn't rush it –

PHILIP: I wasn't. She *will* drag it.

WILLIAM: Now, Joyce, you really mustn't drag it –

JOYCE: I never do. That's just his stupidity.

PHILIP: *(Rising angrily.)* It isn't. It's your-

WILLIAM: *(Very forcefully.)* Stop it, stop it, stop it! Now if one of you would condescend to rush a little less.

PHILIP and JOYCE both sit at their pianos.

then no doubt you'd keep together, be in time,

HELEN enters in simple but striking evening dress.

in exquisite unison, in beautiful harmony, and you'd both be happy and we'd be happy. Whereas –

HELEN: William, you always go on too long.

WILLIAM: *(Rather annoyed.)* How do you mean – I always go on too long?

HELEN: You shouldn't go on with that *Whereas.* Nobody wants your *whereas.* And it's pompous. You're rather inclined to be pompous, you know.

WILLIAM: *(Horrified.)* Pompous! My dear Helen, I'm the last pompous man who ever lived.

JOYCE: You're *all* pompous.

HELEN: Perfectly true, Joyce, dear. They *are* all pompous. But when William has a grievance, I think he's really above the average in pompousness.

PHILIP audibly guffaws. WILLIAM glares across at him.

WILLIAM: If you're going to snigger and provide her with an appreciative audience, she'll go on for hours.

HELEN: Audience! That reminds me. *(To the audience, with tremendous charm.)* I'm so sorry about all this, Do excuse use, please.

WILLIAM: *(Growling. Pats her on the shoulder.)* I've said that already.

HELEN: *(Sweetly.)* Possibly, but perhaps when a little charm is added to the apology –

WILLIAM: *(Cutting in.)* Charm! If there's one quality more contemptible than another in your contemptible bag of tricks, it's this famous feminine charm. As soon as I see that rotten little piece of scented silk run up as a flag, I know that honesty and decency are about to be scuttled.

PHILIP: And I agree.

HELEN: *(Turning to PHILIP.)* Only because you haven't any, Philip dear.

PHILIP: Oh – I don't know about that.

HELEN: *(Smiling sweetly at PHILIP.)* No, Philip, you don't know about it.

WILLIAM: *(Staring at her, then turning her round to face him.)* Now what's matter with you?

HELEN: *(With wide-eyed innocence.)* Nothing that I know of, William. Why?

WILLIAM: Because you're behaving very badly, that's why. You come on here, looking – I must admit – very delightful, shining and smiling upon us like a May moon –

HELEN: Thank you, my pet.

WILLIAM: I'm not your pet. And keep away, keep away!

HELEN: Oh – why?

WILLIAM: Because – well, it's less confusing and easier for me to say what I have to say –

HELEN: Then don't say it. Nobody cares.

WILLIAM: And what I say is that you come on here and instead of trying to help us out of our little difficulty, you at once make everything worse. Now why – why – do you go and make everything worse?

HELEN: Shall I tell you?

WILLIAM: *(Exasperated.)* I'm asking you to tell me. Though I doubt if you know.

HELEN: Oh yes, I do. It's perfectly simple. You see, being a woman I must be noticed and appreciated. We take a great deal of trouble over our appearance – about twenty times as much trouble as you do, for instance – and we insist upon first being noticed and appreciated. Now if you'd said, at once, that I was looking very nice, or if you'd only smiled at me, that would have been quite enough. Immediately I'd have felt full of goodwill and kindness and helpfulness, and I'd have tried to do my best for everybody. But first of all I must be noticed and appreciated.

WILLIAM: That seems to me all wrong.

HELEN: Yes, but then you happen to be a man and I happen to be a woman.

WILLIAM: It shouldn't make so much difference.

HELEN: But it does.

WILLIAM: Well, does it? I know women who aren't like that.

HELEN: Yes, and how much time do you spend with them?

JOYCE bursts out laughing.

WILLIAM: *(Speaking to JOYCE.)* I think you'd better start playing again.

HELEN: *(Rising.)* No, not yet.

WILLIAM: Why not?

JOYCE stops playing.

HELEN: We ought to look into this a little more, this man-and-woman business.

PHILIP: *(With gloomy approval.)* Yes, it needs looking into.

HELEN: Of course it does. Now it's no use taking ourselves, is it?

WILLIAM: *(Brightening at this.)* Not a bit. Lot of talk about ourselves – only leads to trouble – scenes, temper and tears – terrible! No use, you see, unless you can be detached.

HELEN: You love being detached, don't you?

WILLIAM: Can't observe properly unless you're detached. That's obvious.

HELEN: All right then, we'll take some other pair.

PHILIP: What about Henry and Muriel?

JOYCE: Dull.

WILLIAM: Very dull.

HELEN: I'm afraid you're right. Well, you suggest nobody.

WILLIAM: Boris and Nina.

HELEN: Oh – no, just a long cat-and-dog fight broken by an occasional orgy.

WILLIAM: *(Thoughtfully.)* True. Though I've always wanted to be in at an orgy. All this writing and talk about orgies, and yet you never seem to catch up with one. Every place I've ever been to, they've always just stopped having them. "You ought to have been here last year," they say. "It was terrible."

PHILIP: I know.

JOYCE: How do you mean, you know?

WILLIAM: Now, Joyce, don't you start all over again. Look at your music or something –

HELEN: *(Triumphantly.)* I know the very pair. Not too dull, not too wild. Very nice and rather typical. Paul and Rosemary.

WILLIAM: Rosemary and Paul. Yes, they might do. Pleasant pair. As you say, nice people. Not very intelligent, perhaps, but I can supply the intelligence-

HELEN: And you've heard what's happening to them?

WILLIAM: No. Not busting up, are they?

HELEN: Sit down and pay attention. You'll see. Joyce, Philip!

They begin playing some broken, discordant music. Curtains open, to reveal room whose few props suggest waiting-room in a solicitor's office. PAUL, in middle thirties, with horn-rimmed spectacles and wearing dark overcoat and muffler (to facilitate quick change.) is moving about like a man kept waiting for an unpleasant appointment. A noise outside, then ROSEMARY's voice is heard off, saying, "Oh in here. Thank you!" She enters also wearing heavy coat, and looking pale and miserable. She stares at him. He looks very embarrassed.

PAUL: *(With an effort.)* I'm afraid this is – er – rather embarrassing – Rosemary.

ROSEMARY: *(With similar effort.)* Yes – Paul – I'm afraid it is.

PAUL: Well, it's not my fault…. I had a note from Coulson asking me to be here at half-past three – to answer some questions about the – the divorce.

ROSEMARY: *(Tiny voice.)* Yes, so had I.

PAUL: *(Relentlessly.)* Oh, I say – monstrous thing for Coulson to do – asking us both here at the same time. Shows you how blankly insensitive these lawyers are. Typical lawyer's trick, this. Damn Coulson!

ROSEMARY: *(Faintly.)* Oh – I don't think – it's perhaps – *(Dies away.)*

PAUL: What?

ROSEMARY: No – nothing…

PAUL: Look here, I'll go and wait out there.

ROSEMARY: No – it-

PAUL: Don't mind a bit.

Goes, crossing in front of her. Just as he has passed, she makes a movement as if to halt him, but then sinks back. He goes out and we hear the door closing behind him. She stares after him, then her face begins working, and then she starts sobbing.

WILLIAM: I say, this is too bad.

Curtains close.

Now, Helen.

The curtains have closed and with the broken discordant music as before.

HELEN: *(Sympathetically and satirically.)* What made it all the worse, of course, is that obviously it was she who had asked their solicitor to send for them both at the same time.

WILLIAM: Yes, but I can't see why she should do that if they were arranging a divorce.

HELEN: Because she was hoping that a miracle might have happened, that, seeing her again, he might have discovered he was still in love with her. We're always hoping for miracles like that. And then – well, you saw.

WILLIAM: Yes, but mind you, if he'd been completely indifferent he'd have stayed in there. He went out chiefly for her sake.

HELEN: She thought he went out because he couldn't even stand the sight of her.

WILLIAM: Quite wrong. What a lot of muddlers we are, aren't we? She ought to be crying over the human race. There *is* something to cry about.

HELEN: *(Very gravely.)* She was crying because once there was love and now there is no love. If we can't cry over the grave of love, what are our tears for? I could cry a little myself.

WILLIAM: *(Anxiously.)* Now, now! Now, now! Don't you start, my dear. Besides, we must keep our detachment, or we'll never learn anything. *(To the pianists.)* Play something quiet but cheerful.

They begin to play, HELEN turns to him and smiles, he takes her hand.

That's better. Let me see now, how did this begin? Where, when and how did Paul and Rosemary first meet?

HELEN: *(Slowly, reflectively.)* She told me once. Her father gave Paul some architectural job, and asked him to come and dine. You'll have to be Rosemary's father. Go on.

WILLIAM: I thought for a moment you said I'd have to be Rosemary's father.

HELEN: That's what I did say. Go on.

WILLIAM: Certainly. Great pleasure. Only not for long y'know.

Goes out Arch left.

HELEN: It takes some girls months, even years, before they know, but she seemed to know at once.

Curtains open, music swells up, disclosing a corner of a drawing-room. Small table with sherry, cigarettes, etc. No chairs. ROSEMARY, looking younger and prettier, is pouring out the sherry. PAUL, who looks younger without the spectacles, comes in, followed by WILLIAM, wearing grey wig and moustache as Rosemary's father. ROSEMARY pours out three glasses of sherry.

WILLIAM: *(In older man's voice.)* Ah – you haven't met my daughter.

They smile and shake hands.

Glass of sherry, eh? *(ROSEMARY hands PAUL and WILLIAM a glass of sherry.)* Thank you, my dear.

ROSEMARY: I thought your idea for it awfully clever.

PAUL: Thank you.

They raise their glasses at the same time and smile at each other significantly over the top of them.

WILLIAM: *(Rambling on without noticing them.)* Yes, yes – I think Weybridge realises now exactly what I've always had in mind. Convenient and cosy are my two watch-words. Easy and cheap to run, but snug. Plenty of weather outside, on the top of that cliff *(Pours out another glass of sherry.)* but none inside, eh, Weybridge?

PAUL: *(Who is lost.)* What? Oh – yes, rather – that's the idea.

WILLIAM: Made a little sketch or two I wanted to show you. Have 'em in my den. This way, my boy.

WILLIAM goes out. PAUL, obviously reluctantly, hands glass to ROSEMARY, three is a pause between them. He turns and goes out. Music plays softly for a moment or two, she stands in a daydream. Then music stops and she comes forward pace or two, and speaks to HELEN.

ROSEMARY: Really I knew them. Or one part of me did.

HELEN: *(With sympathy.)* I know.

ROSEMARY: That part of me which seems to stand back always and isn't caught up with every moment.

HELEN: Yes, the part that can see far ahead, in a dim sort of way, and seems to know what's coming.

ROSEMARY: That's exactly it, Helen. But how does it work? I mean, it's just as if behind the little *Now* there's the big *Now*, in which all at once you've met a man and loved him for years and lost him. And how can that be?

HELEN: I don't know, darling. I don't believe anybody knows.

Curtains close. WILLIAM enters briskly as himself through curtains.

WILLIAM: I know. It's a question of movement along the fourth dimension –

HELEN: What is?

WILLIAM: These two Nows – two different kinds of time. Now imagine yourself travelling with the speed of light – and eighty-six thousand miles a second – along the fourth dimension –

JOYCE: No.

PHILIP: No.

HELEN: No thank you, William.

WILLIAM: I thought you wanted to know.

HELEN: Not just now, thank you. Some other time. Now I wonder when Paul realised he was falling in love with Rosemary?

WILLIAM: Does is matter?

HELEN: Of course it matters.

WILLIAM: Well, he told me it was about the third or fourth time he went there. They were just saying good-bye in the hall.

Curtains open. HELEN waves WILLIAM off rostrum. The inner stage is now set as an entrance hall. PAUL, dressed in light overcoat and carrying hat, is about to say good night.

ROSEMARY: *(Lightly.)* You know, if your taxi is ticking its life away outside, you needn't wait for Father. He may be ages digging out that old photograph, but he can easily post it to you.

PAUL: *(Rather nervously.)* Well, the taxi is there, so I suppose I'd better go. *(He hesitates, then , with a rush.)* I wondered – well, the fact is, I've been working too hard lately to go out much, but a – er – client gave me two seats for the Haymarket for next Thursday, and – er – I wondered – whether you'd like to come along with me. We might have some supper afterwards if you like – and – er – dance –

ROSEMARY: *(Slowly.)* Thursday? Yes, I'd love to.

PAUL: We'll have to meet at the theatre, if you don't mind as I'm afraid I shan't have time to dine.

ROSEMARY: No, of course not. We can find out what time it begins, can't we?

PAUL: Yes, I don't think they make any secret of that. Well – Thursday then –

They shake hands, he hesitates.

I suppose you'll probably go out every night – with fellows who are rolling in money – but to me Thursday will be quite an occasion.

ROSEMARY: *(With apparent calm.)* Oh – I'm looking forward to it too.

PAUL: I – Good night.

Goes out.

ROSEMARY: *(As he goes.)* Good night.

Then, after a short pause talking with great urgency to herself.

Thursday, Thursday, Thursday. I'll have to put Alice off, of course, but she won't mind. Also, the Kershaws can't come to tea because I may not get back from the hairdresser's in time, but I can easily – and – oh! – some shoes – I'll go down on Wednesday with Alice and buy the shoes. That black bag's filthy but it'll have to do. Unless I can get a blue one – like Alice's – she said it was quite cheap – where was it? Somewhere in Regent Street.

WILLIAM rises, points to HELEN.

I might look at them while I'm getting the shoes. But perhaps after all it might be better to wear the white, though it'll be creased in the theatre and might look terrible afterwards,

WILLIAM is trying to attract HELEN's attention.

and that means wearing my rotten old red velvet coat – I might have it cleaned, but they're horribly slow at that place –

WILLIAM: No, no, no.

Curtains close.

Can't have any more of that. Drive a man barmy! *(Looks at HELEN, who is calm and smiling.)* How long would she go on like that?

HELEN: Hours and hours probably.

WILLIAM: Good God! But the evening she's going to have simply won't be worth all that agonising. Better to stop at home.

HELEN: Nonsense!

WILLIAM: Did you go through all that?

HELEN: Certainly – still do, sometimes.

WILLIAM *and* PHILIP: *(Shaking their heads.)* Simply isn't worth it.

HELEN: We think it is.

JOYCE: And so – really – do you.

WILLIAM: You know – I believe the secret of you women is – you've got far less individual conceit than we have.

JOYCE and HELEN: But – of course.

JOYCE: That's why we take so much trouble with ourselves.

WILLIAM: On the other hand, as a sex, you seem to have an enormous collective conceit.

HELEN: How do you mean?

WILLIAM: – Well, you're all convinced that though individually you may not be up to much, Woman herself is a tremendous treat. That's why if a man starts falling out of love with one of you, you always believe it's because he's falling in love with another one.

JOYCE: And nine times out of ten, at least, we're right!

WILLIAM: It's a sort of trades union conceit. We can't do without a member of the union. And very annoyed you are too when we prove we can.

HELEN: When you can ignore us, you've said good-bye to all hope of magic.

WILLIAM: Magic of a kind. Often a witch's brew. But we can do without your magic, because we're all sons of Adam, who did without it once. But you're all the daughters of poor Eve, who was never by herself, but found Adam already there –

HELEN: And ever since Eve we've felt socially responsible and even as guests we're still anxious hostesses.

PHILIP: *(Calling out.)* Too much talk!

He nods to JOYCE and they burst into loud dance music, which quietens down as WILLIAM speaks.

WILLIAM: *(Turning and going upstage with his back to the audience, puts on a pair of spectacles, turns and comes downstage again.)* Now this is where I might indulge in one of these philosophical disquisitions on Jazz and the spirit of the Age, which were so popular a few years ago.

HELEN: *(Takes off his spectacles, puts them in his breast pocket.)* This *is* a few years ago, but you're not here to philosophise but to dance.

Takes his hand, leads him up on to centre of rostrum. The music is loud again. PAUL and ROSEMARY enter from alcove, they go on to rostrum, both couples start dancing. PAUL in dinner jacket, ROSEMARY in evening dress.

WILLIAM: *(As they dance.)* Having a grand time, isn't she?

HELEN: Yes. So is he. Both of 'em just working up to something drastic. Lovely.

WILLIAM: Might be lovely. *(Pause.)* Might not. Can't tell. *(Pause.)* Never understand why you women always want to help on the biological process. Pairing everybody off as if you were all Mrs. Noah and it had started to rain.

HELEN: We know what life's about.

WILLIAM: My pet, you haven't the foggiest idea.

WILLIAM bumps into PAUL at the end of the dance.

WILLIAM: *(To PAUL.)* Sorry.

Music stops and the four stop. PAUL and the two women clap enthusiastically, WILLIAM perfunctorily. They join up now apparently standing on edge of dance floor.

HELEN: You know William, of course, don't you? Paul, Rosemary.

WILLIAM: *(To ROSEMARY.)* Enjoying yourself, I can see that.

ROSEMARY: Yes, I am, aren't you?

WILLIAM: Not much.

ROSEMARY: Oh, what a shame! I like this place. *(Looks about happily.)*

WILLIAM: *(Looking about unhappily.)* I don't. It frightens me.

ROSEMARY: Some of the people do look pretty awful.

WILLIAM: And some look awfully pretty. But that's not it. Consider the social and philosophical background-

ROSEMARY: I don't think I want to very much to-night.

WILLIAM: *(Almost as if announcing a lecture.)* Jazz, Swing, and the Spirit of the Golden Age-

HELEN: *(Breaking off talk with PAUL.)* No, William, not to-night. And the Cabaret will be starting soon. Naked young women.

WILLIAM: *(Gloomily.)* And the dirty songs at the piano.

Dance music again, not too loud.

PAUL: *(Happily.)* Rosemary!

ROSEMARY: *(Happily.)* Yes, Paul? *(Taking his hand.)*

PAUL: Let's dance.

They start dancing round and about.

WILLIAM: What's the matter with 'em now?

HELEN: It's the first time he's ever called her Rosemary and the first time she's ever called him Paul.

Alcove curtain held open, the other two, still dancing, smile and go off.

And you needn't look so glum about it. That's a very important moment. Don't you remember the first time I ever called you William?

WILLIAM: No. And I think I've had enough of this schoolgirl stuff. It's like being forcibly fed with golden syrup.

HELEN: You're envious really, y'know.

WILLIAM: *(Horrified.)* What – of that – mushy idiocy! *(Burlesquing their eager happy look and tone.)* Paul!

PHILIP: Rosemary!

HELEN: *(Coolly.)* Not of what he's doing, but of his state of mind. And now you're going to see the next stage. Do you remember what the next stage is?

WILLIAM: *(Cheering up a little.)* Yes. Bed.

HELEN: No. These aren't that kind. Think now. He's taken her out for several evenings – dining – dancing, to a play or a film – and they're not shy any longer but are beginning to talk.

WILLIAM: Yes, I know now. They're beginning to talk their heads off, and everything that each of them says, the other thinks is wonderful. The way they have the same tastes, the very same likes and dislikes – it's miraculous.

HELEN: She'll have to cheat a bit, of course.

WILLIAM: *(Sardonically.)* Oh, of course!

HELEN: But not as much as you think.

WILLIAM: Look at the way you pretended to like chess and be interested in politics.

HELEN: *(Scornfully.)* Oh! – chess and politics, there's a limit. But she won't have to cheat very much, she's still an impressionable and rather unformed sort of girl, and his very feeling for her, and her response to it, do really bring her unconsciously into line with his point of view.

Curtains open to disclose scene arranged to represent corner of drawing-room. PAUL sits in chair, ROSEMARY on stool. Both in evening clothes, very eager, inwardly excited. Note: During this scene HELEN quietly goes out, to make her change.

PAUL: *(Eagerly.)* I never knew you'd been there.

ROSEMARY: *(Same.)* Yes, I absolutely loved it. I've always been hoping to go there again.

PAUL: So have I. By Jove, if we could only – *(Breaks off, then resumes.)* And the castle, you know, is one of the most amusing pieces of baroque I know.

ROSEMARY: Yes, isn't it? I adore baroque.

PAUL: Well, I wouldn't go as far as that. It's *amusing.*

ROSEMARY: That's what I mean, Paul. It's terribly *amusing.* That's all, of course. No more than that. Not like – well –

PAUL: Let's say, Perpendicular Gothic or French Renaissance.

ROSEMARY: Of course not. They're absolutely wonderful. I've nearly finished that book you lent me on the French Renaissance. Completely enchanting. Have you played the Sibelius records yet?

PAUL: *(Sitting forward.)* Yes. I put them on to-night, just before I came out. You're right, of course. He's head and shoulders above all the rest.

ROSEMARY: *(Joyfully.)* Oh – I'm glad you feel like that about him, Paul.

PAUL: Yes, he gives me just the same feeling you described – sort of – you know, cold and stern yet with a kind of deep warmth inside –

ROSEMARY: That's it exactly. It's absurd saying you don't understand music-

PAUL: And it's absurd saying you don't understand architecture. Rosemary. Some people have a natural good taste, a flair, and you're one of 'em. And I haven't met many.

They exchange a smile and lean to each other.

ROSEMARY: Won't you have another whisky and soda – ?

PAUL: No, thanks. I must go in a minute.

They look at each other and smile.

WILLIAM: *(The interested spectator, after a pause.)* Well, what about it? Come on. Everything's all set.

PAUL: *(Slowly, shyly, looking away from her to out front.)* It's queer, you know.

ROSEMARY: What is, Paul?

PAUL: The way you go on perhaps for years not meeting anybody who's really your own kind, who likes the same things you like, who can have fun with you or be serious, just as the mood takes you both, until you begin to think you're an odd kind of bird and almost alone in the world…

WILLIAM: Extraordinary how people can imagine they're so different from the crowd. *(Turns to PHILIP at piano.) Paul and his odd kind of bird!* One of the most commonplace fellows I know! Scores just like him eating biscuits and cheese in every club dining room.

PHILIP: Sh – Sh – Sh – *(Points to stage.)*

PAUL: *(As before.)* And then, quite suddenly, you meet somebody…

ROSEMARY: *(Fervently.)* Yes, I know.

PAUL: As we met.

ROSEMARY: Yes. And that's the nicest thing anybody's ever said to me.

PAUL: *(Putting out a hand.)* Rosemary!

ROSEMARY: *(Giving him her hand.)* Dear Paul!

They kiss.

He has pulled her towards him and she is now in his arms and he is kissing her. They are enthusiastic but look a trifle awkward.

Curtains close.

WILLIAM: Yes, yes! Yes, yes! They'll be hours now excitedly explaining their uniqueness to each other.

JOYCE: *(Stoutly.)* Quite right too!

WILLIAM: *(Surprised.)* Joyce, Joyce!

JOYCE: Well, that's how they feel, and they're quite right.

WILLIAM: Yes, yes, Joyce. Nobody's blaming them. All very natural and pleasant, only of course we don't want to be in at it. All rather cloying and tedious to the onlooker. Where's Helen?

PHILIP: She went out during that last scene.

WILLIAM: *(Calling.)* Helen – Helen.

HELEN: *(Off, just behind nearest curtain.)* Shut up, I'm here.

WILLIAM: What are you doing there?

HELEN: Turning myself into Paul's mother. They're engaged now and Paul is going to introduce Rosemary to his mother. A big moment.

WILLIAM: Undoubtedly a big moment. And I think Rosemary's father ought to put in an appearance.

HELEN: *(Urgently.)* No, that's not necessary. Now don't be silly, darling.

WILLIAM: *(With dignity.)* There is nothing silly about it.

He goes out.

Curtains open showing scene, corner of another drawing-room with a settee. PAUL and ROSEMARY are standing together, looking rather anxious.

PAUL: But you dear delightful idiot, what have you to be anxious about? I tell you, she'll adore you. After all, I ought to know. She's my mother.

ROSEMARY: I know, darling. That's just it.

PAUL: The only thing you've got to be afraid of is that very soon if we're not careful, she'll settle down to tell you what I was like when I was cutting my first teeth or going down with whooping cough.

ROSEMARY: Oh – I don't mind that. In fact, I'd love to know what you were like when you were tiny. That's the point about being in love. You want to know *all* about the other person.

PAUL: I'd hate to know about you at the age of two. I wish mother'd hurry up. Though we were rather early.

ROSEMARY: *(Nervously.)* I think she's here.

He gives her a reassuring pat and she gives him a rather desperate quick smile. HELEN now enters as PAUL's mother, wearing different dress, grey wig, spectacles perhaps, and proceeds to give a performance as a solemn matron.

HELEN: I'm so sorry. Well, Paul! *(Smiles and he kissed her cheek lightly.)*

PAUL: Mother, this – is Rosemary.

HELEN: *(With marked change to effusive tone.)* Well, well, well! So this is Rosemary. *(Shakes her head and smiles at ROSEMARY.)* You've given me a real surprise, my dear. I'd begun to think Paul was a born bachelor. And now – here you are. *(Embraces and kisses ROSEMARY.)*

ROSEMARY: *(Shyly.)* Yes – and – I'm very, very happy.

HELEN: I'm sure you are. And I know Paul is too.

PAUL: Tremendously happy, Mother.

HELEN: *(Smiling.)* And if he's happy, you may be sure I am, having spoilt him all his life.

ROSEMARY: *(Smiling.)* He doesn't seem very spoilt.

PAUL: *(Very playfully.)* Just you wait! Eh, Mother?

HELEN: *(Archly.)* Yes, indeed. Though I may be able to show Rosemary one or two little tricks – to keep you in order.

Mime talk between HELEN and ROSEMARY. All three smile at each other, rather fatuously.

PHILIP: *(Across to JOYCE.)* Oh – Lord. I hate this dialogue.

JOYCE: I know. Loathsome! But it's about what they'd say.

Enter WILLIAM breezily in make-up as before as Rosemary's father.

WILLIAM: Well, well, well! Here we are, then.

ROSEMARY: *(Astounded.)* But – Father – what are you doing here?

PAUL: This is a surprise, sir.

HELEN: *(After glaring at WILLIAM.)* My surprise this time.

WILLIAM: Yes, yes, quite right. Her surprise. Most amusing!

PAUL: Yes – but – how did you-?

WILLIAM: *(Bluffly.)* Oh, your mother'll explain.

HELEN: *(After another glare at WILLIAM.)* You see, dear,
Rosemary's father and I are old friends.

WILLIAM: *(Bluffly.)* That's right. Old – old – friends.

HELEN: So I told him over the telephone he'd better come
along and give you both a surprise.

WILLIAM: And here I am, giving you a surprise. *(To PAUL.)* Well,
I expect Rosemary and your mother will have lots to talk
about – so suppose we leave 'em to it. Eh?

HELEN: No, no. You men stay here while I take Rosemary with
me and get to know her properly. *(Takes ROSEMARY's arm.)*
I'm sure you must have a lot to say to each other.

They turn to go together.

WILLIAM: *(Bluffly.)* Yes, yes, naturally. Young man marrying my
only daughter.

HELEN: Yes, well – have a nice intimate man's talk together.
Come along, Rosemary.

*Women go out. WILLIAM and PAUL sit on sofa. Both men look stiff
and uncomfortable and should be deliberately wooden in attitude
and speech.*

WILLIAM: Humph! All right to smoke?

PAUL: Oh – yes, of course. Sorry. Cigarette?

WILLIAM: *(Producing case.)* No thanks. Never smoke 'em. Cigar.

PAUL: No thanks. Can't cope with cigars. Wish I could.

*Both men light up and look straight in front of them throughout the
following dialogue, which should be slow and wooden.*

WILLIAM: I used to smoke a lot of cigars one time.

PAUL: Did you?

WILLIAM: Yes, I did. Used to get 'em by the thousand direct
from Cuba. Wonderful cigars.

PAUL: I'll bet they were. Best place for cigars, of course.

WILLIAM: Only place for cigars, really.

PAUL: *(Pause.)* Know much about the South African market, sir?

WILLIAM: No. Never touch it. Why?

PAUL: Nothing really. Just wondered. Client of mine seems to have made a lot out of it, that's all.

WILLIAM: I believe you can. Must be in the know, though. *(Pause.)* D'you ever go out after wild duck – ?

PAUL: No. Friend of mine does.

WILLIAM: Does he? *(Pause.)* What's his name?

PAUL: Sanderson.

WILLIAM: Not old Billy Sanderson, used to be out in Malaya?

PAUL: No, this chap's about my age. In the City. He's very keen on wild duck. *(Pause.)*

WILLIAM: It's a wonderful sport. *(Pause.)*

PAUL: I tired my hand at trout – trout last year.

WILLIAM: Did you? *(Pause.)* Dry fly?

PAUL: Yes.

WILLIAM: I never could get on with it. Needs too much practice for me.

PAUL: Does really. I wasn't much good.

WILLIAM: No, neither was I. *(Pause.)*

HELEN now appears outside rostrum. If practicable she should look her ordinary self.

HELEN: *(Scornfully.)* A nice intimate man's talk together, eh? Just like two people made of wood, sitting there grunting at each other! What do you think you're doing?

WILLIAM: *(To PAUL, hands his cigar to him to hold for a moment.)* Excuse me a moment, my boy.

PAUL: *(Who doesn't see HELEN.)* Certainly.

He remains in wooden attitude, while WILLIAM comes forward to talk to HELEN. He takes off his wig and moustache to show that he is now his ordinary self.

WILLIAM: What's the matter?

HELEN: Is that your idea of a nice intimate talk between a father and his prospective son-in-law?

WILLIAM: Yes.

HELEN: *(Indignantly.)* But – it's just nothing. Cigars and wild duck!

WILLIAM: A bit impersonal, of course.

HELEN: A bit impersonal!

WILLIAM: You can see the reason, can't you?

HELEN: No, I can't.

WILLIAM: Just shows how insensitive you women are.

HELEN: *(Aghast.)* What?

WILLIAM: *(Coolly.)* Yes, insensitive. We can't get up to your loquacious tricks, pouring out floods of horribly intimate stuff, displaying our underclothes.

HELEN: Who wants you to display your underclothes?

WILLIAM: The fact is, we're shy.

HELEN: But what is there to be shy about?

WILLIAM: This biology we're suddenly caught up in. He's shy because very soon he's going to take my daughter away and share a bedroom with her. And I'm shy because I know he's going to –

HELEN: Yes, yes, yes.

WILLIAM: We're the shy sex, you know. Always were. Now I'll get back and finish this off.

Puts on moustache and wig and goes back to sofa. PAUL hands back cigar. The two men play just in same manner as before. WILLIAM settles down in middle of sofa. HELEN goes out to change back into Paul's mother.

PAUL: How do you like this car you're trying?

WILLIAM: Very comfortable, but find her a bit sluggish so far.

PAUL: Engine needs running in, eh?

WILLIAM: Probably. But don't think she's very nippy. *(Pause.)* You fairly busy now?

PAUL: Yes. We're competing for that big Birmingham job.

WILLIAM: Hope you get it.

PAUL: We stand a fair chance. But that's really my partner's pigeon.

WILLIAM: Yes. I suppose you'll manage to get away all right after the – er – wedding?

PAUL: Yes. I've fixed that all right. Hope to manage a month.

WILLIAM: Good! Any idea where you're going?

PAUL: Not quite decided yet. Might motor across France and end up at the Italian lakes.

WILLIAM: Good trip. Sorry I can't be with you. *(Guffaws awkwardly.)*

They look at each other. PAUL laughs awkwardly.

(Shy and solemn now.) I know you'll try and make her happy, my boy.

PAUL: It won't be my fault if she isn't, sir.

WILLIAM: No doubt. Won't be hers, though. Happiest little thing you ever saw. Not like some of 'em, always whining and moping. Miss her, y'know, my boy. Miss her like the devil. However, there it is, there it is.

PAUL and WILLIAM rise. HELEN as PAUL's mother and ROSEMARY enter. They look happy and thick as thieves.

HELEN: *(Gaily.)* Now, you two. I know you're having a wonderful talk and telling one another all your secrets Don't stop. But there are drinks in your room, Paul, and I thought you'd like to go along there.

WILLIAM: Good idea.

PAUL: Yes, rather. How's it going. Rosemary?

ROSEMARY: Grand!

HELEN: Passed with honours, didn't you, dear? Now, off you go.

The men go out, WILLIAM to change back at once to ordinary self. As PAUL passes ROSEMARY he pats her arm. The two women get into a feminine huddle, very confidential and close, and talking rapidly.

HELEN: Yes, dear, I think you're very wise to take a nice little flat at first.

ROSEMARY: I thought a little flat would be best, at first. Afterwards of course –

HELEN: Afterwards, of course, when you've settled down properly then perhaps Paul might build you a house about twenty or thirty miles out. *(Looks to her and smiles.)* But at first, I know you'll both be happier in some convenient little flat in town. Paul's very fond of the country, of course-

ROSEMARY: I am too. I love the country.

HELEN: I'm sure you do. And of course for young children I think the country's perfect. But you've no need to think about that yet. *(Smiles.)* In the meantime, you're quite right to want a nice little flat. Not a service flat, eh?

ROSEMARY: No, I don't think so.

HELEN: Saves trouble with maids, of course. And cooks.

ROSEMARY: But they're so terribly expensive, aren't they?

HELEN: Most of the ones I know are, but there may be cheaper ones now, though what the food and service will be like I don't know. And Paul's rather fastidious about food, you know. Which reminds me, Rosemary, don't try and make Paul give up his club. I know he's so fond of it.

ROSEMARY: Oh – I wouldn't dream of it. Of course not. He'll want to see other men. But I thought if we had a nice little flat somewhere fairly central –

HELEN: Of course, you're absolutely right. You couldn't do better, at first, than start with a nice little flat, preferably somewhere fairly central. If you could find a reasonably cheap service flat, of course –

WILLIAM enters from alcove.

WILLIAM: I say!

ROSEMARY: Oh – we'd take it like a shot, if it wasn't too dear. Because after all, it would save trouble with maids and cooks.

WILLIAM: I say!

HELEN: That's the point! As long as the food and service are not too bad. Paul's rather –

WILLIAM: *(Almost in despair.)* Look here!

HELEN: *(After giving him a sharp look.)* My dear, I'm sure I've kept you too long from Paul. Run along to his room, where I was showing you the photographs, and you'll find him there.

ROSEMARY: *(Rising spontaneously.)* Oh – I'm so happy.

HELEN: I know you are, Rosemary, and I think you're every right to be, for you're a very lucky girl.

The two women kiss, ROSEMARY exits. HELEN looks at WILLIAM, pushes the sofa upstage with her foot, in irritation, the curtains close.

WILLIAM: *(Going up on to rostrum and speaking through curtains.)* I'm sorry – I say – I'm sorry. *(To PHILIP.)* I believe she's annoyed.

PHILIP: I know she was.

JOYCE: She was furious – and quite right too. You deliberately broke into her scene.

WILLIAM: But she interrupted me when I was Rosemary's father. Still I'll try again. I'm sorry. Hearing me, of course, but not answering. I'm sorry. You don't call that conversation, an exchange of views, opinions, ideas, experiences, do you? You were going round and round in a tiny circle. You were simply making cooling noises at each other.

JOYCE: *(Rather sharply.)* Of course they were. They knew that.

WILLIAM: Well, but what's the point of it?

PHILIP: I've been wondering for years.

HELEN enters from the alcove as herself.

HELEN: Don't be so dense. A girl has just met the mother of the man she's going to marry. A woman has just met the girl her son is going to marry. An ordeal for both of them.

WILLIAM: Yes, I can see that, dense as I am.

HELEN: Well, then they discover, to their great relief, that they're ready to like each other. The ordeal's over. It's going to be all right.

WILLIAM: And so instead of exchanging experiences, opinions, ideas...

HELEN: They'll do that much later on.

WILLIAM: They make a lot of nice agreeing noises together, eh?

HELEN: That's it. Women can't jog along on parallel lines as men seem able to do. They're always either going away from each other or coming together. And these two were coming together, and proving it. See?

WILLIAM: Yes. But what a life.

HELEN: Of course, it's ten times harder than being a man. But far more amusing, I fancy. *(Hesitates.)* Now this is rather awkward.

WILLIAM: Why what's wrong?

HELEN: We have to be two different characters soon – guests at the wedding reception-

WILLIAM: Oh, have we? That's all right. I shall be Major Spanner, back from the East and an old friend and admirer of the bride. No trouble about that.

WILLIAM exits.

HELEN: Now, Joyce dear, I think we ought to show Paul and Rosemary just for a minute before the wedding. Something romantic – young – touching –

JOYCE: *(Rising.)* Yes.

HELEN: A rainy evening in Spring – wet lilac – and the moon lighting up her upturned face –

PHILIP: *(Rising.)* Then you'll want some music.

HELEN: Essential.

HELEN exits.

JOYCE: Chopin I think.

PHILIP: Certainly. One of the Nocturnes?

JOYCE: No. The Fantasy Impromptu Middle Section.

PHILIP: All right, but don't go wrong with the triplets in the left hand.

JOYCE: No, of course not. Yes, Chopin coming through some mysterious lighted window. Didn't you always think, when you were young, that there was something magical about those houses where somebody was playing a piano?

PHILIP: No. I didn't.

JOYCE: You didn't? Why, I used to feel there must be something terribly special about the people in that house – that they were living an enchanted life that I'd never know. What's the matter with you?

PHILIP: *(Sighs.)* I suppose the trouble is I just don't think big, beautiful thoughts.

JOYCE: Oh, you're hopeless. *(JOYCE goes back and sits at piano left.)*

PHILIP: Well I think we're all set. Lights. *(Sits at piano right.)*

Lights dim on stage. Some moonlight comes on. PAUL and ROSEMARY enter from alcove wearing light raincoats, walking close and lovingly. They stop in a moonlight spot.

ROSEMARY: Darling!

PAUL: What, darling?

ROSEMARY: The lilac.

PAUL: Yes, marvellous.

Softly the Chopin music begins. They listen rapturously.

ROSEMARY: Chopin. Perfect!

PAUL: Perfect. Only three days now, darling.

ROSEMARY: Only three days.

PAUL: I love you.

ROSEMARY: I love you.

They kiss, the moonlight spot fades. They exit.

The Pianists begin a quiet amusing version of the Wedding March. The first Pianist comes up to full strength as the lighting comes up too. The curtain is drawn to reveal the inner stage set as corner of a large room where wedding reception is being held. There are one or two small tables, with champagne, glasses, food, etc. A lot of noise off, both direct and recorded – chatter, noise of plates and glasses.

HELEN enters as Mrs. de Folyat, a handsome vivacious widow of about thirty-five with an intense arch manner, with champagne glass in their hand.

WILLIAM now enters as Major George Spanner, a military rather wooden, bronzed man about forty, who is slightly tight in a rather depressed fashion, and is also busy removing bits of confetti from his clothes.

HELEN: *(Shouting.)* I beg your pardon?

WILLIAM: *(Shouting.)* Sorry. What did you say?

HELEN: *(As before.)* I said "I beg you pardon".

WILLIAM: *(As before.)* Certainly – certainly –

HELEN: What time is it?

WILLIAM: Sorry – can't hear you.

HELEN: *(Top of her voice.)* I said – What time is it?

It happens as she says this that the noise has suddenly stopped, so that it sounds very loud indeed. WILLIAM glances suspiciously at her before looking at his watch.

WILLIAM: Twenty to four.

HELEN: What a ghastly hour! Let me see, aren't you Major Spanner?

WILLIAM: Yes. Sorry – I don't remember-

HELEN: No, we weren't introduced. Somebody pointed you out to me. I'm Mrs. de Folyat.

WILLIAM: Oh yes. How d'you do?

HELEN: Do you think it all went off very well?

WILLIAM: Suppose so. No judge really. Don't care for all this business. Beastly functions.

HELEN: Definitely. Let me see, you're out East, aren't you?

WILLIAM: Yes. *(Pause.)* Rubber.

HELEN: That must be wonderful.

HELEN is waving off to somebody again.

WILLIAM: It was once. But ever since the bottom dropped out of the market it's been terrible.

HELEN: *(With vague enthusiasm.)* Yes. But the life there – the colour, the romance, the mystery! The temple bells. The sense of eternity. Do you practise yoga?

WILLIAM: *(Horrified.)* God lord! – No! I'm not in India by the way. Straits Settlement. Fifteen hundred miles away from India.

HELEN: Is it really? But then I suppose it's all much bigger out there than one imagines.

WILLIAM: Oh – enormous. People here have not the faintest notion. They ask me to look up fellas who are two thousand miles away from my place.

HELEN: *(Who has been glancing about her.)* Do they really? I wonder why?

She waves as if good-bye to some people who are leaving and makes this very big.

WILLIAM: *(Disturbed and looking to where she is waving.)* Well, because they don't realise these fellas are two thousand miles away.

HELEN: *(Confidentially.)* I think I shall slip away now. This seems a good chance. *(She comes forward to front of rostrum.)*

WILLIAM: *(With a quick glance round.)* Yes, rather. I was just going out. Join you, I think.

He joins HELEN. The curtains close. Once outside they halt, relieved, as if they had sneaked out of a hotel room. It is now presumed they are in a street.

HELEN: *(Taking deep breath.)* Ah! – it's so good to be in the fresh air again.

WILLIAM: Yes. Frightful row in there. Hate those scrimmages. Taxi!

HELEN: *(Archly.)* Are you bride or bridegroom?

WILLIAM: *(Astounded, pause.)* What?

HELEN: I mean, one of her friends or one of his?

WILLAM: Oh, one of hers. Don't know him at all. Known little Rosemary since she was a child. Friend of the family. Rosemary's grown up to be a very fine girl.

HELEN: Has she? Taxi!

WILLIAM: *(With genuine enthusiasm.)* Yes, decidedly. No doubt about that. Weybridge is a very lucky fella. Hope he realises it.

HELEN: Major Spanner, I do believe – *(Breaks off.)*

WILLIAM: *(Intimidatingly wooden.)* What?

HELEN: No, no, I don't know you well enough. I musn't say it. As a matter of fact I don't know her at all. And I've only recently met Paul Weybridge. He's an architect, you know.

WILLIAM: Yes, so I gather.

HELEN: And a very clever one. He's been adding a wing to my little place in the country, *quite* brilliantly.

WILLIAM: He has, has he? Taxi! *(Waving his stick.)*

HELEN: I couldn't stop help thinking it a pity that a man who has obviously such a tremendous future should go and –

WILLIAM: What?

HELEN: Now, now, Major Spanner, you mustn't tempt me to be indiscreet.

WILLIAM: *(Bewildered.)* Didn't know I was doing so.

HELEN: Besides, it's quite clear I can't expect any sympathy from you.

WILLIAM: *(Stiffly.)* Now look here, Mrs. de Folyat, if you're suggesting he oughtn't to have married because his wife isn't good enough for him –

HELEN: Now I never *said* that. I merely hinted that perhaps –

WILLIAM: Because if so, I'll give you my opinion, as a man who's seen a good deal of the world.

HELEN: And what is your opinion, Major Spanner?

WILLIAM: *(Stiffly.)* That that little girl – Rosemary – is worth ten of him – yes, ten of him. Taxi! Ah, got it. This one, I think.

They step off rostrum and exit.

Lights dim and music begins with final theme of the Act. Curtains open to reveal inner stage set as balcony of hotel in Southern Europe. Moonlight spot comes on. Back of scene is dimly lit, large bedroom window. PAUL in a dressing gown and ROSEMARY in a wrap come out of the long windows, stand close together, looking out into what is obviously a wonderful moonlight night. The music plays softly before they speak, and continues softly throughout.

ROSEMARY: I feel that you and the night are almost one:

    I seem as near to you when I stare into the night,

    Losing myself in the green ivory world

    The moon has carved, as when I felt your heart

    Dividing each precious moment with my own!

    And when you are so close my eyes have lost you

    To my lips, I seem to float in the wide night

    And behind my eyelids rises another moon.

PAUL: *(After a pause.)* Men are restless and nearly always alone.

    Going off in pursuit, nosing along a trail,

    Following a rumour of gold to the waterless hills.

    Now here comes to an end for me many a trail

    That never had a thought in it of women and love.

    Now there is nothing I wish to find.

He puts his arms round her.

ROSEMARY: There should be words that ring our joy like bells.

    But I know none. There is sorrow in all words.

PAUL: If my heart still drums it is to stop my ears,

    Because even to-night from somewhere beyond the moon

    Still roars into the abyss the cataract of time.

ROSEMARY: Then take hold of this night and keep it fast

    Never, never forget it.

PAUL: I shall not forget.

He holds her against him, and she leans her head against his shoulder. HELEN enters dressed as herself.

HELEN: *(In happy excitement.)* Now I'm a woman too, and not a mere voice,

    And blast all supercilious commentating:

    Come on, give me that Mediterranean moon,

    And the right man, and I too can kiss

    And rave the very stars out of the blue.

Moonlight comes full on her too now. She calls sharply.

William, you idiot!

Then in soft cajoling tone.

Oh, Bill, my sweet, come on!

WILLIAM enters as himself again.

WILLIAM: *(In fine form.)* And here I am. Hey – spill that moonshine! Spill it and spread it, boys. Ah, that's better.

With moonlight full on him, he looks across at HELEN.

God, what a night! And Helen – what a girl.

HELEN: You fat, conceited and adorable fool. You've had Paul and Rosemary to thank for this.

WILLIAM: *(Grandly.)* And Adam and Eve and the angel who sometimes nods.

HELEN: And lets us slip under his sword at Eden's Gate.

Music, pause.

PAUL: Rosemary!

ROSEMARY: Paul!

Music, pause.

JOYCE: Philip!

PHILIP: Joyce!

Music, pause.

HELEN: *(The light spreading to them.)* William!

Music, pause.

WILLIAM: Helen!

They crash into triumphant music. PAUL and ROSEMARY are close together. HELEN and WILLIAM extend their arms to each other. PHILIP and JOYCE stare happily across as they play.

End of Act One.

ACT TWO

PHILIP and JOYCE begin playing a fairly brisk overture. After about a minute and a half of it, however, it begins to flag and suddenly JOYCE stops altogether and looks angry. After plodding a bar or two by himself, PHILIP also stops. JOYCE rises.

PHILIP: What's the matter?

JOYCE: *(Angrily.)* You know very well what's the matter.

PHILIP: I don't.

JOYCE: Of course you do.

PHILIP: *(Annoyed now.)* I tell you I don't. All I know is that you suddenly stopped playing.

JOYCE: And I stopped playing because I couldn't stand it any longer.

PHILIP: Couldn't stand what?

JOYCE: Couldn't stand the sight of you there, obviously with no interest whatever in what we were playing, just bored and not making any effort to hide it. I suppose if it had been Margery Walker you'd been playing with, your eyes would have been half out of your head and you'd have been bouncing all over your piano.

PHILIP: *(With irritating air of patience, rises.)* Would you mind telling me what on earth Margery Walker has to do with it?

JOYCE: Oh – don't be so pompous!

PHILIP: *(With same manner.)* I'm not being pompous. I'm merely asking a reasonable question. What has –

JOYCE: *(Furiously.)* Oh – shut up!

PHILIP: *(With injured dignity, sits.)* Certainly. Certainly. Only too delighted.

He brings out of his far pocket a copy of a newspaper and very ostentatiously leans back and buries himself behind it.

JOYCE: *(After a moment.)* How can you sit there – pretending to read a newspaper – !

PHILIP: *(With irritating air of calm.)* I'm not pretending to read. I *am* reading. I notice here, for instance, that a man called Worsnop has just found on his estate several Roman coins. The coins, it says, were in an excellent state of –

JOYCE: I haven't the least desire to hear anything about your ridiculous coins.

She goes back to her piano and sits.

PHILIP: Thank you!

He begins reading again. She looks across at him in angry despair. WILLIAM now enters smoking a pipe and carrying a copy of The Times. He looks rather grumpy. JOYCE brightens up at the sight of him.

JOYCE: Hello, William!

WILLIAM: *(Not interested.)* Hello!

JOYCE: *(With forced brightness.)* Any news?

WILLIAM: *(Beginning to open paper.)* I haven't really looked at the paper yet.

JOYCE: I don't mean in the paper. I mean, have *you* any news?

WILLIAM: *(Blankly.)* Me? Oh – no – nothing at all.

He sits and begins reading his paper. JOYCE looks in despair from him to PHILIP and then plays several hideously-sounding chords. WILLIAM and PHILIP together appear from behind their papers and look at her with silent reproach. They begin reading again. HELEN enters, briskly and cheerfully.

HELEN: *(Crossing over to WILLIAM.)* William!

WILLIAM: *(Looking up without interest.)* Yes, my pet?

HELEN: *(Rather like a guide-lecturer.)* Pay attention. Now, we're going forward several years in the history of Paul and Rosemary. Last time we saw them, you remember, they were on their honeymoon. Five or six years have passed since then. Rosemary has had a baby, now a very nice little boy between three and four, called Robin.

PHILIP: He doesn't come into this, does he? I mean, you don't show us little Robin bringing his parents together again in the end, do you?

HELEN: *(Severely.)* No, of course not. You see that sort of thing at the films, not here.

PHILIP: Yes, dear, I know, but when you said they now had nice little boy, I began to be worried.

HELEN: You needn't worry. And by the way, I'm not really talking to you, I'm talking to William.

WILLIAM: *(Looking up blankly from paper.)* Yes, my love, I'm listening.

HELEN: Move your chair round a bit or you won't see anything.

WILLIAM: Certainly, certainly. *(Moves his stool behind piano, preparing to read again.)*

HELEN: So now, after missing these first years of marriage, we now find Paul and Rosemary comfortably settled in London. And here is an average evening.

Curtains open to disclose inner set, as corner of a sitting-room. PAUL is buried in the evening paper, while ROSEMARY is fidgeting between writing a letter, doing a little sewing and reading a book. Both are rather more mature than when we saw them last. WILLIAM and PHILIP are also reading their newspapers and pay no attention whatever to the scene, to the disgust of HELEN and JOYCE.

ROSEMARY: *(After pause.)* I saw Diana Ferguson this morning.

PAUL: *(Muttering.)* Don't know her.

ROSEMARY: Yes, you do know her. She says she's expecting her husband back from India at the end of the month.

PAUL merely grunts. She looks at him in disgust, then tries again.

ROSEMARY: They're taking a house in South Devon for his leave. Then she wants to go back with him this time. And I must say I don't blame her. Do you? *(Pause. Waits for a reply and doesn't receive one, keeping her temper with some difficulty.)* Is there anything particularly interesting in that paper, dear?

PAUL: *(Blankly, looking up.)* What? – no.

Curtains close.

HELEN now notices that WILLIAM is not looking at all.

HELEN: William, you're the limit!

She goes over to him and snatches the paper away from him. He stares at her in blank astonishment.

WILLIAM: Now don't be silly, Helen. I'm reading that paper.

HELEN: You were, but now you've stopped. I don't believe you noticed Paul and Rosemary at all, did you?

WILLIAM: Well, I'll tell you –

HELEN: Did you?

WILLIAM: No, I didn't.

HELEN: You were too busy staring at that newspaper. What's in it.

WILLIAM: Nothing. Absolutely nothing to-day. Very dull.

HELEN: I take the trouble to show Paul and Rosemary having a typical evening –

WILLIAM: *(Warming as he goes along.)* Yes, yes, but I don't want to see them. Let's leave them alone. That's what's the matter with the world now. Everybody interfering with everybody else. Everybody wanting to know what everybody else is doing and saying and thinking. Nobody's left alone. Not for a single half-hour is anybody left alone. Well I say, leave them alone. Refuse to indulge in this universal idiotic and shameless curiosity. Just hand me my paper, will you?

HELEN: Why? It's only crammed with information about other people, news of somebody else's business, all arranged *(Hands paper, which she has crumpled, back to WILLIAM.)* to satisfy an idiotic and shameless curiosity.

WILLIAM: *(With cold dignity and folding his newspaper.)* It's one thing to acquaint yourself with what is happening in the world and quite another thing to poke your nose into other people's private affairs. However, if you won't see it, you won't. *(Change of tone.)* Now, I suppose you want me to have a look at this pair of yours, several years of marriage, just to show me how dissatisfied she is.

HELEN: If you'd seen and heard –

WILLIAM: I saw and heard enough. She's not really dissatisfied with him – although she thinks she is – but she's dissatisfied because she can't have her cake and eat it –

HELEN: *(Cutting in, vehemently.)* If there's one thing I loathe it's that bit of misery about not being able to have your cake and eat it.

PHILIP: You all do.

WILLIAM: Yes. So she'll begin taking her dissatisfaction out of him. And it's not his fault.

HELEN and JOYCE: Of course it is.

HELEN: Just stuck there, with his head in the paper.

WILLIAM: But he has to read the paper some time and probably it happens that he's been busy all day.

HELEN: And probably not. But that's not the point. The point is he's beginning to treat her as if she weren't really there. All she wants is a little politeness, a little interest, a –

WILLIAM: *(Cutting coolly, puts pipe in his mouth and newspaper under his arm.)* I know what she'd like. Now I'll show you . *(He claps his hands.)*

Curtains open to same scene as before.

ROSEMARY: *(Sitting eating chocolates.)* I saw Diana Ferguson this morning.

PAUL: *(Putting aside paper at once.)* Did you, darling? When's her husband coming on leave from India?

ROSEMARY: At the end of the month.

PAUL: *(Brightly astonished.)* No!

ROSEMARY: Yes. She's awfully excited.

PAUL: Of course. He must be too. I know *I'd* be almost off my head with excitement if we'd been separated so long. They ought to take a furnished house somewhere for his leave.

ROSEMARY: *(Triumphantly.)* That's just what they have done. In South Devon.

PAUL: In South Devon? Oh, they ought to have a grand time there. I know we should. *(They lean to each other and smile.)*

ROSEMARY: She wants to go back with him this time. And I must say I don't blame her. Do you?

PAUL: No, I don't. Just imagine if it were us. How lucky we are to be able to be together without either of us making any sacrifices. *(Blows kiss to her.)*

ROSEMARY: Yes, darling. *(After smiling at him.)* But I'm keeping you from your newspaper.

PAUL: Oh now. *(Throws newspaper over his shoulder.)* I'd much rather have a good talk about us, and especially about you. *(Leans forward, regarding her lovingly and kisses her.)*

Curtains close.

WILLIAM: And that's quite enough of that. Now, Helen, that's what she'd like – or what she thinks she'd like, and, honestly, what do you think of it?

HELEN: I've always tried to be honest with you, Bill, haven't I?

WILLIAM: Except when we're quarrelling – yes.

HELEN: So, I'll admit that for an ordinary conversation – not a special occasion, mind you, making it up or celebrating an anniversary –

WILLIAM: No, no – an ordinary conversation at the conjugal hearth.

HELEN: It did strike me as being a wee bit fatuous and sickly.

WILLIAM: Exactly. Like sitting down after dinner and eating two pounds of chocolate creams.

HELEN: But it isn't the absence of that stuff that is making her feel dissatisfied. What she feels is that he's beginning to be bored with her.

WILLIAM: Now why? A man comes home tired at the end of a hard day, and naturally he wants to take it easy and –

HELEN: Yes, yes, we know all about that, and even women can understand it, seeing that they often have even harder days and aren't allowed to take it easy and sprawl and yawn in everybody's face. But what infuriates a wife is that sort of thing.

HELEN exits.

WILLIAM: What sort of thing?

JOYCE: Watch and you'll see, William.

Curtains open to same scene. ROSEMARY is reading a book this time.

ROSEMARY: And I must say I don't blame her. Do you? *(Pause as before.)* Is there anything particularly interesting in that paper, dear?

PAUL: *(Looking up blankly.)* What? No. *(Half stifles a yawn and returns to reading.)*

ROSEMARY: *(After another pause.)* Did anything amusing happen at the office to-day, Paul?

PAUL: *(Indifferently.)* No, can't remember anything.

She looks at him despairingly but he doesn't even see it. After another, pause, to establish atmosphere of boredom, HELEN marches in, looking very trim and gay.

HELEN: *(Briskly.)* Hello, Rosemary. 'Lo, Paul! Just looked in to ask you about Saturday.

PAUL: Saturday by all means, Helen. By the way, a most amusing thing happened at the office this morning. We've got a new client, a Mrs. Dowson, who's actually very rich, but looks a queer, shabby old thing. We've also got a new charlady whose name happened to be Mrs. Rowston. *(Laughs.)* Well, this morning this Mrs. Rowston comes in for the first time, and of course the clerk thinks the name she gives is Mrs. Dowson, treats her with enormous politeness, can't understand why she keeps mumbling something about cleaning and keeps apologising abjectly because my partner and I aren't about.

He laughs, so does HELEN. ROSEMARY does not laugh.

HELEN: *(Clearly forcing her appreciation.)* What a priceless thing to happen!

ROSEMARY: It doesn't amuse me very much, somehow. The only difference between the two women was that one had a lot of money and the other hadn't any. And I don't think that's funny.

PAUL: Oh – nonsense, Rosemary. *(Pats her on the shoulder.)* That's taking it altogether too seriously.

HELEN: Did you read that extraordinary case of the woman who had two flats and lived a completely different life in them?

PAUL: *(Eagerly.)* Yes. I was just reading about it now. Fascinating business. I don't think she was mad though, do you?

HELEN: No. I believe there was a man in it somewhere.

ROSEMARY: Where is this woman?

HELEN: In all the papers to-day.

ROSEMARY: *(To PAUL.)* And you said there wasn't anything interesting in the paper you were reading.

HELEN: *(In ordinary tone.)* All right, Rosemary, I think that's enough. You see, that's what I mean. If a man's tired, all right, let him be tired. It's a bit dull for wives, who've been messing about at home all day, if husbands come back in the evening fit for nothing but sprawling and yawning.

ROSEMARY: But we'll make the best of it so long as they are genuinely tired, and not simply bored. But you saw what happened. As soon as another woman, an attractive woman, of course, came in, he was up and sparkling, trying to be amusing, ready to show off as hard as he could –

PAUL: I really can't see that just because I show a little ordinary politeness to a friend – a friend of yours as well as mine – you should work yourself up into a jealous fury.

ROSEMARY: I wasn't jealous, and it just shows how stupid you are to imagine I was. I was annoyed because you could take the trouble to entertain Helen when you'd just proved very plainly you couldn't be bothered to entertain me.

WILLIAM: *(Whistles and beckons them up to him.)* I see the point.

HELEN: He sees the point. *(To audience.)* We're getting on.

WILLIAM: *(Turning to PHILIP.)* But after all, when somebody calls, you have to exert yourself a little, for the sake of ordinary social decency –

PHILIP: And I agree – *(He breaks off because both women are shaking their heads.)*

ROSEMARY: I must say William, I expected something better than that from *you* –

PAUL: *(Bitterly.)* Not from *me*, of course, being only your husband.

WILLIAM: "A wife", said Dostoevsky, after covering himself with glory at shooting gallery, when his wife had been angry with him for trying to shoot at all – "A wife," he observed profoundly, "is the natural enemy of her husband."

PAUL: And I know exactly what he means.

PHILIP: So do I and I wish I didn't.

HELEN: And I never heard anything more ridiculous. I'm surprised at you, William.

ROSEMARY: So am I.

JOYCE: I thought he was intelligent.

WILLIAM: I am intelligent and so was Dostoevsky.

ROSEMARY: *(Bitterly.)* The point is, having another woman there he was no longer bored.

HELEN: Perfectly obvious and perfectly maddening.

JOYCE: *(Rising.)* Haven't we all seen it over and over again?

PHILIP: *(Also rising angrily.)* Because you're so childish. You want everything at once.

PAUL: You can't have it both ways.

WILLIAM: *(Angrily.)* Oh – don't begin about that cake.

The men all laugh together at this. The women have all spoken at once, they give each other apologetic little smiles and apologise profusely to each other. Then glare at the men. The women have drifted back and grouped themselves round the piano left. The men begin speaking at once.

PHILIP: It's perfectly simple and I'll explain.

PAUL: What I mean by not having it both ways is –

WILLIAM: Wanting to have your cake and eat it means this –

The women all laugh as the men did at this. The men stop and apologise in a hearty, masculine style to each other.

PHILIP: Sorry, old man! You were going to say – ?

PAUL: Not at all, old boy. My fault. Interrupted you both.

Then men group themselves round and lean against piano right; they remain in a huddle.

WILLIAM: That's all right, my dear fellow. You go ahead.

JOYCE: *(In dry, hard tone.)* Lord help us! When you take a good cool look at them, you wonder why you ever bother. They're so damned idiotic. *(Savagely burlesquing them.)* No, not at all, old man. Go on, old boy. Urr!

PHILIP: One of us had better speak for the lot.

WILLIAM: Good idea! What about you, Paul?

PAUL: No, you're the chap, William. Your job, old boy.

WILLIAM: *(Muttering.)* All right, old boy.

HELEN: *(Coolly.)* They're like schoolboys who've been allowed to sit up late and guzzle and swill as much as they liked and so have all gone to seed.

ROSEMARY: They don't even try – as we do – to keep young outside while letting themselves grow older inside.

HELEN: Just overgrown, sagging, ruined schoolboys.

WILLIAM: *(Rising slowly.)* Ladies, after we have fallen in love with you we feel that existence would be intolerable if you are not by our sides, so we marry you. What happens then?

ROSEMARY: You take us for granted and are bored.

WILLIAM: That is how you see it, but not how we see it.

PHILIP and PAUL: Hear, hear!

WILLIAM: If necessary, yes, with sprawling and yawning. With you we feel we need no longer pretend, for we are at home. There is something in most women, however, that feels itself defeated by the ease and familiarity of marriage. *(He stands on stool and assumes the air and deportment of a political speaker.)* It is not that you dislike the cosy domesticity, the slippers and dressing-gown atmosphere. But at any moment when you feel so inclined you think you are entitled to be regarded as a person clean outside this atmosphere, a strange, exciting creature, a figure of romance.

ROSEMARY: *(Pointing to WILLIAM.)* But that's the point. We are strange, exciting creatures and what's wrong with you men is that you stop thinking we are, and then you diminish us. We grow angry because there is a light in us and you will no longer let it shine for you.

She returns to the piano.

PAUL: But the light has been turned into the domestic lamp and firelight. Your trouble is you want to be courted as well as married.

HELEN: And why not?

WILLIAM: Because – and this is one of the cakes you can't both have and eat – to our way of thinking one relationship cancels out the other. Husbands take wives for granted. Of course they do. They married them in order to take them for granted. But wives take husbands for granted just as much, and that, ladies and gentlemen, is our case.

WILLIAM drops off stool. PHILIP shakes him by the hand. PAUL does the same. They go into a huddle round the piano again.

ROSEMARY: It doesn't suit women to be taken for granted. *(Stamps her foot.)* It withers them.

JOYCE sits at the piano and plays a few mournful chords.

HELEN: What's that?

JOYCE: It's the beginning of a lament for women.

JOYCE plays very softy throughout women's speeches.

HELEN: *(Grouped near JOYCE with ROSEMARY.)* Who was the last to enter the Paradise of Eden – and the first out?

ROSEMARY: The fool who can light up at a single kind word and bleed at a glance.

JOYCE: Who buys a new hat and hopes against hope.

HELEN: *(In a grander style and going up on to centre of rostrum.)* I sing – after the manner of Walt Whitman, who nevertheless, has always seemed to me an insufferable old bore – I chant the theme Woman. Not Woman and the joys of the open road, for no woman ever had an open road. All roads are narrow, dark, bristling and dangerous to a woman.

Not woman and the happiness of loafing, hanging about, watching other people work and producing nothing but noble platitudes, because no woman is allowed – by herself or by anybody else – to indulge in such idle antics.

Some men are handsomely paid and kept in comfort to prove and preach that the ultimate force in the universe is nothing but Love, and they may or may not believe it. But all women, even the stupidest and ugliest that nobody cares about, act as if this were true. *(Comes down to piano and leans against it.)* And much good it does them.

ROSEMARY: It is terrible to be a woman and know in your heart how dependent you are upon other people, how you wait and wait for some fool of a man, who doesn't happen to have anything better to do, to bring you completely to life.

JOYCE: There are too many of us, that's the trouble.

ROSEMARY: A hurried, indifferent kiss, a hint of yawn, from some man who isn't really very different from millions of other men, and ice is packed round your heart.

JOYCE: What we need is ice packed round our heads. *(Finish of music.)*

HELEN: After being a woman, to be a man must be like having a long rest, a sort of convalescence –

PHILIP slides into piano chair and interrupts with some loud, sharp chords while the women look at him.

PHILIP: *(Piano silent.)* Convalescence! You can't imagine what it's like being a man. It's like this. *(Plays some loud, restless, strident music.)* I tell you – it's hell. *(Plays softly now, but with loud chords between speeches.)*

WILLIAM: In the fields you see the cows staring at nothing with their great soft eyes, placidly grazing and chewing, cosily manufacturing to-morrow's milk. Look further, into some lonely field or dark shed, and you will hear unhappy snorts and grunts and see a majestic but restless form, a creature passionate and bewildered, with a ring through his nose. *(Pause.)* The Bull! And that is Man.

PAUL: *(Quick leap on to rostrum.)* Man, fixed for ever in his terrible dualism, the war between the spirit and the senses that no woman can understand. Man who grasps at the moon, and finds himself eating green cheese. Man, who cannot be lulled by the rhythms of the fat earth and who is haunted by the Paradise you hardly remember.

PHILIP: *(Sadly.)* After all, it is better to buy a hat and hope a bit than to buy dozens of drinks and know there is no hope.

WILLIAM: When a pair of lovers declare themselves, one of them thinks he is juggling with the sun, moon and stars, while the other is busy working out how much it will cost to keep a housemaid in one of those nice new bungalows along Elm Avenue. It is safe to prophesy which one of these two will come a cropper first. The chaps who saw themselves keeping the sun, moon and stars going are bound to come down with a bump. The ladies – God bless them – have never left the ground.

PAUL: Man – alternating between Don Quixote and Don Juan –

PHILIP points to WILLIAM indicating that the women are not listening.

WILLIAM: *(To PAUL.)* I don't think they're listening, my dear fellow. Better get back on the job.

PAUL: What? Oh, yes, certainly. *(He goes back into the inner stage, sits in arm-chair.)*

WILLIAM: *(Crossing to HELEN and ROSEMARY.)* Come along, you two. Never should have stepped out of the scene like that y'know. Spoils the illusion.

HELEN and ROSEMARY go up on rostrum, take up their former positions.

HELEN: I'll just say good-bye to you both, and then you show how annoyed you are with him, and we'll carry on from there.

Well I must run along, children. Oh – what about Saturday? *(HELEN and PAUL rise.)*

ROSEMARY: *(Coldly.)* Paul can go if he likes – but I'm sorry – I can't.

PAUL: But you said –

ROSEMARY: I promised to spend the afternoon with Father. You go. I'm sure you'll find it very amusing.

HELEN: Settle it between you and give me a ring, one of you, in the morning. 'Bye, darling.

ROSEMARY: Good-bye, Helen.

PAUL: I'll see you out.

PAUL goes out with HELEN. ROSEMARY now looks furious, takes up her book and hurls it down in chair.

ROSEMARY: *(Muttering angrily.)* Oh! damn – damn – damn!

These get softer as she drops into chair. PAUL enters and offers her cigarette box.

PAUL: *(With forced cheerfulness.)* Cigarette, darling?

ROSEMARY: *(Very cold and distant.)* No, thank you.

PAUL: Anything the matter?

ROSEMARY: No, why should there be?

PAUL: I dunno – I just wondered. I thought you were very keen on going with them on Saturday.

ROSEMARY: *(Miles away.)* Did you?

PAUL: Well, you said you were.

ROSEMARY: I haven't the least desire to go with them. I loathe the Sunderlands anyhow. I've always thought your friend Helen had a very queer taste in people.

PAUL: *(Raising his eyebrows.)* My friend Helen, no, eh – ?

She does not reply.

She used to be your friend too. In fact you knew her before I did.

ROSEMARY: I only knew her through William. And I *adore* William. I don't dislike Helen, but I think she has some very queer friends and I'd just as soon she didn't bounce in and out like that, even if you have to make such a fuss of her.

PAUL: *(Very innocently.)* Fuss of her! What fuss did I make of her?

ROSEMARY: If you join them on Saturday, you'll be able to have a whole day of it, with funny stories and charwomen and women who live in two flats at once and everything.

PAUL: Look here, I didn't care a tuppence about Saturday but if you insist upon taking that tone about it, all right, I *am* going.

ROSEMARY: I should. It'll be a nice change for you after being so bored at home.

PAUL: *(Angrily now.)* Now when have I ever said I was bored at home?

ROSMARY: You didn't need to *say* anything.

PAUL: Well, what have I done then? What's the matter?

ROSEMARY: *(Stormily.)* Nothing. *(Close to tears.)* Everything.

She goes out, we hear loud door-slam. Curtains close.

HELEN: Well, there they are then.

WILLIAM: Yes, and I was working out their future. I see three stages waiting for them. First, a stage of constant and bitter quarrelling. Secondly, a stage in which each seeks satisfaction elsewhere. Thirdly, a stage of final separation or a real reconciliation and the beginning of a decent adult life together.

HELEN: Very good, darling. I couldn't have done it better myself.

WILLIAM: You couldn't have done it as well as myself.

HELEN: Yes I could. Actually, you've left out a stage. You see, with some couples like Paul and Rosemary, there's another stage that comes before the constant quarrelling; in this period each partner finds a friend of the same sex that the other partner very much dislikes. It might be called the Unwise Friendship Stage.

WILLIAM: You're right. *(To audience.)* She *is* right, y'know. Very clever woman. Most of 'em, especially Englishmen, dislike clever of course. *(Pause.)* An *amiable* clever woman is an absolute treasure. *(WILLIAM takes her hand, brings her downstage.)* Thank you. You've probably been wondering what our relationship is – haven't you? It's very interesting.

And perhaps later on – well, we'll see. *(To HELEN.)* You're dead right, of course.

HELEN: Rosemary will suddenly become friendly with some terrible woman whom Paul can't stand.

WILLIAM: And Paul will pick up a pal who's poison to Rosemary.

HELEN: It seems accidental – and yet – I don't know –

WILLIAM: The subconscious does it, I think. It deliberately singles out the type that the other partner loathes. *(Pause.)* Well, it's up to us, I suppose.

HELEN: Certainly. What are you going to be?

WILLIAM: I shall be one of those self-made City bachelors. They're always dining in very expensive restaurants and they put up the money for bad musical comedies. Wives hate them, because they imagine that these fellows have flats somewhere crowded with show-girls drinking champagne-cocktails and playing strip poker.

HELEN: *(Interested.)* And have they?

WILLIAM: No, it's all an illusion. Nevertheless, the instinct of the wives is right, because these chaps are fundamentally anti-domestic and try to turn the husbands back into bachelors. That's me, then. And what about you?

HELEN: I shall be Mrs. Ambergate – Gloria Ambergate. I'm separated from my husband – he probably cleared out with his typist – and now I've got a down on all husbands and am very, very sorry for the poor wives. And she's gone in for New Thought and Higher Thought and Astral Planes and Auras and Vibrations and she sees everybody's personality in terms of colour. And she has a general deep soulfulness from which the coarse scoffing male is excluded.

WILLIAM: I know the type. But Rosemary would never put up with her.

HELEN: Oh yes, she would – for a time. Just because she was sorry for her. It often happens among women. Being members of the gentler and more sympathetic sex –

WILLIAM: *(Astonished.)* Members of the what?

HELEN: *(Shouting.)* The more sympathetic sex – idiot.

WILLIAM: Yes, I see. Well, that's us, then.

HELEN: *(To the pianists.)* And you two ought to find Leitmotivs for –

WILLIAM: Jimmy Mowbray.

HELEN: Gloria Ambergate.

HELEN and WILLIAM exit.

PHILIP: Oh, I've got mine. *(Pause.)* This is Jimmy Mowbray. *(He plays snatch of cheerful, rather vulgar dance tune.)*

JOYCE: And this is Gloria Ambergate. *(Plays a snatch of cheaply "soulful" music.)*

PHILIP: Good. Now we can make 'em into something.
Short prelude to Scene illustrating this stage of Unwise Friendships.

JOYCE: Alternative title: What on earth Do you See in Him – or Her?

Finish of music they bow to each other. Curtains open to show same set. PAUL enters with tray with cocktail shaker and glasses. Telephone rings, which PAUL answers in dumb show during last bars of music.

PAUL: *(As music ends.)* Ha, ha, ha. Of course it's not too early. Come along at once, all right then. Good-bye for now.

ROSEMARY enters and sits with a book.

Will you have – er – have a cocktail?

ROSEMARY: No thank you. You know I hardly ever have a cocktail. I think it's an awful waste of making them. And why *three* glasses? *(She opens book.)*

PAUL: *(Uncomfortably.)* Well – as a matter of fact – Jimmy Mowbray rang up to say he might look in.

ROSEMARY: *(Disgusted.)* What again? He'd better come and live here, hadn't he?

PAUL: *(With great dignity.)* Mowbray happens to be a client of mine.

ROSEMARY: That has nothing to do with it, and you know it hasn't. And what you can see in him I can't imagine.

PAUL: Oh – he's not a bad fellow.

ROSEMARY: He's *terrible*. And Sybil Stinnes says he has a flat crowded with chorus girls drinking champagne-cocktails. Really, Paul, I thought you'd better taste than that.

PAUL: *(Irritably.)* Oh – don't be so snobbish. Jimmy Mowbray may not be your type –

ROSEMARY: My type! He's not anybody's type outside a race-course and non-stop variety. He's –

PAUL: *(Cutting in sharply.)* Jimmy Mowbray's quite a decent, amusing sort of fellow – who might turn out to be a very good client –

ROSEMARY: And then again might not. I wouldn't trust a man like that a yard. Still, I suppose if he wants to turn this house into his cocktail-bar I mustn't complain.

PAUL: *(Pleasantly.)* Oh – you couldn't complain. You wouldn't know how to.

ROSEMARY: Thank you. *(Giving him a wounded stare.)*

ROSEMARY goes to telephone and begins dialling. JOYCE plays Ambergate theme softly. ROSEMARY speaks into telephone with marked sweetness. PAUL sits and picks up paper from table; begins to read it.

ROSEMARY: Oh – is that you Gloria? Rosemary… Yes, I suppose it might be telepathy.

PAUL throws paper down on table.

Yes, as soon as you like… Good. *(Puts down telephone.)*

PAUL: *(Glaring at her.)* Was that your dear friend Gloria Ambergate?

ROSEMARY: Yes. She's coming across to spend the evening here.

PAUL: *(Angrily.)* If that awful woman comes here, I'm going straight out.

ROSEMARY: *(With mock innocent air.)* I thought you were probably going out anyhow, with your nice friend Mr. Mowbray. Weren't you?

PAUL: *(Rather confusedly.)* He suggested our dining somewhere – but I hadn't said definitely I would.

ROSEMARY: *(Same tone as before.)* Well, now you can, and that'll be very nice for you.

PAUL: I warned you before. If you must see that frightful half-baked woman – and what on earth you can see in her beats me – please don't ask her here when I'm about. I *loathe* the woman. Really, I'm surprised at you, Rosemary. A year or two ago, you couldn't have spent an hour with a woman like that, and now –

ROSEMARY: *(Vehemently.)* Yes, now – when I have to watch you being dragged off every other night by that – that –

Sharp ring of bell off. PAUL rises and hurries out. ROSEMARY glares after him, then hastily takes up shaker and smells it in disgust, then hastily puts it down and assumes an air of distant dignity. WILLIAM enters as Mowbray.

WILLIAM: *(Who has entered laughing.)* Ah! Good evening, Mrs. Weybridge.

ROSEMARY: *(Coldly.)* Good evening.

WILLIAM: Wonder if I might snatch your husband – dine with me to meet another friend just back from South America – just the kind of bloke to amuse Paul. Quiet bachelor evening. Steak and a decent bottle o' wine, y'know – an' perhaps finish our cigars at a variety show.

PAUL: *(Who has been pouring out drinks.)* Cocktails? Rosemary?

ROSEMARY: *(Distantly.)* No thank you.

PAUL: *(Handing one over.)* Mowbray?

WILLIAM: *(Taking it.)* Ta! Well, down the hatch!

PAUL: Dry enough for you?

WILLIAM: Oh, yes. Do with a dash p'r'haps. Like a dash myself.

PAUL: Ah – sorry about that.

ROSEMARY: *(Distantly.)* And what is a dash?

WILLIAM: Dash? Don't you know what a dash is? Where have you been? It's absinthe.

ROSEMARY: *(Condemning it.)* Oh – absinthe.

WILLIAM: *(Not noticing her attitude.)* That's it. Absinthe makes the heart grow fonder, eh? *(Guffaws.)* Well, I won't say No to another, old boy.

PAUL pours out another drink.

Had a hard day to-day. Market's all over the place. Still, never say die. *(Gives ROSEMARY a hearty pat on the back.)* Met a bloke at lunch to-day who's bringing that musical show over from New York – and blow the expense *(takes a drink from PAUL.)* – y'know the big smash hit there – *Got What It Takes* or something. Says if he can sneak most of it past the Lord Chamberlain, it'll make London's hair stand on end. He's importing all the original girls. *(Nudging PAUL with elbow.)*

ROSEMARY: *(Coldly.)* I would have thought we'd enough chorus girls here without bringing some all the way from New York.

WILLIAM: That's just your innocence, Mrs. Weybridge. These American kids have got something. Ask your husband. Well, down the hatch.

Another sharp ring at bell. PAUL makes as if to go but ROSEMARY rises and goes herself.

PAUL: *(Dropping his voice.)* We'd better push off in a minute, Jimmy. This woman's terrible.

WILLIAM: What woman?

PAUL: You'll see.

WILLIAM: Isn't time for it now, but remind me when we get out to tell you the story of the widow and the piano tuner. It'll kill you. By the way, this bloke you're going to meet – like most of these lads just back from the pampas or whatever they are – is a bit hot and might want to start a pretty thick sort of evening. Have to sit on his head a bit. You don't want any young female society to-night, do you?

PAUL: No, definitely not.

WILLIAM: Same here. Last week-end was bad enough and I've a business to look after. *(Takes another drink which PAUL has poured out.)*

227

HELEN enters as Gloria Ambergate, followed by Rosemary. HELEN contrives to register her disapproval of the two men and the cocktails at once.

PAUL: Oh – good evening. Mrs Ambergate.

HELEN: How d'you do?

ROSEMARY: Gloria – this is Mr. Mowbray

WILLIAM: How d'you do?

HELEN: *(Coldly.)* Good evening,

PAUL: Cocktail, Mrs. Ambergate?

HELEN: *(Sitting.)* Oh – no, thank you. I can't take alcohol in any form.

WILLIAM: *(Taking drink offered by PAUL to HELEN.)* Can't you? It's about the only thing I can take nowadays. *(Laughs.)* Well, Weybridge, better push off, eh?

PAUL: I'm ready. *(Drinks up and puts glasses on table.)*

WILLIAM: Well, the skin off your nose. *(Drinking to HELEN.)* Good night, Mrs. Weybridge.

WILLIAM exits.

ROSEMARY: Don't be too late, Paul.

PAUL: No, I won't be. 'Night Mrs. Ambergate.

HELEN: That man, Rosemary – who is he?

ROSEMARY: He's a client of Paul's. You can say what you like about him. I loathe him.

HELEN: I'm so glad, dear. I was sure you must. He's a dreadfully undeveloped type. *Earthy* – quite earthy. With a muddy brown aura. I wish you could have been at our lecture last Wednesday. Mdme Rubbishky gave us a *wonderful* talk on I AM THE GREAT ALL –

ROSEMARY: On what?

HELEN: *(Solemnly.)* I AM THE GREAT ALL. And so *profound* – so *stimulating* and yet at the same time so essentially *simple*. We are all of us the Great All. And the Great All is all of us. The whole *thing* was there.

ROSEMARY: I'm not sure I believe in all this, you know.

HELEN: I didn't expect you would, dear, not yet. Perception comes with suffering and loneliness of spirit. You'll see.

ROSEMARY: *(Dismayed.)* But I don't want any suffering and loneliness of spirit.

HELEN: It won't be so bad for you, dear, as it was for me. You'll have friends – certainly *one* friend, darling – who can help and guide. As soon as I saw that man here to-night, and saw him taking your husband away, I knew at once that soon you'll need a friend very badly. I could *feel* a downward, earthward influence –

ROSEMARY: But what kind of influence is that, Gloria?

HELEN: It's downward – earthward, dear – pulling down. I've always been able to feel it, even before I knew what it meant. Chiefly among men, of course. And I've always *known* it was antagonistic. But I myself rejected the influence. I said "You cannot pull me down, I am *all* spirit", I said. – And, of course, I was.

PHILIP: I say, Helen, is there much more of this horrible stuff?

HELEN: *(In ordinary tone.)* Yes Philip. Hours and hours.

PHILIP: Then let's cut to midnight. Lights!

Lights blackout. Clock chimes twelve. As lights go on again ROSEMARY is discovered slumped down in her chair, half asleep, and HELEN lying on the floor with her head on a chair.

HELEN: …And four Hindu disciples living in the spare room. Good gracious – twelve o'clock already. We've had such a wonderful lovely satisfying talk, it's just given the evening great golden wings – and – pouf – it's just flown away. *(She rises, ROSEMARY giving her a helping hand.)*

ROSEMARY: *(Stifling a yawn.)* Yes, hasn't it?

HELEN: *(Solemnly.)* But I do hope nothing has happened to your husband, dear.

ROSEMARY: Of course not. Why should it? Just a moment, I'll put the light on. *(Exits.)*

HELEN: *(Moving to the door.)* It's all very well saying, of course not, my dear. But I can't forget the night I was sitting up late with poor Mildred Fothergill. We heard the ambulance ringing right outside her window, and the telephone went a voice said "Come at once, Mrs. Fothergill". But, of course, it was all over by the time she got to the hospital. Mr. Fothergill had departed for the Astral Sphere, and had not even insured himself properly.

Lights on the stage black-out and come up to Full again. We hear the clock strike one o'clock. ROSEMARY has now changed into a dressing-down to indicate time lapse. She enters, goes to window and looks out. She seems agitated, now moves to table and is about to pick up telephone but decides not to. Just as she is about to sit down the telephone rings urgently.

ROSEMARY: *(Rushing to telephone.)* Yes, yes…? *(Then sharply.)* No, we're not… Well, I ought to know whether we're the gasworks or not. You've got the wrong number, that's all… *(As she puts down the receiver, she mutters to herself.)* Silly idiot…

An ambulance bell now rings furiously. This disturbs ROSEMARY and she moves restlessly about the stage.

Enter WILLIAM from alcove.

WILLIAM: What's the matter with her?

JOYCE: Paul's late, so now her imagination will get to work. We all do it.

ROSEMARY: *(Lights fade and ROSEMARY picked out in a single pink spot.)* …the hospital, please driver – and hurry – it's terribly urgent – yes, nurse, I'm Mrs. Weybridge, take me to him – oh! – yes, I'll be brave – I will be brave. *(Then in worrying tone like that in Act One.)* I'd have to ask Father to come up to look after things- and I couldn't let Robin stay here – perhaps he and Nannie could go to Alice's for the week – and as soon as I'd got them off I'd have to order my black – and then to sell this house – then try to find a little cottage in the country – and then Robin would have to go away to school – but we'd share our little cottage during all his holidays. *(Sighing very dreamily now.)* Yes, dear, it's years ago now, and they realise that my Paul was a great architect – and they want me to unveil a memorial to him – it will be a beautiful experience but, of course, sad too. *(The lights begin*

*to come now, ROSEMARY moves upstage to sit down. She is dabbing
her eyes with a handkerchief.)*

*We hear PAUL outside, he is whistling the Mowbray theme, but she
does not hear him. He enters.*

ROSEMARY: *(With joy and surprise.)* Paul! *(Rising.)*

PAUL: I'm sorry, my dear. You shouldn't have waited up –

ROSEMARY: *(Severely.)* Where have you been?

WILLIAM: The eternal question. *(Pause.)* And now I understand
why they always put it so angrily.

PAUL: Mowbray took me to his club – and we began playing
snooker – and then I couldn't get a taxi. You know how it is,
my dear. What have you been doing?

ROSEMARY: Listening to Gloria for hours and hours –

PAUL: *(Laughing to himself.)* Oh! Bad luck.

WILLIAM: *(Turning to JOYCE.)* I wonder if the chump realises
this is his chance. He's had as much as he wants of Jimmy
Mowbray and she's had far more of Gloria Ambergate. I
wonder if he realises this. Oh dear, it doesn't look as if he
does.

*PAUL is pouring himself a glass of whisky from the bottle but this
bottle only contains sufficient for one glass, therefore he has tipped
the bottle up and is draining it.*

PAUL: *(Drinking.)* You know very well, Roseemary, that's a
terribly dreary woman.

ROSEMARY: I know – but I'm sorry for her, though I admit she
can be an awful bore. But she's lonely. Not like your friend
Jimmy Mowbray, who's so pleased with himself.

PAUL: Well I'll admit that Jimmy is a bit much at times. But Oria
Glambergate – is a tearily dreary –

ROSEMARY: Paul, I believe you're tight.

PAUL: *(Swaying about and toying with his glass.)* If I say I am,
you'll believe I'm not, which wouldn't be quite true. But if I
say I'm not, then you'll think I'm very tight, which would be
quite wrong. Better ignore the whole thing.

WILLIAM: Now, what's her reaction going to be? She might burst into tears. She might lose her temper and throw something at him. She might rise haughtily and sweep out of the room. Or she –

ROSEMARY suddenly bursts out laughing. It is quite warm and friendly laughter. He seems to her, at this moment, very funny.

JOYCE: *(As ROSEMARY's laughter is quieter.)* This is his chance.

WILLIAM: Of course it is. He's only to drop down and put his arms round her and babble any nonsense and she's his again.

JOYCE: *(Scornfully.)* But he isn't go to. *(Pause.)* You men!

WILLIAM: *(Sadly.)* Pompous vanity is our weakness.

PAUL: *(With foolish dignity.)* Glad you're amused.

ROSEMARY: *(Still ready to be reconciled.)* Paul, don't be silly.

PAUL: After spending five hours exchanging idiocies with that woman, you can ask me not to be silly.

ROSEMARY: Oh – you are a fool!

Exits. We hear door being slammed. He stares after her half bewildered, half angry, then stares blankly out front. There is a little broken music.

WILLIAM: Let's hide the poor chump.

Curtains close.

HELEN enters from alcove as ordinary self. WILLIAM takes her arm and brings her downstage.

HELEN: We shall have to look at them now, somewhere in the middle of the next stage.

WILLIAM: *(Reflectively.)* Now wait a minute. Constant quarrelling is bad for both, of course, but I think that in this quarrelling stage the woman is better off than the man.

He says no more because HELEN begins straightening his tie, brushing his hair back and generally trying to smarten up his appearance. She takes him by left ear and turns him to JOYCE.

HELEN: And that's supposed to be a clever one. Imagine what some of the rest are like!

JOYCE: He just doesn't know, dear. How could he?

WILLIAM: *(Severely and rather annoyed.)* Instead of indulging in idle antics, I will produce a reason or two for my statement. The woman is better off because – first – an emotional outburst, a scene is less repugnant to her than it is to the wretched man, who will go to almost any length to avoid one. Secondly, the woman has a superior technical equipment and knows instinctively how to put the fellow in the wrong and keep him there, and has a diabolical skill in detecting the weak joints in his armour.

HELEN: The said armour consisting of solid plates a foot thick of masculine vanity, conceit and self-complacency. While the poor woman, her heart thumping away, her tummy tying itself into knots, has no armour and feels completely naked.

PHILIP: But I thought you liked to feel naked.

HELEN: *(Doing a funny walk.)* Five minutes after he has stamped out of the house the man begins to forget about the quarrel, and by the time he has plunged into the day's business it no longer exists for him. But the woman lives with the quarrel all day and half the night, as if she were wrestling with a giant scorpion. She hears the angry voices hour after hour. Her whole world looks as if it had been torn into quivering strips by an earthquake. The very chemistry of her entire being...

WILLIAM: *(Catching hold of her hand and kissing it.)* Yes, yes, yes, my pet. An excellent speech. How well you do these things. We all enjoyed it. But I think we ought to be getting along. Let's have another look at them.

HELEN: Here they are then. Typical.

Curtains open. We now see the same room, but the table has been removed and in its place is a modern desk. There is a different picture on the wall, something which suggests the study of an architect. PAUL is sitting at his desk and making a few casual notes; he is not working very hard and after a moment or two ROSEMARY, looking rather pale and strained, enters and begins rather elaborately looking for something.

ROSEMARY: *(After a moment, very politely.)* I'm sorry to disturb you.

PAUL: *(With strained politeness.)* No, that's all right. Can I – ?

ROSEMARY: *(Still looking vaguely.)* No. No. *(They get weaker.)*

She exits and after a moment or two she returns. This time she comes to centre, looking as if she has been in the room for hours.

You haven't seen my scissors – the large pair – have you?

PAUL: *(Half rising, very politely.)* No, I'm afraid I haven't. Can I – ?

ROSEMARY: *(Looking round vaguely.)* No. No. Sorry to disturb you, that's all.

PAUL: *(Sitting down again.)* No, that's all right. *(Goes on with his work.)*

ROSEMARY gives him a sharp contemptuous look and goes out.

WILLIAM: I didn't quite see the point of this dodging in and out.

HELEN: She's giving him a chance to be human again and to say he's sorry, and then of course she'll say it's all her fault. But meeting this heavy politeness, she knows that the quarrel is still on.

WILLIAM: Why has the man to say he's sorry first? He nearly always has, you know.

HELEN: Yes, but once he does, the woman is nearly always ready to be downright abject.

WILLIAM: Quite so. But why has he to start the ball rolling?

HELEN: It's a kind of tradition with us.

WILLIAM: *(Pause.)* That is very curious.

ROSEMARY enters again and this time stands rather rigidly looking at him.

Back again. Different technique this time.

HELEN: Yes. She's still giving him a chance, but now she's hardening rapidly. The excuse to talk to him will be a telephone conversation that she's saved up for this moment.

ROSEMARY: *(In cold, polite tone.)* I forgot to tell you that Mona Roberts rang up to ask if we'd dine with them on the fifteenth. Do you want to go?

PAUL: *(Rising slowly and taking off his spectacles.)* Not particularly, I think he's rather a bore. But – you like her, don't you?

ROSEMARY: *(Same tone.)* Yes, but I can see her some other time. It's not essential that you should go and be bored.

PAUL: No, if you want to go –

ROSEMARY: I know how easily you are bored.

PAUL: *(Heavily.)* Was that necessary?

ROSEMARY: Oh – don't be so pompous.

PAUL: *(Still heavily.)* Really, I don't see why I should be accused of being pompous just because I try to be decently polite.

ROSEMARY: *(Cold, contemptuous.)* Don't you?

PAUL: *(With more warmth.)* No, I don't.

ROSEMARY: Well, what am I to say to them about the fifteenth?

PAUL: *(Impatiently.)* Oh – say what you like. What do I care!

ROSEMARY: What do you care about anything?

PAUL: What does that mean?

ROSEMARY: *(Contemptuously.)* What do you think it means?

PAUL: I don't know.

ROSEMARY: No, of course, *you* wouldn't.

PAUL and ROSEMARY turn their backs to each other. WILLIAM and HELEN rise. They look at PAUL and ROSEMARY in astonishment.

WILLIAM: *(To HELEN.)* Y'know what's wrong with this is our horrible modern poverty of language. It's sheer misery to feel such sudden hate and despair and yet be so inarticulate.

HELEN: I agree. They'd feel ever so much better if they could let it rip.

WILLIAM: Then we'll let it rip for them. We'll make an Elizabethan job of it. Hold tight, girl! Blow, winds, and crack your cheeks.

HELEN: Rage, blow! You cataracts and hurricanoes –

There is a roll of thunder and a blackout. HELEN and WILLIAM exit. PAUL and ROSEMARY come downstage. Curtains close. PAUL sits stool right and ROSEMARY on stool left. There are now lightning flashes and thunder. WILLIAM and HELEN enter from their respective alcoves with cloaks. They come to centre on rostrum, the lightning and thunder stops and two blue spots come on them.

HELEN: *(In grand manner.)*

Oh – that I should be tied to such a pudding bag

Of dreary Vanity and duller wit. A thing

Made up of braces, collar studs and starch,

With hardly more red blood in it than drips

Out of the poor frozen joint from Argentine.

WILLIAM: Imagine a cat five feet four inches high,

Take away dignity and let it rage

With deep inferiority – and that's a wife.

HELEN: Why – hot-water bottles of the cheaper sort,

Bargains from Boots, bring me more comfort.

Two and fourpence at the nearest Odeon

Bring more romance or cheerful entertainment.

WILLIAM: *(Pointing to HELEN.)* You're Madame Nature's grim old conjuring trick.

Every man's disappointment – girl into wife.

I married a loving, ripe and merry lass,

To find myself keeping, at a rising cost,

A bitter woman who hates the sight of me.

HELEN: *(Coming to centre and standing in front of WILLIAM.)*

And why? Because I had a lover once

And how he's disappeared, and in his place,

For me to live with, are a costing clerk, a

Lecturer, a stomach and a thirst.

HELEN comes down to piano left. WILLIAM comes down to piano right. PAUL and ROSEMARY rise. JOYCE and PHILIP rise.

HELEN: *(Pointing to WILLIAM.)* Oh, hateful, pompous clown!

WILLIAM: *(Pointing to HELEN.)* Oh, damned, malicious shrew!

ROSEMARY and PAUL point at each other also JOYCE and PHILIP do the same, all bitterly quarrelling.

There is a crash of thunder and the lighting is held until the curtain has fallen.

End of Act Two.

ACT THREE

PHILIP and JOYCE begin playing and go on brilliantly for a minute or so. The he stops and, after a moment or so, she stops too.

JOYCE: *(Annoyed, leaning on piano.)* What's the matter, darling?

PHILIP: Well, nobody's coming on or anything. What happens now? You see, it's exactly what I said. They can't make a third act out of it. All the critics will say, "Not really a play at all, and even so it goes to pieces in the third act."

JOYCE: Well, you're quite wrong. *(Sits at piano again.)* The third act's all right and it's starting now. Listen!

Plays a few bars of pseudo-Oriental, mystical music.

PHILIP: What's that muck for? *(Pause.)* Are they bringing on a bogus Oriental illusionist?

JOYCE: *(As she plays softly.)* No, this is the fortune-telling music. Madame Aurora who's just returned from the East –

PHILIP: Probably Clacton-on-Sea.

JOYCE: – to read palms and gaze into crystals.

PHILIP: Rosemary's consulting her, I suppose?

JOYCE: Yes. *(Music stops.)* She and Paul have now arrived at the third stage, when each feels the other is hopeless and is ready to be consoled by somebody else. And so of course Rosemary's having her fortune told.

PHILIP: Using her husband's money to find out if there is any other chap on the way.

JOYCE: What a noble mind you have, maestro!

JOYCE commences to play again in which PHILIP joins her in a mocking manner and curtains open to disclose corner of Mdme Aurora's sitting-room, with a few cheap pseudo-mystical decorations. ROSEMARY in outdoor clothes sits at small table with crystal on it, opposite HELEN as Mdme Aurora. She wears Oriental shawl, with grey hair showing under it, probably large spectacles. Music dies away.

HELEN: *(In thick common voice, looking at ROSEMARY's hand.)* Yes, dear, I see you're married. Two children –

ROSEMARY: *(Hastily.)* One.

HELEN: *(Quickly.)* That's right, dear. One. I'm afraid you're not very happy. Nothing like so happy as you thought you was going to be. Of course, your trouble is you're a lot more sensitive than people think – you're a very loving, sensitive nature , it's 'ere as plain as a pikestaff – an' what's the result? The result is people close to you 'urt your feelings when they 'ardly know they're doing it. An' what else? You go an' trust people – for you've a trusting nature. I can see that – an' then they go an' let you down. Isn't that right?

ROSEMARY: Yes, it is. I can't imagine how you can see me so clearly.

HELEN: It's a gift, dear. Very few 'ave it, an' even then it needs a lot of development. *(Coughing.)*

ROSEMARY: Could you – tell me what's going to happen?

HELEN: *(Taking and staring at ROSEMARY's right hand.)* I see a tall man coming over the sea with love for you in his 'eart. You'll meet 'im soon, quite soon, an' he'll make you very happy. I see a journey – and a strange bed.

ROSEMARY: What sort of strange bed. *(Withdraw her hand.)*

HELEN: *(Darkly.)* Never you mind about that, dear. *(With marked change of manner.)* And that'll be seven-and-sixpence, thank you, Mrs. – er –

ROSEMARY: *(Hastily.)* Oh yes – of course. *(Rises and exits right.)* Thank you so much. Good morning.

HELEN: *(Rising as ROSEMARY goes.)* Good morning.

Curtains close. PHILIP with one hand plays quick harsh music.

PHILIP: *(Pleased with himself.)* Not bad, eh? Taxis. Street scene.

JOYCE: What about this? *(Plays a heavy thumping tune in march time.)*

PHILIP: Now what's that?

JOYCE: Major Spanner on the way.

PHILIP: Who's Major Spanner?

JOYCE: *(Loudly and cheerfully.)* He was the wedding guest, you remember, who'd known her for a long time and didn't

239

think Paul good enough for her. An awful chump, if you ask me, but nearly every woman's got one of these faithful hounds tucked away somewhere. Keep the street music going.

As he does, ROSEMARY enters. She goes to centre below rostrum, looks at her watch, then glances at the space above footlights as if it were a shop window, catches sight of something that interests her, tries it on, so to speak, then rejects it and is just turning away, giving another glance at her watch, when WILLIAM enters as Major George Spanner, bronzed and trim, just back from the East. He suddenly recognises ROSEMARY with delight. They talk in front of the imaginary window through which we see them.

WILLIAM: *(With enthusiasm.)* Why – Rosemary.

Music stops.

ROSEMARY: *(Almost equally pleased.)* George Spanner! How nice to see you again!

WILLIAM: Wonderful to run into you like this! Just goin' to ring you up, matter of fact.

ROSEMARY: *(With mock severity.)* You haven't been back ages and never told me?

WILLIAM: Of course not, my dear Rosemary. I only got in last night.

ROSEMARY: You didn't come to England at all, did you, on your last leave?

WILLIAM: No. Haven't been here since your marriage – you remember?

ROSEMARY: Yes. And I've missed you, George.

WILLIAM: Ho, ho! Like to believe that, but sounds a bit steep. I mean, young married woman and all that.

ROSEMARY: But you're one of my very oldest friends, George, and of course I've missed you.

WILLIAM: *(Soldierly embarrassment.)* Very decent of you to say so, Rosemary. Of course, I've missed you no end. Fact is, that's why I stayed out East last leave. Felt I couldn't face it here with you – well – er – tied up elsewhere sort of thing.

ROSEMARY: George, is that true?

WILLIAM: Word of honour. I shouldn't have mentioned it, of course. You fault it slipped out. Let's forget it.

ROSEMARY: *(Smiling at him.)* But I don't want to forget it.

WILLIAM: Look here, I suppose you're busy and crowded with engagements, eh? No chance of joining me in a spot of lunch, eh?

ROSEMARY: I'd love to.

WILLIAM: *(As they begin to move away to left, takes ROSEMARY's arm.)* Good show! Now look here, I'm out of touch, and you know all the places. Where do you suggest we go?

Exit alcove left. As they move away, PHILIP supplies a little more street music. This dies down when they have gone. HELEN enters. She is wearing a Mrs. de Folyat day dress but not the wig or make-up.

JOYCE: I'm sorry, Helen, but I think that outfit's all wrong for you.

HELEN: *(Speaking to JOYCE.)* It's not meant for me. This outfit is for Mrs. de Folyat – you know, the rich widow who talked to Major Spanner in the wedding reception scene. She's given Paul another commission, after leaving him alone for several years, and now she's getting her claws into him. Paul and Rosemary are in the third stage now, you know.

JOYCE: Yes, I know. But what's she after, this Mrs. de Folyat?

HELEN: Anything she can get, I think. But nothing very serious. If she can detach an attractive man from his wife and keep him playing around and coming to her for sympathy, she's quite happy. A sort of collector.

JOYCE: I know. And how I hate 'em!

HELEN: Yes, but men often like them.

JOYCE: Men'll like *anything.*

PHILIP: And so will women.

HELEN: I must see how the Spanner affair is progressing. *(Goes up on rostrum. Looks through curtains, addresses JOYCE.)* Yes, yes. I think at any minute now she may throw a biscuit or a bone at his doglike devotion.

Curtains open to disclose corner of restaurant. Table for two at end of meal, just when cigarettes are lighted. ROSEMARY and WILLIAM sit each half-facing audience, the table having corner, not side, to front.

WILLIAM: *(Who has had a good meal, holding photo frame.)* Yes, this photograph you once gave me – you remember it, eh?

ROSEMARY: Yes, but that was ages ago. I'd only just left school. You don't mean to say *that's* the photograph –

WILLIAM: Yes, it is. Had this neat little folding – er – frame arrangement made for it, and taken it everywhere. Been in some dashed queer places *(Puts photograph in his back pocket.)*, I can tell you.

ROSEMARY: But, George, that's terribly touching. I'd no idea –

WILLIAM: No, no, of course not. I couldn't expect you to have. But – er – well, I don't mind telling you now, Rosemary, it was quite a blow – had to take it right on the chin – when I came home last time and found you'd just got engaged to Weybridge. *(Pause.)* Because I had made up my mind to ask you! – Because I was going to say something pretty fierce to you myself.

ROSEMARY: *(Softly.)* I'm sorry, George. *(Pause. Puts out a hand and he pats it enthusiastically.)* Go on. Tell me some more.

WILLIAM: *(Pats her hand again, more heavily.)* Isn't much to tell, really. Except this. Shouldn't have said anything now if I'd known you were happy. But now I know you're not, it's different. *(Pause. Fiercely, leaning back in chair.)* Good God, a wonderful little girl like you not being happy!

ROSEMARY: *(Half-laughing.)* But you're forgetting. I'm not a little girl and haven't been for years. Not only am I married but I'm a mother – nearly a matron.

WILLIAM: Nonsense! To me you're a little girl – *(Pats her hand.)* – *my* little girl.

ROSEMARY: Really, George *(Pats his hand.)*, I believe you've been taking a course of something. You say all the nice things I want to hear.

WILLIAM: *(Taking his hands from under hers, pats her hands again.)* You won't be like this, though it's got to be said. You're not happy, are you? Weybridge doesn't realise what a lucky fella he is.

ROSEMARY: *(Quietly, sincerely now.)* It doesn't seem to be working, somehow.

WILLIAM: Queer thing. At your wedding do, some fool of a woman – a friend of his, of course – told me what a clever fella the bridegroom was. And I as good as told the woman there and then that in my opinion you were worth ten of him. *(Pause.)* I've been uneasy in my mind ever since.

ROSEMARY: *(Affectionately.)* Poor George!

WILLIAM: *(Fatuously.)* Well, that's something. But – er – is that the best you can do?

ROSEMARY: *(In half-comical whisper.)* No.

WILLIAM: *(Doglike devotion in his stare, takes her hand and kisses it.)* A wonderful little girl.

Curtains close. HELEN enters wearing no hat and a light coat or something to suggest outdoors. PHILIP plays some music.

HELEN: *(Near entrance, calling.)* Here I am, Paul.

PAUL enters in ordinary lounge suit without hat or overcoat. He carries a note-book with him. It is essential she should look a rich, attractive woman.

HELEN: Now then, this is what I mean. Would it be possible to enlarge the wing that way? No, you can't see it properly from here. This is better. *(Takes his arm and leads his a few paces, keeping her hand inside his arm.)* Now you see what I mean?

PAUL: Yes, it could be done.

HELEN: Mind you, Paul, I wouldn't dream of letting anybody but you lay a finger on the house. You do understand that, don't you?

PAUL: Yes. That's very good of you.

HELEN: *(Turning so they face each other.)* Paul – don't be so professional.

PAUL: *(Smiling.)* Sorry, Frances. But you see, it was a professional question you were asking me.

HELEN: Oh – but I can't divide relationships into compartments like that. Don't forget *(Moves closer and smiles seductively at him.)* I'm a woman.

PAUL: *(Smilingly.)* I'm not likely to forget that, me dear Frances. *(In mock whisper.)* In fact, if I didn't think there were at least a couple of your housemaids watching us through a bedroom window, I'd probably behave – this very moment – very unprofessionally indeed.

HELEN: You talk as if architects could be struck off the register, like doctors.

PAUL: Oh – no, we can be trusted. If you don't make it too hard for us.

HELEN: *(With change of attack.)* Paul, I think you're looking tired.

PAUL: I have been rather hard at it lately.

HELEN: Of course. A man in your position and with you genius has to *give* and *give.* We all understand that. But it's obvious that wife of yours isn't looking after you at all.

PAUL: Well, as you know, we don't get on – and of course, now she isn't very much interested in my welfare.

HELEN: *(With fine show of indignation.)* Paul, I think it's *monstrous!* To have no *intellectual* companionship, no deep store of sympathy, at home – that's bad enough – in fact, for a man of your kind it's the worst thing of all – but on top of that simple to neglect the most obvious duties a woman has towards a man – oh! –

PAUL: *(Uncomfortably.)* Well – there it is. *(About to change the subject.)* Do you think you'd like – ?

HELEN: *(Breaking in, impressively.)* Paul, I think I ought to meet your wife. Remember I haven't seen her since your wedding and don't know her at all. You ought to bring us together.

PAUL: *(Alarmed.)* I don't think that would work very well, would it?

HELEN: My dear. *Please* remember I'm a sensible woman of the world – and don't get into a silly masculine panic. There won't be any scenes. I'm a client – we've something to talk over – so you ask me to your house. *(Taking his arm again.)*

PAUL: All right, only don't blame me if you don't enjoy yourself.

HELEN: Of course, I'll enjoy myself. Better make it lunch, though, not dinner. Just the three of us. I'll look at my book and see if we can fix a date.

They go out the way they came in. JOYCE plays a few harsh chords.

PHILIP: What on earth is that?

JOYCE: *(Grimly.)* Just a brief sketch of the music for that lunch.

PHILIP: Is it going to be like that?

JOYCE: It'll be worse than that.

Enter WILLIAM as himself.

WILLIAM: Getting a bit tired of Major Spanner. Not a character that gives a fellow much scope. Where's Helen? Still doing Mrs. What's-her-name?

PHILIP: Yes. Mrs. de Folyat wants to meet Rosemary, so Paul's got to arrange a lunch.

JOYCE: If he'd any sense, of course, he'd have refused. The two women'll sit there, hating each other, and he'll be wretched. However, I like this third stage, with philandering just round the corner. I'm getting quite interested now.

WILLIAM: *(Addressing audience.)* Not enough comment now, in my opinion. It's rapidly degenerating into ordinary theatrical muck.

PHILIP: That's what she likes.

JOYCE: It's what everybody likes. Let's see how they're getting on at that lunch.

WILLIAM: I'm against it. Leave 'em alone.

JOYCE: Just have a peep.

WILLIAM jumps on rostrum and stealthily peeps through curtains into inner scene, then comes away.

How's it going?

WILLIAM: *(Sombrely.)* Light thickens and the crow makes wing to the rooky wood.

PHILIP: Hamlet?

WILLIAM: Macbeth. And it's extraordinary – the way Shakespeare –

JOYCE: *(Impatiently breaking in.)* Oh, never mind about Shakespeare now – I want to see what's happening at that lunch. It'll be over soon.

WILLIAM: Over now, I think.

WILLIAM exits. Curtains open and show corner of dining-room. HELEN is just going. PAUL is in centre standing. ROSEMARY and HELEN both have their backs to each other.

HELEN: *(With false gush.)* Thank you so much, Mrs. Weybridge. It's been such a pleasure coming here and meeting you, especially after I've heard so much about you from your clever, clever husband.

ROSEMARY: *(With obvious false geniality.)* Awfully good of you to come, Mrs. de Folyat. I hope you'll come and dine with us sometime.

HELEN: That would be *lovely.*

PAUL: I'll see you down to your car *(Crossing after her to left.)* and then I must get back to the office. 'Bye, darling.

Follows HELEN out.

ROSEMARY: 'Bye, darling.

ROSEMARY watches them go.

Of all the false, faked-up, smarmy, poisonous man-hunters! It wouldn't be so bad if he'd found himself a *decent* woman.

PHILIP: *(Turning to JOYCE.)* You women always say that, don't you?

JOYCE: Yes. We do –

ROSEMARY has now gone to telephone and is dialling.

ROSEMARY: Is that the Sahibs Club? Is Major Spanner there, please?

Curtains close. PHILIP is playing de Folyat music. JOYCE comes in with the Spanner tune.

PHILIP: Don't come in with that awful Major Spanner tune now. I'm playing the Mrs. de Folyat music.

JOYCE: I know you are, dear. But I don't particularly like the way you are playing it.

PHILIP: I was playing it very well.

JOYCE: Rather too well, I thought. I believe you are beginning to take an interest in that frightful woman,

PHILIP: I am. Very attractive type. And probably cleverer than she looks.

WILLIAM enters.

WILLIAM: Well, I lay six to four against her.

PHILIP: I'll take you. It's money for nothing. Paul hasn't a chance against that woman.

WILLIAM: Hasn't he? Well, I think she's going to learn that the situation is not quite as simple as she imagines. The relation between husband and wife, even though they may be quarrelling all the time, is never simple, and I think we'll find that Mrs. What's-her-name – de Folyat – doesn't realise that and so plays the wrong card.

JOYCE: I am delighted to hear it.

WILLIAM: Well, let's see. But give her every chance. *(To pianists.)* Music, atmosphere.

Curtains open. WILLIAM exits alcove. PHILIP and JOYCE play de Folyat music.

Scene shows corner of Mrs. de Folyat's sitting-room, similar to ROSEMARY's, but harder, brighter colours. HELEN as Mrs. de Folyat, in loose, semi-evening gown, is seeing that the right drinks – brandy, whisky, etc., are on low table and is all-expectant. She has a final glance at herself, and PAUL enters dressed as before. JOYCE leans on her piano. HELEN, arranging flowers, turns to meet him.

PAUL: I came along as soon as I could. I was kept at the office until nearly nine.

HELEN: *(All solicitude.)* Poor boy! But have you had anything to eat?

PAUL: Yes, I had a quick bite to eat at the club on the way here.

HELEN: *(Moving to table.)* Drink then, eh? Whisky, brandy? This brandy's supposed to be rather wonderful. *(Pours out glass.)*

Let me give you some. And sit back and relax. You poor
boy, you must be so tired.

PAUL relaxing, while she gives him a liberal helping of brandy.

HELEN: There, darling! *(Coming to behind sofa with the glass.)*

*Puts cushion behind PAUL. As she stands near him, he takes her hand
and she immediately leans over and kisses him, then fondles his face
for a moment and lefts glass for him to drink. She sits centre of sofa.*

PHILIP: She knows her stuff all right.

JOYCE: *(Sharply.)* Sh – sh. *(PHILIP stops playing.)*

*PHILIP leans on his piano. They now look very cosy and relaxed.
PAUL sips his drink.*

PAUL: You're perfectly right, Frances. This is a wonderful
brandy.

HELEN: Well, my dear, I always take a little trouble and try and
get the nest of everything. I may not always look it, but,
believe it or not, I'm rather a clever woman.

PAUL: *(Smiling, takes her hand.)* You're a fascinating woman, and
that's even more important. *(Kissing her hand.)*

*HELEN puts her head on PAUL's shoulder who is lying back with
his arm round her.*

HELEN: *(Smiling at PAUL.)* Well, we had our lunch.

PAUL: *(Not quite happy.)* Yes, we had our lunch.

HELEN: And of course, being a man, you loathed every minute
of it, didn't you?

PAUL: Yes, 'fraid I did.

HELEN: *(Soothingly.)* Never mind. All over now. But, of course, I
had to see for myself.

PAUL: And what did you see? *(Into his glass.)*

HELEN: My dear! Why, of course, you're quite right.

PAUL: *(Rather stiffly, lowering his glass.)* What do you mean?
About Rosemary?

HELEN: Of course. Everything you told me about her – as well
as everything you meant to infer – was, of course, absolutely
right. She's completely wrong for you.

PAUL: *(Tonelessly.)* Yes. *(Puts glass on floor left of sofa.)* I suppose she is.

HELEN: But – I – mean – I saw that in two minutes. I can quite see how it all began, of course. A nice, fresh, little thing. But now, you're quite right. You're growing all the time. She can't develop. In fact, like most women of her type, she's narrowing instead of broadening. It's not even a matter of being really *aware* – of being shall we say – intellectual – but, of course, she's not even moderately intelligent. In fact, let's admit t, she's *stupid.*

PAUL: *(Who has liked this less and less.)* You know, you really saw Rosemary at her worst to-day. I mean, we've been having rows and so on – and then I think she spotted something.

HELEN: Oh – but then – as I say, it didn't take me two minutes to *see.* She is *stupid.*

PAUL: *(Angrily.)* She isn't stupid.

HELEN: My dear Paul, there's no need to be cross merely because I'm agreeing with everything you've told me about her.

PAUL: *(Sulkily.)* I never said she was stupid.

HELEN: Not in so many words, perhaps. It takes a woman to do that. But you've told me she doesn't make an effort to understand you – she doesn't try to develop. And now that I've seen her for myself I'm merely telling you in one word – why – because she's –

PAUL: *(Crossly.)* Yes, yes, yes. You said it before.

HELEN: Paul. What's the matter?

PAUL: *(Turning to face her.)* I suppose the matter – is that I don't enjoy listening to you sneering at my wife.

HELEN: *(Annoyed herself now.)* Sneering! When I'm only –

PAUL: *(Cutting in sharply.)* I know. You said that before too. Well, no doubt it's all very illogical, inconsistent and absurd, after the rot I've talked, but there it is – *I don't like it. (With forced change of manner.)* I'm sorry, Frances, I've had a long day and I'm probably rather tired. I think I'd better go.

HELEN: *(Coolly rapidly.)* I think you had. I also think you're behaving very stupidly.

PAUL: No doubt that's the trouble with us Weybridges – we're *all* stupid people. Thank you for the brandy. Good night.

He hurries out. Curtains close. WILLIAM exits. PAUL wearing light overcoat enters as if walking home. We hear him muttering angrily to himself. PAUL goes up on to rostrum. Moonlight spot comes on.

PAUL: Damned cheek talking about my wife like that! Just damned cheek. Rich, spoilt woman – say anything.

PAUL takes same position in moonlight spot as in Act One, then listens.

ROSEMARY: *(Voice off.)* Darling…the lilac…

Chopin music as before. PAUL hears it.

ROSEMARY: *(Voice off.)* Chopin…perfect…only three days…I love you.

PAUL: Rosemary!

Lights stay down but music soars as he hurries out. Curtain draws on right alcove, where PAUL is discovered still in his raincoat. Holding telephone, he is speaking into it eagerly.

PAUL: Rosemary, listen, darling… Oh, it's you, Nannie. Could I speak to Mrs. Weybridge, please. Gone away, well, if there's a note you'd better read it to me… Gone away for the week-end, perhaps longer, all right then, Nannie. If she does ring up would you tell her I've gone away too, and I might be back on Monday, and I might not.

Some music. Curtain closes on alcove. Fade-in ordinary lighting.

PHILIP: It's too bad she wasn't there, just when he was ready to make it up.

JOYCE: *(Rising.)* Doesn't surprise me, though. That woman at lunch was the last straw, so she telephoned Major Spanner to take her away somewhere, for a nice little bit of consoling romance.

PHILIP: *(Showing more interest and rising.)* Oh – that's it, is it? They've taken to the road, have they, probably under a false name? Fun in a Tudor Trust House, eh? Though I have my doubts about the Major.

JOYCE: Oh, I don't know. I'm beginning to fancy the Major, though I think he'd need a lot of training. Not a week-end man at all.

PHILIP: The blatant cynicism of you women – ugh!

JOYCE: *(Indignantly.)* And after the things I've heard you say –

Curtains open showing corner of private sitting-room in very Olde Worlde Inne. ROSEMARY in day clothes is sitting on sofa, looking rather forlorn and dubious. She sits still throughout outside dialogue.

PHILIP: There we are. Ye Olde Tudor Inne with plaster beams.

JOYCE: And he's taken a private sitting-room with the best double bedroom adjoining it. Well, well, well!

WILLIAM enters as Major Spanner, in dinner jacket. PHILIP and JOYCE retire to pianos and sit. Spanner has traces of a cold, which gets worse throughout the scene.

ROSEMARY: But, George, you've changed.

WILLIAM: *(Startled.)* Changed? Same man you've always known. Loved you for years.

ROSEMARY: No, I mean your clothes.

WILLIAM: Oh yes. Always like to change. Make a habit of it. Keeps a fella from getting slack, y'know.

ROSEMARY: *(Half vexed, half laughing.)* But we want to be slack. That's why we've come here. Besides I didn't bring any evening things with me.

WILLIAM: Oh – I see. Look odd, will it?

ROSEMARY: Of course it will. We'll have to have dinner up here.

WILLIAM: *(Rather disconcerted.)* Oh – will we? Oh, I say, I've just commandeered a good table down there. Slipped down for a short drink before feeding. *(Sneezes, then sniffs a little.)* Fact is, that bathroom's damned draughty and I didn't notice it in time. Have to be careful after all these years in a hot climate.

ROSEMARY: *(Vaguely.)* Yes, of course. Well, you'd better slip down again and tell them we'll dine up here.

WILLIAM: You don't think it would look odd, do you? I mean, you know what these people are. *(Pointing to the door.)*

ROSEMARY: *(Rather impatiently.)* Well, if you like you can dine down there by yourself and I'll just have something on a tray up here. I'm not very hungry anyhow.

WILLIAM: Oh, aren't you? Oh, I say, that's rather a shame. Food here's pretty good, too. That's how I remembered the name of the place.

ROSEMARY: I don't care. I didn't come here for *food*.

WILLIAM: *(Rather embarrassed at this.)* No, of course not. Neither did I, of course. Happy, little girl?

ROSEMARY: Yes, of course, darling. I've been enjoying the lovely peace of it. To be quiet – with peace all around – lovely.

WILLIAM: *(Dubiously.)* Yes, quite. Mayn't last, though.

ROSEMARY: *(Startled.)* Why?

WILLIAM: Got a big table all laid out down below *(Leaning towards her.)* and the head waiter told me it's for a crowd of Air Force blokes who make a night of it here every Friday. Probably won't be much peace and quiet when those lads get started. Ho – ho!

ROSEMARY: Yes, but I didn't mean *that*.

WILLIAM: No, of course not. Quite understand what you mean.

ROSEMARY: *(After pause, wistfully.)* George, do you really love me?

WILLIAM: Why, Rosemary, little girl, you know I do. Haven't I carried that photograph of you with me everywhere for years. Got it here now, matter of fact. *(Pats his back pocket.)*

ROSEMARY: You don't want it now because you've got me. *(After staring at him speculatively.)* You know, George, darling, I hope you realise that a photograph is one thing and a real live person is quite a different thing. I mean, are you quite sure it's me – me myself – you really want?

WILLIAM: Why, of course, Rosemary darling. I tell you, I've dreamed of this for years.

ROSEMARY: *(Stifling all doubts.)* Darling! *(Holding up her face.)* Kiss me!

WILLIAM: *(Moving to her.)* By Jove, yes. Just a second. *(Suddenly stops and turns away, then violently sneezes.)* Oh – damn! Sorry! *(Sniffs and blows his nose hard.)*

ROSEMARY: *(Not holding up her face now.)* Have you got a cold?

WILLIAM: *(Annoyed and apologetic.)* Yes. Beginning to look like it. Damn that bathroom! Felt a touch somewhere too, coming down in the car. That's why I wanted the window closed, but you wouldn't hear of it.

ROSEMARY: *(Rather coldly.)* I'm sorry. I didn't realise you were so susceptible to colds.

WILLIAM: Well, a fella can't be years in a hot climate and then come back to this cold, damp hole – without – *(Just catches another sneeze, then sits on sofa and looks at her gravely.)*

ROSEMARY: *(After a pause.)* What's the matter, George? Is it – something about us?

WILLIAM: *(Solemnly.)* Oh – no. But I've just realised I didn't pack my little glass thing. For the nose, y'know.

ROSEMARY: *(Sadly.)* No, George, I don't know.

WILLIAM: *(Solemnly, sitting very close to her.)* Sort of nasal douche, y'know. Harley Street fella told me never to be without it here at home. First sign of a cold you fill it with a solution of common salt and bicarbonate, then use it night and morning. *(Goes through motions of douching.)* Loosens and dissolves the mucus, he said.

ROSEMARY: *(In a tiny voice.)* Did you say the mucus, George?

WILLIAM: *(Solemnly.)* Yes, Rosemary. And I've gone and forgotten the thing and it's too late now to buy one.

ROSEMARY: *(Sadly.)* Yes, George, it's too late now to buy one.

He gives another violent sneeze, fiddles with his shirt cuff, takes out his handkerchief, mops his face, and now she suddenly bursts into a fit of hysterical laughter, rocking and snobbing with it while he sniffs and pats his nose and stares in amazement at her. After several moments of this –

WILLIAM: *(Puzzled.)* Look here, are you laughing or crying?

ROSEMARY: Both! Both! *(Rising with decision.)* Listen, George, do you know what we're going to do?

WILLIAM: *(Surprised sniffing.)* Well, yes, I suppose –

ROSEMARY: *(Briskly.)* No, you don't, so I'm going to tell you. One of us is going to drive back to town to-night, now, and the other is taking the early train back in the morning. Now, if you like you can stay here and enjoy your cold and let me go back in the car now. Or –

WILLIAM: But – but – *(Just stifling a sneeze.)* – I mean to say – what – thought we were –

ROSEMARY: No, we're not, my dear. I like you very very much, but all the rest of it is simply off. My mistake. And don't pretend not to be relieved because I know very well you are and not just because you've got a cold either. And if we both stay we'll only quarrel and feel silly afterwards. Now, do I go back in the car to-night or do you?

WILLIAM: Well – if it's all the same to you – I think I'd like to get back – because if my cold –

ROSEMARY: I know – your little nose thing. That's settled then. Run down and get something to eat and I'll pack for you. Go on, there's a lamb. *(As she almost bustles him out.)* And George! Remember! We've never been here. It never happened. All a dream! Oh – what name did you put in the hotel register?

WILLIAM: *(Almost off, still trying to sneeze.)* All I could think of was the name of an old C.O. of mine – terrible old stickler *(Sneezes.)* Smith.

WILLIAM goes out. ROSEMARY sits on sofa, half-laughing, half-crying. Curtains close. Bar or two of music with Spanner theme suggested.

JOYCE: All he wanted was to go on with his nice, safe little doglike devotion. A photograph to wag his head over when he'd had a few drinks, and not a real woman.

PHILIP: He's probably got two or three little brown wives in Banji-Banji. But I thought that bogus romantic devotion was just what you women wanted.

JOYCE: Not at all.

HELEN enters through curtains and comes to centre of rostrum.

HELEN: What we women want is something quite simple, and it's you men who make it all seem complicated. What we want is simply to be intensely real living people to the men we love. Nothing fancy at all – we get over that a year after we've left school – not strange, romantic glamorous figures – but just attractive and desirable real people. And your trouble is, whether you're romantic, sensualists, Don Quixotes, Don Juans, it's all the same – you won't let us be real people. You'll turn us into anything, dolls, goddesses, drudges, symbols, phantoms, rather than recognise us as our simple selves. And that's the honest truth.

Lights are now fading. Curtain on alcove left drawn, showing ROSEMARY telephoning like PAUL in the previous scene. JOYCE plays.

ROSEMARY: *(At telephone.)* Oh, Nannie, is Mr. Weybridge there? I see… All right, Nannie…

She begins dialling savagely to the sound of staccato music; playing stops.

Is that Fletcher, Fletcher and Coulson. Is that Mr. Coulson there, please?

Mrs. Weybridge. Say it's rather important… Oh, Mr. Coulson, could I see you as soon as possible? Well, it is, really… Well, it's – it's – *(Hurriedly, but rather louder.)* – it's about a divorce –

Music starts a little mournful. Close of curtain alcove left.

HELEN: And there you are. That separated them.

Playing stops.

JOYCE: It's just the sort of dam' silly thing that would.

PHILIP: No doubt, But may I point out one important fact? If she hadn't been in such a hurry to ring up that solicitor –

JOYCE: *(Cutting in.)* Yes, yes, we know. But she felt she had to do *something*. I understand exactly how she felt.

PHILIP: There you are. You women –

HELEN: *(Cutting in.)* Yes, we'll admit it's when we feel thoroughly upset, we are inclined to do the first thing that comes into our heads.

JOYCE: Oh Lord – yes!

PHILIP: Quite so. Whereas – if you'd only take it easy, just turn things over, enjoy a little quiet reflection –

JOYCE: *(Cutting in.)* You've been taking it easy, turning things over, and enjoying your little quiet reflection ever since I've known you.

PHILIP: I prefer to ignore that type of remark.

JOYCE: *(Mocking his tone.)* He prefers to ignore that type of remark.

PHILIP: *(Annoyed.)* Oh – shut up!

HELEN: Hoy – hoy! It's not you two we're doing but Paul and Rosemary. Now, of course, it was months – and horribly dreary months – before they found themselves together in the solicitor's office.

JOYCE: Yes, it would be. But don't show us any of those dreary months.

WILLIAM now enters as himself.

WILLIAM: No, no, we can imagine. *(Sits on rostrum.)*

HELEN: In any case, they ought to be back in that solicitor's office by now. Joyce – Philip.

HELEN joins WILLIAM. Curtains open to reveal exactly the same solicitor's office scene as in Act One. PAUL moves about as before. ROSEMARY's voice is heard off, as before, saying "Oh, in here. Thank you!" and she enters as before, wearing the same clothes. PAUL is looking out of window and turns. She stares at PAUL. He looks embarrassed. All as before.

PAUL: *(With an effort.)* I'm afraid this – er – rather embarrassing – Rosemary.

ROSEMARY: *(With similar effort.)* Yes – Paul – I'm afraid it is…
(Sits and looks away.)

PAUL: Not my fault… I had a note from Coulson asking me to
be here at half-past three – to answer some questions about
the – divorce…

ROSEMARY: *(Tiny voice.)* Yes, so had I.

PAUL: *(Restlessly.)* Oh, I say – monstrous thing for Coulson to
do – asking us both here at the same time. Shows you how
blankly insensitive these lawyers are. Typical lawyer's trick,
this. Damn Coulson!

ROSEMARY: *(Faintly.)* Oh – I don't think – it's perhaps – *(Dies
away.)*

PAUL: What?

ROSEMARY: No – nothing…

PAUL: Look here. I'll go and wait out there.

ROSEMARY: No – it…

PAUL: Don't mind a bit…

*They stare at each other uncertainly and miserably. Lights on inner
stage and pianos and fore-stage now begin to fade. JOYCE rises from
piano and begins to move towards back. PHILIP does same.*

JOYCE: It's just as it was before. In another minute he'll go out,
and that poor girl will start crying –

PHILIP: And if we're not careful, we'll find ourselves arguing
about it as before, and then we'll be shown how they first
met, and it'll all go round and round.

JOYCE: It's not good enough.

PAUL: *(Quietly but indignantly.)* I couldn't agree with you more.

ROSEMARY: *(Rising, same tone as PAUL.)* It's really Helen's fault
– and William's –

PHILIP: *(Voice beginning to fade.)* Well, my dear, let them settle it.

Moves to right alcove, and exits.

JOYCE: *(Voice fading.)* And themselves – if they can.

She exits from left alcove. Curtains close. WILLIAM and HELEN are now lit as if in firelight, with the rest of the stage dark. HELEN speaks quietly, as if concluding a long story.

HELEN: So there they were. Paul, like a fool, went out, and poor Rosemary sat there crying. Of course, she'd asked the solicitor to send for them both at the same time, in the hope that seeing her again he might have discovered he was still in love with her. *(Pause.)* William, are you listening?

WILLIAM: Yes, I'm listening. But I'm thinking too.

HELEN: No doubt. But I don't believe you were listening.

WILLIAM: Yes, I was. The last thing you said was that she hoped he was still in love with her. Well, he is. And he's only got to run into her anywhere outside that solicitor's office, and he'll show her he is.

HELEN: I'll tell her about that. Then she'll make sure he does run into her. But what were you thinking about – those two?

WILLIAM: No. About two other people.

HELEN: *(Who knows at once.)* Oh!

WILLIAM: *(Slowly.)* Two people – rather older and more mature – and perhaps cleverer in some ways – than those two, who also fell in love, got married, and went galloping away to happiness – only, of course, to find the usual hurdles and jumps and obstacles – losing the first excitement of possession, disagreeing about friends…

HELEN: *(Quietly.)* Complaints about being taken for granted or neglected, and jealousy when other men and women were specially attentive –

WILLIAM: *(Quietly.)* And then a whole fog of cross-purposes –

HELEN: And each of them wearing their pride like blinkers –

WILLIAM: And so, instead of clearing the hurdles and reaching the long flat stretch where they could canter home in trust and affection, they turned aside, they broke – they got divorced.

HELEN: *(With controlled emotion.)* One of them – didn't seem to mind very much – behaved as if it were true what he'd said when – when they were quarrelling – that marriage wasn't right for him –

WILLIAM: He was a fool – and a liar. But he didn't know enough then. And those were the silly easy days when people were busy deceiving themselves. Now he knows that life is hard, and the years are slipping by, and soon the nights will be longer and lonelier and friends will vanish and where there might have been love to the end, not excitement and passion and possession, not rockets and stars but the steady glow of the fire, there will be darkness – and nothing. *(Pause.)* She can't understand that yet.

HELEN: *(Half-laughing, half-crying.)* Oh, can't she? You ask any woman living alone!

WILLIAM: But she needn't live alone.

HELEN: She prefers to.

WILLIAM: *(Pause, turning to HELEN.)* I'm giving myself a last chance, Helen.

HELEN: Why do you say that?

WILLIAM: Because – this being friends, all so gay and matey and cool – doesn't work any longer for me. I've tried hard but I can't make it work. So if this is all, I'm going away.

HELEN: *(Hastily.)* You're not going without me.

WILLIAM: *(Joyfully.)* Helen! *(Turning to her.)*

HELEN: No, wait, William. I agree with everything you've said, and I've felt it too. But it's not good enough. I'm a woman – and not an insurance against a lonely old age. Say it – or never talk like this again.

WILLIAM: *(With great sincerity. Pause.)* My dear, I love you – I love you with all my heart – and I ask you to forgive me – and marry me again –

HELEN: Oh – my darling – there's nothing to forgive – and I love you too – and, of course, I will –

They embrace, and then after a moment she withdraws and looks at him, half-laughing, half-crying.

But darling, making all that fuss and getting divorced – and then marrying again – they'll say we don't know our own minds –

WILLIAM: *(Sturdily.)* Well, we do.

HELEN: *(Same tone as before.)* They'll laugh at us.

WILLIAM: *(Roundly.)* Let 'em laugh.

They rise. Curtains open on inner stage. Great burst of laughter from all four on inner stage, with all lights coming on full – showing a back wall of drawing-room and a buffet table, with drinks, food, and the four – PAUL, ROSEMARY, who are now in evening dress standing in front of it. The side curtains of alcoves are also drawn aside to show flowers or lighted decorations. The laughter is friendly and not at all malicious.

PAUL: Well, you're a bright pair. Ask us here to celebrate with you – and then go off into a corner.

He gives WILLIAM a glass, PHILIP hands glass to HELEN.

WILLIAM: *(Grinning.)* Sorry, old boy!

ROSEMARY: And you haven't even congratulated Joyce and Philip.

HELEN: *(To PHILIP.)* I hope you'll be very happy, Philip. I'm sure you will.

PHILIP: Thank you, Helen. I had to do something to make her play in tune.

WILLIAM: *(After drinking.)* I don't know that in the long run marriage makes anybody very happy. But then the single life doesn't make anybody very happy either. The fact is, nobody in his senses *can* be happy.

HELEN: Don't start philosophising now.

WILLIAM: No, my love. *(To JOYCE.)* My congratulations, Joyce!

JOYCE: Thank you, William! I'm so tired of seeing him look bleary-eyed that I decided I'd better marry him to try and clean him up.

WILLIAM: *(Sternly.)* For that, get back to your piano.

JOYCE comes down to piano left.

HELEN: *(To PHILIP.)* And you to yours.

PHILIP comes down to piano right. They all have drinks now.

ROSEMARY: *(Holding up glass.)* Well, here's to all of us!

JOYCE, PHILIP and PAUL: Well, here's to all of us.

They all toast each other and drink, the three couples look and smile at each other.

WILLIAM: Mind you, the sexual life, as even Shelley had to admit, is a cheat.

JOYCE: *(Sardonically.)* Are you telling me?

WILLIAM: *(Munching away at a sandwich which ROSEMARY has handed him.)* It's been a cheat ever since Paradise.

PHILIP: It has.

HELEN: It takes us women in, just as it does you men.

ROSEMARY: Worse, I suspect.

WILLIAM: *(Broadly now.)* But to share the cheat together – with humour and kindness –

HELEN: *(Smiling at him.)* With trust and deepening affection –

WILLIAM: Is to put up a tent not too far from the shining gates.

ROSEMARY: That's true. And I only hope you'll all be as happy as Paul and I have always been.

PHILIP and WILLIAM take a drink.

PAUL: *(Too heartily.)* Well, I suppose we've been extraordinarily lucky – but there it is – never even a really serious misunderstanding.

ROSEMARY: *(Sweetly.)* We said from the first we'd take care never to quarrel –

HELEN: Well, I must say, my dears…

WILLIAM: *(To HELEN with irony)* I don't think we can do better than follow their wonderful example.

At this PHILIP and JOYCE sit at their pianos and begin playing, while HELEN and WILLIAM toast each other and move up on to the rostrum to meet PAUL and ROSEMARY.

End of Play.

OTHER J.B. PRIESTLEY TITLES

**The Art of the Dramatist:
And Other Writings on Theatre**
9781840022940

Dangerous Corner
9781840022513

Eden End
9781840022544

Johnson over Jordan
9781840022483

When We Are Married
9781849431163

Cornelius
9781849435000

J B Priestley: Plays One
9781840022926

J B Priestley: Plays Two
9781840022933

J B Priestley: Plays Four
9781849432177

WWW.OBERONBOOKS.COM

Follow us on www.twitter.com/@oberonbooks
& www.facebook.com/oberonbook

www.ingramcontent.com/pod-product-compliance
Ingram Content Group UK Ltd.
Pitfield, Milton Keynes, MK11 3LW, UK
UKHW020721280225
455688UK00012B/447